BOB FLAME
ROCKY MOUNTAIN RANGER

Revised Edition

By

DORR G. YEAGER

AUTHOR OF
"Bob Flame, Ranger," etc.

ILLUSTRATED

ROCKY MOUNTAIN NATURE ASSOCIATION
ESTES PARK, COLORADO
Published in cooperation with the
Estes Park Museum Friends and Foundation, Inc.

Published by
The Rocky Mountain Nature Association
48 Alpine Circle • P.O. Box 3100
Estes Park, CO 80517
800-816-7662 • rmna.org
in cooperation with the
Estes Park Museum Friends and Foundation, Inc.

First edition 1935
Revised edition 2010

ISBN 978-0-930487-85-0
LCCN 2009935104

Editor: John Gunn
Editorial Assistance: Nancy Wilson
Cover Design: Ann Green

CONTENTS

Dorr G. Yeager

FOREWORD

J ust as "Bob Flame, Ranger" told an accurate story of the National Park Ranger in Yellowstone, so does "Bob Flame, Rocky Mountain Ranger" give a true picture of the men in this park, perched atop the Rockies and straddling the Continental Divide. Yet, upon reviewing the manuscript before it is sent to the publishers, I know that I have failed in what I have attempted. I have failed in that insufficient emphasis has been placed upon the bravery and hardiness of the Rangers of Rocky Mountain. It would take a better writer than I to picture to the reader the dangers and hardships of their everyday work and the cheerfulness with which they undertake them. I have written of mountain men who, it seems to me, have something in common with the mountain men of the early fur trade days. Those of an earlier time blazed the trails for progress and those of the present day are keeping those trails cleared that a nation may enjoy its playgrounds.

D. G. Y.

Rocky Mountain National Park,
June, 1935

Barney

PREFACE

I grew up a National Park Service kid, which was one of my father's gifts to me. To the world he gave the four *Bob Flame* books to encourage young people to embrace national parks and their rangers. Pa also contributed several novels about wild animals to help young people understand and respect the world of nature. One of his animal books was translated into Dutch. My father was forever an encourager. He surely would be pleased to see *Bob Flame, Rocky Mountain Ranger* back in print.

Pa also was a classic romantic. As the great dictionary author Noah Webster might say, he enjoyed real happenings and adventures as exciting as those in romance literature. I was blessed to be his daughter, and to benefit from his paradoxical nature. My father was practical and professional. He also was a dreamer of dreams. How else can you explain a man who composed books telling his own personal stories while penning tales of the wild animals that shared the life of this career ranger-naturalist? I am a huge fan of Pa's writings, even though an occasional word written in another era might now be considered inappropriate.

When I was growing up, we had a photograph on the wall of a small grizzly cub standing at an old hand-crank telephone, as if the animal were making a call. That bear was Barney, a cub my father had rescued on ski patrol at Old Faithful in Yellowstone National Park and carried in a backpack to park headquarters in Mammoth. With great relish he told of fashioning a baby bottle from an aspirin bottle and an eyedropper, and getting up several times a night in a frigid cabin to heat canned milk for the little cub. He said, "I have always claimed that I am the only person to carry a bear around Yellowstone loop, especially on skis." Another favorite picture of mine was of Pa sitting under a tree with Barney on his lap.

My father was a collector of critters. Barney was only the first. As a youngster, I recall a succession of them: the raccoon that hissed at people, the skunk we never saw because it was nocturnal, the spider monkey that rode around on Pa's shoulder, the succession of dogs large and small, and my horse Baba, a gift from my father to my sister and me.

My father was an advocate for wild animals. His books *Scarface* and *Chita* focused on the nearly hunted-out grizzly and mountain lion populations in Rocky Mountain National Park. He wrote articles urging protection of coyotes and bats. Of the latter, he wrote, "Unfortunately, superstition has put these little flying mammals in such a bad light that they are usually placed in the category of witches and ghosts. There is nothing mysterious about bats. They are simply small mammals… They fly at night, not because they are searching for sleeping human victims, but because they, like owls, can see best at night…"

My father was a builder. He constructed efficient, professional teams in the Park Service and built "stuff," including a corral for the horse and much of our home in Alamo, California, where I spent part of my youth after we returned from Zion and Bryce Canyon national parks and Pa worked in the Regional Office in San Francisco. I remember many times helping him hold boards or tools when he was working. He helped build a small cabin cruiser that he used to explore the waters of the Sacramento River's delta country. In many of his letters to me in college, Pa would say he could hardly wait for me to get home so we could go out on the boat. I think it was his place of refuge from phones and demands.

My father was a gardener. One of our evening rituals in Alamo was walking through his old-fashioned rose garden, checking on the plants and learning the history of each. I was expected to learn their botanical names, as well as the names of all the different conifers he had planted around the property after their service as Christmas trees. As a botanist, he expected people to know the names of things. It was only in his last years that I discovered that his specialty was mycology, and I lament all the wild mushrooms I might have eaten had I known this earlier.

After he retired from the Park Service, my father began to explore new means of expressing his creativity. He painted water colors (badly), made jewelry of silver and turquoise (some of it passing fair), and made pottery dishes, which I still use and cherish, although they lack uniformity – no two are alike. Perhaps that is a metaphor for my father. He was unique. He loved trying new things, exploring new places, dreaming new dreams. He even tried to convince my mother to move to Alaska after his retirement so he could pan for gold.

My father was a philosopher. In re-reading the letters he wrote me during my first summer away from home (working in Olympic National Park) and later in my early college years, I realize that many gifts of wisdom came with those missives. There was a letter in which he cautioned me against letting a supervisor spoil my summer. "Don't let her get your goat. Pay attention to what she says in correcting your work, but let the other remarks go in one ear and out the other… It's an experience to work with someone like that because it makes a normal person appear so nice by comparison." I always suspected he retired early from the service because he was a field man who tired of being a bureaucrat behind a desk.

I think my favorite letter was one he wrote me when I was feeling lonely and homesick. "I suppose that everyone is lonesome to some extent, not lonesome for company because as you know, one can be lonesome as the devil in a crowd. But one can be lonesome for places, lonesome for understanding, and even lonesome for solitude… About all I can tell you is that I know exactly how you feel. Hope by the time this reaches you the sun is shining again." In another one, when I was having boy troubles, he pointed out that I might have a number of loves in my life, and perhaps more than one at a time. The letter concluded, "Never close your eyes and your heart to the future."

Whenever I was around my father, I tried to remember

that advice. I will always remember him cruising down the hall in the retirement home on his motorized scooter, wearing the junior ranger hat I had given him for his 92nd birthday. Until his final stroke, he never closed his heart to the future. He lived to be 94, and died, most appropriately, on Earth Day. We scattered Pa's ashes on one of his favorite fishing lakes. I like to remember him as being not unlike the great grizzly, Scarface, the hero of one of his animal novels.

The last grizzly speaks:
I am the last; all others gone.
I alone salute the dawn.
From my wind-swept mountain den
I look upon a world of men.
Highways winding far below
Where once roamed only buffalo.
In retrospect I seem to see
The days now gone – that used to be.

– From the introduction to *Scarface*

PATRICIA YEAGER WASHBURN
ESTES PARK, COLORADO
JULY, 2009

INTRODUCTION

For many youngsters, being a park ranger is a dream job. They imagine wearing a badge, being skilled as mountaineers, able to hike the trails, ride horses, scale mountains, fight forest fires, protect wildlife and save people's lives.

In the mid-1930s, when author Dorr Yeager wrote *Bob Flame: Rocky Mountain Ranger,* what rangers did on a day-to-day basis was a mystery to most people. Rarely did the average tourist actually meet them. Yes, it is true, park visitors saw people dressed like rangers giving talks at campfire programs, but these professionals were better known as "ranger-naturalists." When arriving in the park, they met "entrance station rangers." Such rangers were friendly; they answered all sorts of questions. But from the start, there were different types of rangers.

Beyond giving information, people wondered, what did rangers actually do? Where were those heroes they'd read about who chased wildlife poachers across the mountains? Whose job was it to save children from raging rivers? Everyone wearing uniforms tended to look alike.

Unless a park visitor suffered an accident, he or she rarely met a law enforcement ranger, a rescue ranger or a fire control ranger. Most of the time, such rangers toiled in the background, patrolling the park, ensuring people's safety, enforcing rules or preparing for emergencies.

When Dorr Yeager wrote *Bob Flame,* the concept of park rangers was new. In less than two decades, they had started earning their reputations by performing rescues, fighting fires, enduring hardships and protecting parks and visitors. Rocky Mountain National Park could be a dangerous place where avalanches happened, blizzards could strike, people got lost and mountain travel was treacherous – sometimes deadly. Wildlife needed protection. Occasionally, visitors needed help.

By telling this story – somewhat fictional, yet based on fact – Dorr Yeager hoped that everyone would appreciate what rangers did day in and day out, heroic or not. He knew it took stamina and hard work to protect the park and its visitors. He understood that being a ranger was a tough job.

Today, modern rangers require even more skills than those exhibited by Bob Flame. Every specialty – from law enforcement to fire management, from search and rescue to wildlife management – demands greater training, broader knowledge.

Not so long ago, I served as a park ranger at Glacier National Park in Montana, performing tasks similar to those tackled by Bob Flame. We "utility" rangers were expected to know how to fight fires, rescue people from cliffs, find lost children, work around the clock without sleep, qualify with firearms, repair a boat motor, make an arrest, write a speeding ticket, give first aid, retrieve keys locked inside cars, investigate crimes, deal with troublesome skunks, sharpen chainsaws, track poachers, saddle a horse, fend off bears, write accurate reports and be ready to go in a heartbeat. The famous Boy Scout motto is "Be prepared." Put simply, rangers live prepared. Bob Flame's spirit lives on.

Thanks to the Next Generation Fund, a major fundraising campaign of the Rocky Mountain Nature Association, a non-profit organization Yeager helped found in 1931 to assist Rocky Mountain National Park, this republishing of *Bob Flame: Rocky Mountain Ranger* may help those who aspire to become a ranger understand what being a ranger was like in early national park history. Still today, it remains a strenuous and exciting profession. Being a regular ranger is not for everyone. But for those who are willing to invest their talent and public spirit, the result may produce stories as rich as those presented by Dorr Yeager in the pages that follow.

C.W. BUCHHOLTZ
EXECUTIVE DIRECTOR
ROCKY MOUNTAIN NATURE ASSOCIATION
ESTES PARK, COLORADO
OCTOBER, 2009

Courtesy P. F. Shope

An Isolated Lake in the High Country

To PEG

Who helped me Write this Book
because
She Wanted to Know More About Bob Flame

Editor's note:Yeager dedicated the 1935 edition to his bride, Eleanor Mills, affectionately known to her friends and family as Peg.

CHAPTER I

MOUNTING UP

IT WAS raining at Old Faithful Ranger Station—a slow steady spring rain that soaked the ground and rotted the snow and turned the already swollen rivers into raging torrents. The rain, combined with the fact that it was Sunday, seemed automatically to give Bob Flame permission to cease activities for the remainder of the day and spend a quiet evening before the log fire that crackled in the huge stone fireplace. For the past few weeks he had promised himself such an evening when it would be possible to put some of his winter equipment in shape for summer storage.

He was shellacking a pair of snowshoes before the dry heat of the coming months would have an opportunity to get in its work on the leather and wood. As he spread the liquid over the tightly stretched webbing, his mind traveled back over the winter just passed. It had been tough—the toughest he had ever known, but all the men had said the same thing and he knew that he had stood up with the best of them. The snow had never been right for skiing and they had floundered for days through the white stuff. In spite of these difficulties he figured that he had traveled over a thousand miles on his patrols—and there was another hundred added to it by his trip to the Ashton dog races.

It was early May in the Yellowstone. The land,

which for seven months had been buried under a deep
snow blanket, was gradually arousing itself from a
mountain winter. It had been a season of hardship for
everything that lived within the boundaries. Tem-
peratures had fallen to record-breaking lows and had
remained there for days at a time. Under the terrific
cold, trees burst with gun-like explosions, and animals
in burrows deep under ground had frozen in spite of
the protection they had sought. Blinding winds and
blizzards whipped the flats and plateaus—winds which
drove men and wild creatures alike to shelter. And
after the winds had come the snow, piling deep in the
lodge-pole forests. Deer and elk perished by the score,
for the white blanket was too thick for them to reach
through to the frozen grass.

But now it was spring, and a warm bright sun beat
down upon the park, dispelling all memories of cold
and snow and forcing the drifts further back each day.

Wilderness creatures began to appear. Chipmunks
and ground squirrels came forth to loosen their taut
muscles after a winter of inactivity. Bears lumbered
lazily across the flats followed by fat waddling cubs.
And while the females sought out tender bulbs and succulent grasses in the swamps the babies fought desperately for a chance to feed from their mothers. Birds
began to make their appearance—warblers in the willows along the creek bottoms, tanagers at the edge of
the forests, and bluebirds flashing their dazzling colors
across the parade ground at Headquarters.

The great herds of elk and deer were gradually
drifting upward, following the snowline as it receded.
They cropped eagerly at the fresh new grass or

browsed on the new shoots of willow. The time of easy feeding was at hand and the animal world seemed at peace. No longer did the deer flee wild-eyed at the sight of a slinking coyote, for now their winter enemies were again able to concentrate their attentions upon mice and other small rodents.

Slowly the aspens were taking on color. They had stood white and bare throughout the past months, but now delicate new leaves began to tint the groves on the slopes. Pasque flowers and anemones became prominent on the drier hillsides, while marsh marigolds bloomed in profusion in the ice runoffs of melting drifts.

Already the big rotary snowplow had smashed its way through Golden Gate and the usual rush of pre-season activity was at its height. Rangers had been assigned to their summer stations on the main loop road and, with the assistance of crews, were rapidly clearing away the collection of accumulated winter debris. In spite of the early season there was no time to lose, for within a short while great throngs of sagebrushers would be camped outside the gates clamoring for entrance. A few lodge and hotel employees were on the scene and more were arriving daily to assist in the preparations for an early season rush.

Bob finished the snowshoe, lit a cigarette and stretched. Well, it was over for another season and soon the dudes would be arriving. He wondered vaguely what sort of an outfit they'd give him this summer as temporary rangers. He hoped that he would be lucky enough to draw at least a few old men. Dick Howe was here already and he would make a good working nucleus. He'd give his right hand to have Tex back. If he got him he'd put the kid on the Shoshone fire patrol. And he mustn't forget the broken lock at Shoshone cabin. They'd lost the key last winter and had to smash it with a rock to get in. And there was a clump of bug trees around Black Sand Basin. Those would have to be cut and burned before the insects emerged and attacked other trees. There were a hundred things to do in the next few weeks.

Suddenly the door of the station opened and a man entered. There was a swish of wet oiled cloth as he slipped out of the coat and tossed it into a corner. Then he strolled over to the fire.

"Hi, kid," greeted Bob without looking up. He knew from the step that it was Dick Howe.

"It's raining," volunteered the newcomer.

"You're kidding me." Bob grinned. He liked this boy. For two years Dick had been with him throughout the summer, but this would be his last. He'd have to start earning a living in the fall, for school days were over. Bob knew why he had pleaded to come in for early work. He wanted to get as much of the park as he could this season. But there was another reason for his early arrival.

"How is she?" he asked the boy.

"Huh? Who?"

"Who, my eye. You know who."

Dick Howe smiled slowly. "She's fine, Bob."

"You know," drawled the other in mock seriousness, "it's quite a coincidence—here she is at Old Faithful Lodge for the summer, and here you are at Old Faithful Ranger Station."

"Yea," agreed the boy, "that is strange, isn't it?"

"And you both got here early."

"Also strange."

Bob shifted his position and looked at the young fellow in front of the fire. "You aren't kidding me a bit, son. Where do you think I thought you've been every evening since you got here. Out by yourself watching the geysers?"

Dick laughed. Although he had not told his station chief that the girl was already at the lodge he had felt that Bob was aware of it. "So what?" he asked still smiling.

"So nothing. What's going to become of it?"

"We're going to get married."

"I'm amazed," drawled the other; "I hadn't dreamed of it. But wait a minute"—he sat up in his chair suddenly—"not this summer. You're going to stay single this summer if I have to hog-tie you."

"Don't get excited. It won't happen till fall."

Bob settled back and studied the fire. He remembered the beginning of this romance between the two. He recalled with crystal clearness a night two years before when this youngster had been taken to the hospital at headquarters with a broken back—broken because he was carrying out orders. He had been sent to run down a bootleg car and the driver had crowded the motorcycle off a narrow stretch of mountain road. And he remembered the frightened face of the girl as she had come to him late that night when she heard the news. She had begged him to tell her the truth; and he had, as best he could, smoothing off some of the rough details. For some reason Bob had never told anyone about that little sidelight. There had been something in the girl's eyes that had sealed his lips, and there had been another something that had told him there was more than friendship between Dick Howe and this pretty girl.

"Well," he said, getting up and tossing another log on the blaze, "power to you, fella. I like you both."

Dick looked enviously at the pair of snowshoes. "Gosh," he said wistfully, "I wish I could get into the service permanently. I'd chuck this law business in a minute if there was any chance."

But Bob shook his head. "Forget it, kid. You're going to get married and it's no place for a woman."

Dick looked puzzled. "Meaning what?"

"Meaning that there are mighty few women who would be happy living for the rest of their lives in a place like this."

"But Jean loves it."

"Yea, I know. But Yellowstone is a lot different in summer than it is in winter. She's a mighty fine kid, and I like her, but you keep her out of it."

Dick grinned. "You sound as if you've had experience. Holding out on me?"

Bob shook his head. "I haven't had experience but I know what I'm talking about. Either marry a woman and stay out of it, or marry the Service and stay in it."

"Maybe you're right," Dick said slowly. "But no matter where I go I'll always wish I was here. Why even back at school, every time I'd open a book I'd see you fellows in snowshoe cabins or on skiis. And I was supposed to be concentrating on law. Nuts!" He kicked the fireplace rocks impatiently.

Bob nodded. He knew how the kid felt. "You love her, don't you?"

"Sure I do!"

"More than anything else?"

"I wouldn't marry her if I didn't."

"Then the best way to show it is to forget you were ever a ranger."

The telephone jangled impatiently—two longs and a short, Old Faithful Ranger Station.

"Answer the phone," grinned the station chief. "Maybe they're calling you to see if you'd take a permanent appointment."

Dick crossed the room and took down the receiver. "Hello. This is Old Faithful—Howe speaking. Yea, just a minute." Then turning to the other: "You, Bob. Headquarters."

The man grunted impatiently. "Now what?" he muttered. "Too early for sagebrushers to complain and too wet for fires. Hello . . . yes . . . hello, Mitch, what's up? How would I like to take a ride? How would you like to jump in the river? I'm not stirring out tonight without a personal note from the President. What? . . . No kiddin'? Okay, but I suppose you know it's raining bucketsful and it's a heck of a note dragging anybody out—all right, see you later."

He hung up the receiver and stood for several seconds before the fire lost in thought. Then he turned a puzzled face toward Dick.

"Wonder what's up. Mitch says they want me at headquarters pronto. Said it was important."

The other grinned. "Nice night for a boatride."

"Yea, sweet. Fifty miles and the roads are like rivers. This is just one reason why you don't want to be a permanent ranger. Imagine leaving Jean on a night like this."

"I just did."

"Yea, and you stay left. Have her over here if you want to, but you stick near the station while I'm gone. Well, here goes nothing." And he disappeared into the next room.

Ten minutes later he reappeared, clad in a heavy slicker and carrying a waterproof bedroll. "I'll go in, but I'm telling you right now I'll not come back tonight. If they haven't a bed for me I'll sleep with the horses. Take care of the dump. I'm off."

Dick walked to the door and watched his chief climb into the car and start the motor.

"Oh, by the way," Bob shouted at him through the rain, "phone the mess shack and tell 'em I took an ocean trip."

Dick waved an acknowledgment and the car shot out of its parking space and roared down the road toward headquarters.

Now that he was actually on his way, Bob centered his thoughts on the mysterious phone call which he had just received. It was not like the office to bring a man in on such a night unless something urgent was at hand, and try as he might he could not imagine what was behind the request. During the summer, when the park was crowded with all classes of people, such calls were not uncommon. Often he had made trips to headquarters after midnight on theft and bootleg cases. Twice he had stayed up the whole night patrolling roads and stopping every car in search of persons wanted. But this was something else. He knew that, for there were no dudes in the area at present and it was too early for "brass hats" to arrive and demand special attention. The memory that Mitch's voice had been jovial cheered him, for he knew the assistant chief ranger well enough to realize that his mood would not be light if serious trouble were brewing.

Bob was thoroughly familiar with the road and he did not hesitate to plow through the submerged portions without slacking his speed. Water sprayed in sheets from under the wheels as he took the puddles. Sometimes it completely covered the windshield but the wiper cleared it with a single sweep. Only once did he slow down, and that was to negotiate a piece of road under construction. He waved cheerfully to the crew foreman going into the night shift, and thanked heaven that he was a ranger in a car instead of an engineer in the rain. Tough job, the engineers had, he thought. No sooner did they get the roads clear of snow than they started in getting them ready for the heavy traffic that would soon be upon them. This road hadn't stood up, and the men were pushing the work day and night in an effort to have it open in time.

Past Madison Junction he sped and into Norris Geyser Basin. Tonight it was a ghostly valley of steam, for every opening was belching forth the vapor in white billowing clouds. As he rounded Dead Man's Turn he remembered the supply truck that had gone off the embankment on just such a night. A dense layer of steam had settled over the basin and the driver, new to the road, hadn't made the curve.

Half an hour later Bob rounded the wide sweeping curve at Mammoth Hot Springs and gradually the lights of headquarters began to twinkle weirdly before him. As he pulled up in front of the gray stone administration building he looked at the luminous dial of his wrist watch.

"Not bad," he muttered, "two hours on a night like this."

The office was dark save for a brilliantly lighted room on the second floor. He knew that someone was waiting for him and he lost no time in entering the building and climbing the stairs.

For a moment the bright lights of the room blinded him and he stood blinking in the doorway. Then a familiar voice came from somewhere within.

"Well look what swam in! Nice night for a ride." It was Mitch's voice.

Bob made a wry face and slipped out of his wet slicker. "Say, listen," he began, "what's the big idea hauling me out . . ." Then he stopped short, for he suddenly became aware that Mitchell was not the only person in the room. Seated near the desk was McMannon, the chief ranger, and beside him was a man whom Bob had never seen before. Seeing his embarrassment, McMannon arose and came foreward.

"Bob," he said, "I want you to know Superintendent Wentworth."

Bob shook hands with the man, lit a cigarette and dropped into a vacant chair. While he was doing so his mind was working rapidly. He had heard of Wentworth, Superintendent of Rocky Mountain Park in Colorado. But what was he doing here? Could it be that Wentworth was going to take over Yellowstone? If that was it, where did it leave . . . No it didn't fit. They wouldn't bring him in for that. Still, they'd been making some funny transfers and changes lately. At length he looked at McMannon in a puzzled manner.

"I suppose, Bob," began the other, "that you've been wondering why we dragged you out on a night like this."

Bob grinned and nodded. "Well, I haven't exactly been able to figure it all out."

"Well, we had a reason," continued the other, "and when we're through I think you'll agree that the trip was justified."

"You wouldn't have asked me to come in if it weren't."

"Right. Now listen. You remember two years ago McDonald went from here to Rocky Mountain?"

Bob nodded. Everyone remembered that. He'd never forget that day at Lake Station when Mac had received the news of his transfer.

"You've been out in the sticks all winter and you haven't had a chance to keep up with the developments in Washington. Since March things have been popping. Have you heard anything about the C.C.C.?"

Bob pondered for a moment. "I've heard a few snatches over the radio. Sort of a national conservation movement, isn't it? To relieve unemployment?"

"Exactly. The C.C.C. stands for the Civilian Conservation Corps. It's an army equipped with shovels instead of guns, if you get what I mean. Briefly, the plan is to put men to work—to get kids in their early twenties off the road and off the streets and get them into something where they can support themselves and help the country.   Understand?"

"Yes, so far."

"The President's idea is to establish camps all over the country, put these boys in them and give them a dollar a day for short hours.   They'll be doing real conservation work—planting trees, preventing soil erosion, cutting fire-lanes—a thousand things that need doing but for which we've never had the money."

Bob nodded.

"They're going to depend upon the national parks to use a lot of these camps.   It's a mighty big project —bigger than any of us realize now.   But to make a long story short, Bradley, assistant superintendent at Rocky Mountain, is being transferred to Washington within a short time to help out with this job of lining up the camps in the various parks.   McDonald is being promoted to take his place."

For a moment Bob's heart stopped beating.   Instinctively he knew that something was about to break —something which vitally concerned him.

"So what?" he asked.

"Well, that leaves Rocky Mountain without a chief ranger."

"Yes."

"The point of this whole conference is this.   Would you consider the chief ranger's job there?"

It was with difficulty that Bob remained in his chair. He tried to hide his emotions but his effort was to no avail for Mr. Wentworth chuckled.

"That's what Mr. Wentworth came up here for— to see you and to find out if you'd take it."   McMannon paused. Then, "McDonald suggested you and I've put in a good word for you."

Bob sighed. "And I cussed the trip in here. Lord, yes, I'll take it—when do I leave?" He looked at Mr. Wentworth.

"How soon could you leave?" asked the older man.

Bob calculated mentally. "Tomorrow noon."

They all laughed; then Wentworth said: "There isn't that much rush. Suppose we say that you drift in by the end of the week. Is that all right?"

"Perfect."

"There will be the usual amount of red tape connected with the transfer, but we felt reasonably sure you'd take it and we can arrange the final details with Washington by wire."

Bob rose from his chair and extended his hand to the Superintendent. "All I can say"—he smiled—"is that I'm mighty grateful and I hope you'll be satisfied with me."

"On the other hand," said the man, "I hope you'll like us and like Rocky Mountain. We don't have as large a layout as you do here, Flame, and you'll undoubtedly find a great many things that are different, but there's a big opportunity to do some pioneering work down there. McDonald has made a good start and I'm sure that you will be able to carry it on."

There was little more to be said and Bob soon took his departure.

"Hey," shouted Mitch as he started down the stairs, "you're not goin' back tonight, are you?"

"Yea, I've got to. Dick's holding down the fort alone."

"Well, it won't run away," urged the other. "Come on over and bunk with me. You can get an early start in the morning."

But Bob shook his head. "Thanks, old man, but I'd better get back. See you later."

Mitch did not urge him further, for he guessed Bob's reason for refusing the invitation. He wanted to be alone to think this thing out, and he felt that he could do it best driving back through the storm.

He did not push the car on his return trip. Instead he cruised along through the rain, doing his best to adjust himself to the new situation. Had he, he asked himself, jumped too rapidly at this thing? Would he have been better off to remain where he was? He was practically assured of an advancement before another year was over. But even with an advancement he would not be as far along as he would by accepting the Rocky Mountain appointment. He recalled a winter night two years before which he and McDonald had spent in the tiny cabin at Park Point. The same subject had come up, and Mac had said, "Believe me, when an advancement of any sort comes along grab it. Who knows when another one will roll your way?" McDonald had done this and he was now, or would be within a few days, an assistant superintendent. Bob remembered a long letter he had received after Mac went to Rocky Mountain. He was not sorry. It was different, but it was foolish to believe that one park held all the advantages.

It did not take Bob long to convince himself that it was a step in the right direction. In spite of this he seemed depressed by a vacant feeling within him as his thoughts drifted back over the trail which he had traveled for two years. He remembered how, as a raw-boned ranger, new to the game, he had gone out on station for the first time. He had gone over this very road, wedged between potato sacks in the back end of a commissary truck. He remembered Hicks who had been his station chief that first summer— Hicks, now chief ranger in Teton. He recalled the big fire of that summer and the torturing ski patrols the following winter. He remembered the old familiar faces—faces he had lived with during those months, men with whom he had slept and eaten and joked, men who had shared the terrific hardships of winter with him, men who had taught him all he knew of this game; he was leaving them.

His throat grew tight and he stepped on the gas. Well, wherever he might go in the future, he vowed that the friends he had made and the experiences which he had had during these first years would always linger fondly in his memory. So much had he to occupy his mind that he awoke with a start to find himself sitting in the parking area at Old Faithful Ranger Station. Dick, clad in pajamas and a sweater, was standing in the doorway holding a gasoline lantern above his head and dodging the raindrops which dripped from the roof.

"What in thunder?" called the temporary sleepily. "I though you were at Mammoth."

Bob grinned and climbed out of the car. "I was, but I'm here now."

"S'matter? They fire you?"

"Yea," Bob said soberly.

"G'wan."

"Fact! I'll bet you a dollar I won't be in Yellowstone this season."

Dick sleepily muttered something about crazy talk and went back to his cot, little dreaming that what Bob said was true.

CHAPTER II

FOUR days later Bob Flame again sat in the office of Chief Ranger McMannon. It had been four days of frenzied preparation for departure. Although he had collected little in the way of personal property during his life in Yellowstone, he had made many friends, and much of the time had been spent in farewells. Those loop stations which were already accessible by car he had visited, shaking hands with the men in turn and sitting in awkward silence, attempting to make cheerful conversation. But his heart was heavy and he never stayed as long as he planned. They were too near him and it was impossible to make light of such a parting. Many of the farewells were without words—simply a firm handclasp and a slap on the back—that was all, but they were full of meaning. Those men who could not be reached by car he called by phone. This was easier and he had spent many minutes with them, recalling old experiences and laughing at their jokes.

On the last day Wilson had come to take over Old Faithful, and it was necessary to show him around the region and explain the many details, for Wilson had never spent more than a day at a time at this point. But Dick was there and Bob knew that after he was gone the two would have considerable chance to go over the ground which he had not covered.

So Bob Flame left Old Faithful. As he pulled out of the station three geysers simultaneously broke into full eruption. It was as if the basin was giving him a parting salute. Here he had really begun his life as a ranger. It was the first station which he had taken over, and it was home to him.

"It was like tearing my heart out leaving that place and saying good-bye to the boys," he confided to Mitchell the morning of the day on which he was to depart.

"Yea, I know."

"No, you don't, fella. You'll never know till you do it. You don't realize the grip this place has on you till you know you're going. I've lived with those mugs for so long that they've become a part of me. Sometimes I even feel that I don't want to go."

Mitchell snorted. "Don't be a sap. You've got to go. It's a big chance for you."

Bob smiled. That was like Mitch. Never thought of himself, or if he did he'd never show it. Mitch outranked him five years in service, but instead of wondering why he didn't get the appointment, he was glad that another fellow had. Something about that thought made Bob swallow hard.

"When you pulling out?" Mitchell asked curiously.

"Just as soon as I can. Mac has some papers for me to sign and some information on government travel. Then I'm leaving."

"Goin' to take your car with you?"

"Yea."

Mitchell pondered for a moment. "Listen. How about giving me a lift to Livingston? I gotta go anyway and I can come back on the bus in the morning."

"Tickled to death," Bob replied enthusiastically. "Come on."

"Suppose we eat lunch here and then roll?"

"Nothing doing, Mitch. I'm not going to risk my reputation by going over to the mess shack with that gang. I'd be sure to make a fool of myself, and I don't want to. We'll eat in Livingston."

"Fair enough. Guess Mac will let me go all right."

Bob knew why his friend had proposed going to Livingston, and he knew that an hour before the thought had never entered his mind. He wanted to make it as easy as possible for Bob. It would be easier to start from Livingston alone than to leave the park and know that everything was behind you. Good old Mitch! He arose and patted him affectionately on the shoulder.

"Nice of you, big boy."

Mitch snorted again. "Nice, hell! I tell you I gotta go anyway an' I might as well save gas."

At that moment McMannon came up the stairs and entered the room. "Why hello, Bob," he greeted. "Ready to shove off?"

The man nodded and turned to look out of the window.

"Say, listen, Chief," Mitchell interrupted briskly. "How about goin' down to Livingston with him? I gotta mess of stuff to do?"

McMannon scowled and started to speak but his

assistant winked and jerked his head in Bob's direction.

The chief ranger nodded knowingly. "Sure," he said. "It's all right with me, but don't forget to make out a leave-slip."

Then he sat down at his desk. "You've never traveled on government status have you, Bob?" he called.

The man turned from the window and sat down in a chair beside the desk.

"No, and I hear it's a lot of red tape."

"Not so much when you get onto it, but you'd better get it down pat because if you make a misstep it's out of your own pocket and not Uncle Sam's. They watch things of that kind like a hawk. Going in your own car, aren't you?"

Bob nodded.

"Good. It's simpler by auto. Nothing to monkey with for trains and pullmans that way. Now listen and get this. First of all, you keep a strict account of all your car expense—gas, oil, flats, repairs, storage— everything. Pay for them, get receipts and when you get down there they'll reimburse you. Understand?"

"Yes."

"You'll be allowed five dollars a day expense money, and that is to cover everything except actual transportation. They'll give you that when you get there, too. Oh yes, another important thing." He handed Bob a small book. "These are tax exemption blanks. Every time you fill up with gas make one of these out. You never pay state gas tax, and this is the gas man's receipt. I don't know of anything else. Is that all clear?"

"It's clear now, but wait till I get out on the road. I'll probably get rattled and give away the wrong blanks."

McMannon laughed. "No you won't. Just remember that you'll pay for any mistakes you make on this trip. When are you leaving?"

"As soon as Mitch is ready."

Mitchell closed the drawer of his desk and put on his hat. "Be right with you, kid. Throw a toothbrush in my pocket and meet you at the barracks in five minutes." With this he dashed through the door and down the stairs.

"Well, Bob, good luck," said the chief ranger, extending his hand. "I'm mighty glad you're going down to take this job. We'll miss you, but it's a big chance. How is it, kind of tough leaving?"

Bob took the hand eagerly. "Boy, you don't know how tough it really is."

"Oh yes I do. I was in the same boat once myself. It'll be tough pulling stakes here, but as soon as you get on the way that will all be forgotten and you'll be able to concentrate on your new work."

"Maybe so," sighed the other, "but right now . . ."

McMannon interrupted him. "Say listen, before I forget it. Watch your step when you get there. All the other parks have the idea that Yellowstone men have a high-hat attitude. Don't let 'em know it, even if you think it."

"But I don't."

"So much the better. Now Wentworth likes you,

and when a superintendent likes you half the battle's won. And remember, the less you say about Yellowstone the better off you'll be. If you've learned anything up here that you can apply to advantage down there, for the love of Mike do it, but don't say we did it that way in Yellowstone. That's poison in another park. Remember, from now on you've got a park of your own, and you'll have to make a transfer of loyalty."

"Okay, chief," Bob said with a grin as he picked up his bag.

"And back up on that 'chief' stuff. I'm not your chief any longer. You're one yourself now."

For a moment the other looked puzzled. Then his face brightened. "Gad, you're right, Mac. Thanks for reminding me. Adios, and take care of yourself."

"Good luck," McMannon shouted after him as he went down the stairs. "And tell McDonald 'hello' for me."

Mitchell was waiting as the car shot around the corner of the barracks, and within a few moments they were streaking it down the road toward the northern entrance.

"You know, Mitch," said Bob as they passed the Mammoth Auto Camp, "I didn't say good-bye to a lot of 'em back there, but it was on purpose. Tell the bunch when you get back, will you."

"Yea, I'll tell 'em—that is," he added as the car skidded around a corner and headed down the straightaway, "I'll tell 'em if I ever *get* back. My gosh, you *are* in a hurry to leave."

Bob slowed down slightly as he passed out of the

entrance gate and struck the oiled highway which connected the park with Livingston.

"Well, that's over," he said softly as he straightened himself in the seat for the drive. "Remember, Mitch, the day you brought me up here?"

Mitchell nodded. "I was just thinkin' about that before you spoke. And remember what you said when you crossed the boundary for the first time?"

"Yea. Funny."

Both men smiled knowingly. Instead of entering it for the first time, Bob was now leaving the park—leaving Yellowstone. The thought was strange to him. He had come, at first, new and inexperienced, and now he was quitting it with sufficient knowledge and training back of him to take over the protection of another park. It still seemed like a dream. For the hundredth time his mind began to wander down the trail of the past two years—a trail blazed with experiences and friends which he could never forget. It was evident that Mitchell read his thoughts.

"Come out of it, kid," he said half gruffly. "That's over with. Talk about the weather."

Bob grinned and squinted at the sky. "It might rain."

"Hope it rains all summer," replied the other. "I haven't gotten over that Heart Lake fire yet."

"Two of us. Remember the lost pack train?"

Mitchell nodded. "Say!" he suddenly exclaimed, "they're goin' to come in handy."

"What?"

"These C.C.C. camps. Listen. Do you know what

it'll mean to have that many men ready to send into a fire?"

"Sure, I've thought of that. But did you ever stop to think that those men have been raised on the city streets, that not one out of ten of them ever saw a forest?"

Mitchell pondered the situation for half a mile. "Yes, but they're men, and that's what's needed usually. But I have a hunch the whole thing's going to be pretty much of a mess."

"Meaning what?"

"Oh, I dunno. Just look what we're up against. Just as you say, hundreds of kids, lots of 'em never been out of the city before. They'll be worse than tourists. The only animals they've seen have been in zoos. I can just picture 'em wanting to ride the bears. And most of 'em have never slept under canvas in their lives. I don't know."

"Well, I still think the President has the right idea."

"Sure, so do I. But there's goin' to be a lot of educating done before they'll be good for much."

Bob shifted the sun-shade to keep the light out of his eyes. "I've been so busy packing since I first heard about it that I don't know much more than I did," he said. "What's the setup?"

Mitchell lit a cigarette and settled back in the seat. "I dunno much about it either. We've got a little advance stuff from Washington, but that's all. As I understand it, the army is in with us on the project. It's not only for national parks, you understand. Camps are going in all over the country. Well, the army will construct and maintain these camps. Army men will be in charge of the boys from the time they leave the job in the afternoon till they go back on the next morning. Then we take 'em over during working hours. We plan the jobs, select our own foremen and see that the work's done. In other words we work 'em and the army feeds, clothes, sleeps and entertains 'em."

"It looks to me," Bob said after a moment, "that it's just as Mac said. It's going to be a mighty good chance to get some of the work done that's been piling up and for which we could never get sufficient appropriations."

"Yea," drawled Mitchell, "but I've got enough to worry about in the summer with dudes, let alone a bunch like this. Well, we'll see. Maybe it'll work out better than I think."

For several minutes the men were silent as the car roared down the highway, circled Emigrant Peak, and on toward Livingston. Then Mitchell spoke again.

"You know," he said, forgetting his recent orders to Bob to forget the subject, "in some ways it seems only yesterday."

How well Bob Flame remembered that spring morning when he had tossed his duffle into the back of Mitchell's car and they had come up this same road together. He recalled it all so plainly now—the manner in which the morning sun had fallen upon the peak which they had just passed, and the objects of interest which his companion had pointed out to him—Yankee Jim Canyon where Freeman had safely run the white water, the old buffalo jumpoff, and Cinnabar where the rails had stopped in the early days. He would never forget the thrill which his first sight of Electric Peak had brought, nor the emotion which swept him as he passed over the boundary for the first time.

"Too bad the East Gate isn't open yet," continued Mitchell. "Would have saved you quite a little."

"Yes," Bob nodded. "It's half a day longer this way but guess I can stand it. Wish you were going clear through with me."

"Don't *I?* Well, maybe I'll see you down there this fall. Always have wanted to take a squint at that place."

"Come on down. I'll show you a real park."

As they entered the outskirts of Livingston Mitchell turned to him suddenly. "Listen, fella. What say we eat at the same place we did that first night?"

"Sure thing," Bob replied with a grin.

They entered the lobby of the hotel and waved good-naturedly to the clerk. During the two years which had elapsed since he first visited the place, Bob had become well acquainted with him, for he had stopped overnight many times.

"Hey, Bob," called the clerk. "Just a minute, I've got a message for you."

"Sure it's for me?" the ranger asked, puzzled.

"I oughta know your name by this time."

"Yea," cut in Mitchell. "Maybe they don't want you after all."

For a moment Bob experienced a dizzy sensation. "What's the news?" he asked.

The clerk consulted a piece of paper. "McMannon just phoned. Said to tell you that a wire had come from McDonald . . ."

"Whad I tell you?" Mitchell grinned.

The clerk ignored the interruption and continued— "from McDonald saying he would meet you at the Forestry Club in Fort Collins Sunday morning. Where's that?" he asked curiously.

"Colorado," Bob replied.

"Gonna take a trip?"

"I've been transferred. Down to Rocky Mountain."

"Never heard of it."

Mitchell motioned hopelessly with his hands. "There you are, son, there you are. Nobody's ever heard of it. I think it's a fake."

Bob grinned. "Well, you're going to hear of it if I have anything to say about it."

"Well, good luck, Bob. Hate to see you go. You've been a good customer."

"Thanks," replied the other as they headed for the dining room. "Maybe I'll be back sometime and buy a room from you again."

After they were seated at the counter he said: "That's darn nice of McDonald to meet me. Now my job is to find Fort Collins by Sunday morning."

"Probably a good thing he *is* meetin' you," grunted the other. "Otherwise you'd probably lose yourself meanderin' around that state and never get to the park."

"And that's no lie," agreed Bob.

After having eaten, the two men walked slowly to the car. Mitchell took out his bag and snapped down the rumble seat. For a moment they stood looking at each other. Then Mitchell held out his hand.

"Well, kid," he said simply, "good luck."

Bob took the hand and wrung it warmly. He tried to speak but words refused to form. In an instant he felt very much alone and he knew that action was the only thing that could keep down the great lump which was rising in his throat. Without a word, he turned abruptly, got into the car and started the motor. With a brief wave he backed away from the curb and swung down the street heading eastward. Mitchell understood this sudden move for, as he watched the car disappear around the corner he, too, felt a lump in his throat.

CHAPTER III

MEETING MAC—AND THE MOUNTAINS!

IT WAS a bleak Sunday morning when Bob Flame left Cheyenne for the short run to Fort Collins. He had hoped to catch a view of the famous peaks of the Front Range, but a drizzling rain had commenced an hour before which made distant visibility impossible. Bedraggled jack rabbits huddled disconsolately under clumps of sagebrush while wet coyotes slunk across the road, their drooping tails dripping little streams of water as they went. It was not a morning to inspire cheer, Bob reflected—not a good morning to start a job; but, in spite of the weather and the poor visibility, he was far from downcast.

The country through which he was passing fascinated him. Bare Wyoming hills rolled monotonously as far as the eye could reach on every side. He had found interest in the old cattle town of Cheyenne, and every mile he had covered seemed enchanted with a mellowness of romantic history which it so rightfully claimed.

Over these sage-splashed hills had roamed war parties of Arapaho, Sioux and Cheyenne. Every inch of the land had been bitterly contested as the whites had driven their savage enemies back. These silent hills could tell weird stories of bloody fights, of unknown hardships and unsung heroes. It was a region which had known Bridger and Sublette and St. Vrain. It had seen these men and their companions fight desperately against terrific cold and the ever-present danger of being ambushed by hostile tribes. But it had also seen revelry of the rendezvous when the cares of the past trapping season were forgotten and the men came to the appointed meeting place to spend the days in trading and gambling and swapping yarns. Indians came, too, eager to dispose of their furs in return for a few bright trinkets. Later, after the fur trade had died out, came the long lines of covered wagons bearing pioneers to settle a western empire—to carve a new commonwealth with courage and brawn. Over these hills gallant blue-clad cavalry detachments had galloped to glory—or to death. Even after the Indians had been subdued there was still war, for the great cattle herds were endangered by the flocks of "hoofed locusts." Battles for the supremacy of the range had been waged between the cattle and sheep men until it seemed that this new land would never know peace. But peace had come at last, and with it prosperity. The splendid paved highway down which Bob drove spoke of a living tomorrow and a forgotten yesterday.

With these many things to occupy his mind, he found the trip to Fort Collins an enjoyable one. So rapidly did the time pass that he started in surprise to find himself within the limits of the little town. He knew the place by reputation, for it was from this school of forestry that so many men had gone into the Service.

After a brief inquiry he located the Forestry Club and, entering the building, he addressed the man behind the desk.

"Is Mr. McDonald here?"

The clerk looked puzzled.

"From Rocky Mountain National Park."

With this the man's face brightened. "Oh sure," he laughed, "Mac. I've always known him by 'Mac' since he was in school here. Almost forgot he had any other name. I think you'll find him in the lunch room."

Bob nodded his thanks and passed into the next room. There was no one at the counter, but in a booth he found a man reading a morning paper and leisurely sipping a cup of coffee. Bob grinned as he looked at the figure in the booth. It was evident that he had not been seen.

"And that, children," he said, "is how grandpa learned to ski."

The man looked up suddenly. "Well, I'm a—" he exclaimed springing to his feet. "Bob, you old such and such, how are you? Boy, you're a sight for sore eyes. Sit down."

"Assistant Superintendent McDonald," Bob grinned, looking across the table at his friend.

"Chief Ranger Flame," countered the other.

Both men laughed.

"Hey, waiter," called McDonald, "bring another cup of coffee." Then he turned to Bob. "Who'd have thought when we were floundering through those drifts on the Thorofare Patrol and sitting in Lake Station listening to Potts and Sedgewick throw the hooks into each other, that we'd ever end up like this?"

"Well, I didn't," Bob declared. "You could have knocked me over with a feather when they called me in and told me."

"I was pulling for you from this end," McDonald said seriously. "I've jeopardized my position and endangered my social standing. What lies I've told in the last month!"

Bob laughed. "Never mind your social standing, it never was too good. Tell me, how's everything—I mean the park?"

"Swell," beamed the other. "It's as different from Yellowstone as day is from night, but you'll like it. Guzzle that java and we'll roll up and look the place over. By the way, you're taking me up, you know."

"I'd supposed so."

"Yea. There was a Forestry Club meeting down here last night. One of the boys brought me down and then he went back."

Ten minutes later the two men emerged from the building and climbed into the car. The rain had stopped and the low-hanging blanket of clouds was rapidly breaking.

"Going to clear," McDonald prophesied as he squinted at the sky. "Good, because I want you to get a clear view of the place as you come in. It's really a knockout."

Bob started the car and, following his companion's instructions, headed down the road, through the town of Loveland and on into the canyon of the Big Thompson River.

The country had changed. From the level farming land in the vicinity of Fort Collins they had come suddenly into a world of brilliant color. Everywhere bright red sandstone rose in cliffs and hogbacks through which the road wound tediously.

"We get this red standstone all along the foothills,"
McDonald explained, "but it gives out a little way up
the canyon."

"Interesting country," commented Bob.

"Sure is. We often come down in this section hunting Indians."

"Doing *what?*"

McDonald laughed. "Hunting Indians. We're all
a bunch of nuts up there when it comes to Indian stuff,
and you'd be surprised the number of things this foot-
hill country will give up if you look carefully."

"This morning," Bob said, "as I was coming down
from Cheyenne, I got to thinking what interesting
stories that country could tell. Full of history."

The other nodded. "So is this. Interested in history, Bob?"

"Always have been."

"Good. See that road turning left?" He pointed
to a side road which meandered off and lost itself beyond the cherry orchards which skirted the road.
"Well, down there about a quarter of a mile are a
couple of old stone buildings. It used to be called
Namaqua and was a stage stop in the early days. Old
Mariana Modina, the first white settler in the region,
started it. Married a Blackfoot woman, and their son,
Louis Papa, is still in the country. An old man now."

As they penetrated deeper and deeper into the canyon the walls rose in sheer perpendicular cliffs until it
seemed that they shut out the sky. Beside the road
rushed the Big Thompson River whose source, according to McDonald, was to be found in the high mountain lakes within the park. As they progressed up the

gorge his companion continued to tell Bob interesting bits of information about the country through which they were passing.

"This region," he said, "was discovered about the same time as Yellowstone. Of course, Longs Peak was used as a landmark by the trappers on the plains in the early days, and it was probably seen by the early Spanish and French exploring expeditions, but not much was made of it until Joel Estes wandered in about 1859. He settled in the region and about ten years later things began to boom."

"Tell me this," Bob said suddenly, "something I've always wondered about. You hear of Estes Park and Rocky Mountain National Park. What's the score?"

His friend laughed. "That's always a pain in the neck, and everyone who comes in for the first time asks the same question. Well, it's this way. There are several big open areas in the Colorado Rockies known as 'parks.' There's North Park and Middle Park and South Park and Estes Park and a lot of others. Because Joel Estes was the first settler they called the open valley up there, as well as the surrounding vicinity, 'Estes Park.' The village took the same name. Then in 1915 Rocky Mountain National Park was established. Get it?"

"I get it now."

"Of course," continued the other, "Estes Park is famous the world over for its scenery, but not so many people have heard of the national park."

After an hour in the canyon they suddenly emerged.

"Wait a minute, Bob," said his friend. "I want you

to see this right. Give me the wheel and you keep your eyes closed till I say open 'em."

Bob did as he was told. After a few minutes his companion stopped the car.

"All right," he said, "take a look."

The scene which greeted Bob made him gasp. They had rounded several rocky shoulders and now, spread out in front of them, was a wide sweeping valley. Behind the valley, the most magnificent range of mountains he had ever seen arose with breath-taking abruptness. The jagged peaks lifted their summits to so great an altitude that many were hidden in the clouds. Along the crest of the chain, snow glistened in the sun. Longs Peak stood like a mighty sentinel, guarding the park and dwarfing even the highest of the other granite masses.

For fully a minute Bob was unable to speak. When he did his voice quavered. "I feel very small," he said simply. "It's the most beautiful thing I've ever seen in my life."

McDonald nodded. He understood that feeling. After he had lived with it for many months the view held the same awing majesty as it had when he had first seen it. He had watched many newcomers to the region who were completely overpowered by the humbling force of the range. The emotional stress had been too great and he had seen men weep like children.

"I know," he said softly. "It gets you."

Bob did not reply. There was something about the scene before him which made words meaningless. He had no method of expression.

"And this is only the first chapter," continued his

companion. "The middle of the book is the Trail Ridge Road, and the final chapter is the feeling you experience when you actually get into the gorges of the back country."

At length Bob found himself. "Why, Mac, I didn't dream anything like this existed. I'm absolutely weak. It's stupendous. Let's go. You drive. I want to look."

The car started on down the road. "You remember Dunraven's experiences in Yellowstone—the one for whom Dunraven Pass was named?" asked McDonald. "Yes."

"He came down here in the 70's and built a hotel near this spot. He was so impressed by the place that he let his enthusiasm run away with him and tried to prove up on a good many thousand acres. But they got wise and nipped the scheme in the bud."

"Well, I don't blame him," smiled Bob. "I'd have been tempted to do the same thing myself."

A mile beyond, the road suddenly rounded another shoulder and he found himself in the main street of the enchanting little village of Estes Park. It was so tucked away under the hills that one would never have dreamed of its existence. Bob looked approvingly at the place which was to be his home.

"Why, it's quite a place," he exclaimed.

"Sure it is. Several hundred live here all winter and in summer it literally swarms with people."

They drove down the long paved street, made a left hand turn to cross Fall River, which meandered its gurgling way lazily through the village, and stopped before a rustic building on the outskirts of town. A flag fluttered listlessly from a pole and Bob realized with a start that this was headquarters.

He recalled the trim appearance of Yellowstone headquarters with its rows of dignified stone buildings. Turning to his companion with a puzzled expression he said, "But where's the rest of it—I mean the quarters and shops and entrance gate?"

McDonald laughed. "You're from Yellowstone all right. I asked the same question when I came. Well, you see it's this way. You aren't in the park yet. In fact, you're about three miles from any of the gateways and the shops and quarters are out at the Utility Area. You'll have to remember, Bob, that Yellowstone got the jump on everyone else. The army built headquarters there and it was handed to us on a silver platter. Here the Park Service has done everything. And remember another thing. We're young. This park wasn't established till 1915."

They climbed out of the car and entered the building. The place was deserted, but Bob detected at once a friendly atmosphere of congeniality. "The boss is in Denver today," McDonald explained, "and there's no one else around. You see, we don't have a large staff. There's the superintendent, the assistant superintendent, chief ranger, park naturalist, and two clerks here. Then out at Utility there's the mechanics and the storehouse gang."

"How many rangers?"

McDonald grinned. "Hold everything. Four."

"Four!"

"Yea. I told you it was different, but when you get into the swing of it, you'll like it. Just because it's small and under-manned some people have the idea that we don't amount to much. But we've got a real job down here and it's all the more important because it *is* under-manned."

He led the way into a small, attractive office on the first floor. "This is yours, Bob," he said, "I herewith turn it over to you—desk, chair and pictures. Take it with love and kisses."

Bob's eyes sparkled. "Gives me quite a kick, having an office of my own."

The other nodded. "I know. You forget that I had exactly the same experiences two years ago that you're having today. I know just how everything strikes you and how you're reacting inside, because I remember how I felt. And I landed on a Sunday, too, and the little slam met me in Fort Collins."

"The what?"

McDonald laughed. "Oh, that's just a pet name for the assistant superintendent. The boss is the grand slam, and the assistant superintendent is the little slam."

There was already mail awaiting Bob and while McDonald busied himself with work which had accumulated during his absence, the new chief ranger looked over the pile of papers and notes on his desk. At length he sat back and examined the walls of the room. In front of him was a large fire map, similar to those which he had used in Yellowstone. He knew where McDonald had picked up that idea. He was about to speak of it to the man in the next room, but he suddenly recalled McMannon's advise and checked himself. Photographs of peaks and glaciers adorned the walls. This park *was* different. Here they dealt in mountains and ice and snow instead of in hot springs and geysers. It would be an entirely new life—and suddenly the realization that he had much to learn came over him. During the past week his mind had been busy making plans for an organization, but he saw now how futile such plans were without a knowledge of existing conditions. How impossible it was to compare the work of any two parks! Like attempting to compare the building of the Panama Canal with the construction of a New York skyscraper. Each park had its problems and nothing but a thorough understanding of those problems, obtained by living on the ground, would solve them.

He lit a cigarette and studied the photographs on the wall. There was a photograph of a man doing rope-work on an especially dangerous climb. He knew nothing of that. Another picture of McDonald standing on the very top of Longs Peak. Bob had never climbed a mountain in his life. There was still another photograph of a man making a sharp telemark curve on skis as he came down an unbelievably steep slope. Bob was used to plodding hour after hour through heavy snow. That was skiing of one kind, but telemarking at a lightning speed was something entirely different.

He was still deep in thought when McDonald came into the room.

"You know, Mac," he said slowly, "I've got a lot to learn?"

"What's the matter now?"

"Nothing, except I just made a discovery." He pointed to the pictures on the wall.

McDonald nodded. "Again 'I know.' When I came down here I'd plowed a lot of miles on skis and I thought I knew how to do it. But that first winter these old-timers taught me what real skiing is. Oh, forget it! It's just different and you'll pick it all up just as I did. Hungry?" he asked suddenly.

"Starved."

"Let's go down and get a bite to eat and then I'll show you around the dump. Here's still another difference. Up there we ate at the mess shack. Down here we're more civilized and eat in town."

Five minutes later they were seated in the dining room of a large hotel on the main street. "Most of the boys eat here," explained McDonald. "Just got into the habit and now it's more or less a bachelor headquarters. Mother, come here," he called to a tall friendly looking woman who had just entered the room and was moving among the tables chatting with her guests. She approached the table where they were seated with an easy air of western hospitality.

"Mother Wilson, this is Bob Flame, the new Chief Ranger."

"Hello, young man," smiled the woman, shaking Bob's hand and taking a seat beside them. "Sit down, sit down, your dinner'll get cold. We've been looking for you. Mac's been talking about your coming for a week. How do you like the place?"

"I just landed half an hour ago," Bob replied, "but from what I've seen of it I wish I'd come earlier."

"Atta boy!" she smiled. "You'll like it. You'd

better like it or we won't have you around. Well, I
must be going. Make yourself at home, Bob. We'd
like to have you eat here, but there's no law compelling
it. Even if you don't, drop in whenever you can."
With this she continued her journey through the dining room.

"I like her," grinned Bob. "Who is she?"

"Just Mother Wilson," was the reply. "Everybody
calls her that after they've eaten here a couple of times.
She's been in the park ever since Longs Peak was a
hole in the ground. Everyone knows her and she'd do
anything in the world for us. She's sort of a patron
saint for the boys around here. If any of us gets sick
she fusses like an old biddy until they bring him down
here, and then she usually takes care of him herself.
She's a good egg. We all take our troubles to her and
she can usually straighten us out."

The meal over, they were once again in the car,
heading south toward the range. Past the office and
through Beaver Point they went until Bob's head was
completely befuddled.

"I know just what you're thinking," McDonald
laughed as he turned off the main road and onto another which ran toward a group of green-roofed buildings. "You're thinking that you'll never get this road
system straightened out. But after a few days of wandering around you'll find your way about all right. This
is the Utility Area."

They entered a large fenced enclosure and, had his
friend not told him, Bob would have known that these
were government buildings. They possessed the characteristic low rustic appearance with the uniform green

roofs and light brown stain.   Again he looked puzzled and again McDonald read his thoughts.

"It's not as extensive a layout as they have up there, of course, but we'll have more sooner or later.   But we have shops and storage sheds and a warehouse and stables and comfortable quarters—everything the others have except they're not quite so large.   The way I feel about it is that we're just beginning and it's a swell chance to do some real pioneer work."

Bob smiled.   "That's what Mr. Wentworth said to me when I met him in Yellowstone."

"Sure.   That's the way we feel—all of us down here. Well here we are."   They had pulled up before a small one story building.   "I want to show you my pride and joy.   Has an equal place with Longs Peak in my affections."

"What?"

"The reddest little firetruck you ever laid eyes on."

"Firetruck?"

"Yea.   Wait and see."   He swung open the doors of the building and they went in.

At once Bob concluded that his friend had spoken truthfully.   It *was* the reddest firetruck he had ever seen.   Not only the reddest firetruck, but the reddest red.

"We designed it especially for use around here," McDonald said proudly.   "Isn't she a beauty?"

Bob looked at the truck and then turned a serious face toward his friend.   "Do they allow it on the road?"

"What d' you mean, allow it on the road.   Of course they do."

"Well, I'll hand it to you," laughed the other. "She's red."

"She comes in mighty handy for getting stuff there in a hurry," went on McDonald enthusiastically. "Especially good for roadside fires. Look her over."

Bob proceeded to examine the truck and the farther he went the more he forgot its brilliant paint. It was thoroughly equipped for every emergency—portable gasoline pumps, revolving searchlights, chemical tanks, as well as a huge water tank containing several hundred gallons. Along the sides were built-in compartments housing picks, shovels, back-pumps, hose and lanterns.

At length he turned to McDonald. "Nice going," he said approvingly. "I'll bet she comes in handy. And I'll even forget the color."

"She's okay. This fire shed is a new idea of ours. Everything's in here for an ordinary fire. These chests," he pointed to a row of rough wooden boxes along the wall, "are filled with tools. The contents is labeled on the outside. If we need ten men on a fire we just shove a ten-man chest into the truck and start rolling. No lost time checking things out of the warehouse. Then the loft is filled with blankets, fire rations, pack saddles, etc. Everything's right here ready to go. Of course on a big fire we have to draw on the warehouse, but that's not often."

They spent half an hour wandering over the area and looking through the various buildings. At the end of that time Bob fully realized that, although small, this park was efficiently equipped, and he had already begun to take a pride in these green-roofed buildings.

"Now," McDonald said, as they completed their tour, "I'm going to take you places."

"Where now?"

"I'm going to take you over the most spectacular road you've ever seen. We're going up the Trail Ridge Road."

"I've heard people rave about that," Bob said.

"Wait," McDonald replied confidently. "Prepare yourself for a thrill."

CHAPTER IV

THE HEIGHT OF THE JOB

THEY parked Bob's car in a large equipment shed and backed out a green government one.

"This is your wreck," McDonald explained as they got under way. "I've used it for a year but I'm getting a new one. She's not much on looks but I've found that it'll get you places. It's geared up and there's a high-compression head on her that'll take the hills as fast as you want to drive. I'll do the driving today because I want you to take in the scenery."

McDonald had said that the second chapter of the book would be the Trail Ridge Road and they had not gone many miles from the Utility Area before Bob realized what he had meant. For a short distance they wandered through open mountain meadows and valleys. Hundreds of deer dotted the sweeping hills, for it was still early in the season and there was abundant feed in the low country. A few scattered elk were seen, but most of these animals had already gone upward, following the snowline as it retreated day by day.

"Nice bunch," Bob commented as they stopped a moment to watch a large herd of deer grazing quietly in an open meadow.

His companion nodded. "They wintered pretty well, considering everything."

45

"Much trouble with coyotes?"

"No. We have a lot more deer than Yellowstone, and a lot fewer coyotes, so we don't have a predatory list. There's no problem here as there is in some of the parks. The coyotes get a few of the weak and sick ones, but they're welcome to them."

"I've always felt," said Bob, "that some people are a little haywire on the killing of coyotes. It seems to me that lots of people, especially Easterners, get just as much thrill out of seeing a coyote as a deer. It's getting so now that deer are pretty common, but it's seldom they see a coyote."

"Glad you're taking that attitude, Bob. Down here we feel that a coyote has just as much right to live as anything else, and we protect them accordingly."

"Most of the elk have gone higher, haven't they?"

"Yes. We don't have so many elk. There are several hundred here, but they were brought in a number of years ago. You see, the old-timers killed off all the original animals and so the park was restocked by the same species as originally lived here."

"Much trouble during hunting season?"

McDonald nodded seriously. "Yes. Lots of it. The deer drift down outside the park and even though it's a state game refuge the hunters do their best to get 'em. We have a merry time around here in the fall. Mostly people from Denver and the valley towns, but there are even a few of the locals who have the idea they've done something spectacular if they go out and get a deer. I can't see it. There'd be as much sport in it as shooting an old cow, but maybe you and I were raised wrong, Bob."

The other smiled and McDonald continued: "It's been especially bad during the depression because it was an opportunity to get free meat, even though it was a bit risky. Oh, you'll have your hands full during the hunting season."

Suddenly Bob realized that they were climbing. By wide sweeping curves which rapidly gained altitude the road had left the valley and was going steadily upward. Every curve brought a new and more spectacular panorama of snow-capped peaks. McDonald watched his friend's expression of amazement as these new vistas crowded one upon the other.

"You haven't seen anything yet, Bob. Wait till you get a little higher."

"It's stupendous," marveled the other. "I never saw such mountains in my life."

The man beside him smiled but said nothing. If there had been any doubt in his mind of Bob's enthusiasm for the new park, it was rapidly vanishing, and he knew that by the time they had completed the trip, Yellowstone would be entirely crowded out of first place in his affections. At length he said: "This is the highest through road in the world, Bob. Nearly twelve miles of it are above timberline and it reaches an altitude of 12,183 feet."

"How high are we now?"

"About eighty-five hundred. We started around seventy-five hundred. Here's Many Parks Curve." He pulled the car up at the side of the road and shut off the motor.

Bob sat speechless beside him. Below him was a series of parks arranging themselves one after the other and separated by glacial moraines. In ages past, tongues of the mighty ice sheets which had moved down from the great mountain cirques had covered the sweeping expanse before them. When they had withdrawn they had left high piles of gravel and boulders along their sides, and where each ice tongue had lain a beautiful mountain park had been formed. Beyond these parks, nearer now, but standing jagged against the sky, loomed the range. Its deep canyons seemed dark and mysterious where trees clothed the slopes. Above the trees—above timberline at the head of the canyons was the birthplace of glaciers. These great amphitheaters of granite which had been filled with ice in years gone by now lay bleak and rugged at the crest of the range. At that distance they seemed devoid of life as if even a tree could not exist amid that wilderness of stone.

Snowfields along the crest sparkled in the sun—snowfields which were deep and would remain throughout the greater portion of the summer. From these snowfields, and down through the gorges sparkling streams rushed, cutting the canyons ever deeper as they went. High as the backbone of the range seemed, Longs Peak towered still higher to dwarf the rest of the mountains. No snow lay on its crest, for there the terrific winds had swept the rocky faces bare.

For a long time Bob sat in silence. Then he said softly, half reverently, "For the benefit and enjoyment of the people."

His friend patted him on the shoulder. "It takes someone in the Service to appreciate what that means," he said. "And it's the same in every park. Somehow it makes you proud when you look at a scene like that to know that you have a part in it.   I've often wondered if the man who wrote the bill which created the first park ever thought how really great the words were that he incorporated in it—'for the benefit and enjoyment of the people.' "

"I've always remembered," Bob said at length, "what you told me that winter day at Park Point Cabin. Remember it had been so tough the day before with the fresh snow that we had to make a pit camp and spend the night out in the drifts.   And do you remember what you said?"

"I probably said 'damn.' "

"You did," Bob admitted, "but you said something more than that.   You said that rangers don't have publicity agents."

"Oh yes, I remember."

"That's always stuck with me, and the more I see of the service the more I realize that you were right. The things these boys go through that no one ever hears about—well, it sort of gets you.   There are a lot of battles that go on inside us that even the superintendent doesn't dream of.   And yet, when you look at a view like this, it's worth all the fights and heartaches, and you know you couldn't give it up."

"We miss a lot," McDonald said slowly.

"Sure we do. I know it. When I go to a city I feel like a hick. I'm not comfortable in a tux and I'm not always sure I'm using the right fork, and sometimes I get frightfully lonely—but it's worth the price. Remember Howe, Mac?" he asked suddenly, "the kid that cracked up on that Thumb Road Patrol?"

"Yes, I remember him."

"I had a long talk with him just before I left. He's pretty much in love with a girl up there, and at the same time he can't get park work out of his head."

"I thought he was going in for law."

"He is. His dad's a lawyer and he wants to take Dick into the firm. Carry on the name and all that stuff. But he'll never make a lawyer. His heart's in the service, not in a law office."

"Where does the girl fit in?"

"That's just the trouble. She doesn't. Dick's about decided to chuck law altogether and take the civil service exam for park ranger. But the girl———. Well, she's an awfully nice kid and I like her, but she'd never be the type for a ranger's wife. She spent a couple of summers in Yellowstone and it all sounds like a romantic dream to her."

"What's the answer?"

Bob shrugged his shoulders. "I don't know. It's up to Dick to find the answer. I gave him my best wishes and condolences all in one, and let it go at that. I've a hunch he'll work it out someway."

They started on again. Presently little drifts of unmelted snow became visible under the trees which bordered the road, and as they climbed these drifts became more and more numerous until the ground was covered.

"How far is it open?" Bob asked.

"Almost to Fall River Pass," replied the other, "and they have a good two week's work before it's clear to Grand Lake. Here's another view for you." He pulled up alongside the stone guard-rail and stopped the car. "That's the Mummy Range. This side is pretty well known and there are some trails into it, but very few people ever go beyond it. There are some lakes on the other side that aren't even on the map, and there's some country that I guess no one has ever seen."

"It's marvelous," Bob murmured as he looked across the wide valley to the semicircle of rugged, snow-capped peaks.

"That's a different range entirely. The one we first saw, with Longs Peak, was the Front Range, and this is the Mummy Range. Some of us like the Mummies even better than the Front."

"Tell me," Bob said slowly, "don't people get lost wandering around through that sort of country?"

McDonald nodded. His tone was serious as he replied: "That's one of the big jobs in summer— hunting people who lose themselves. Usually, of course, they find their way back, if they don't lose their head, but sometimes we spend days combing the mountains for them. And even then there are some who have never been found. In Yellowstone you had to keep 'em from walking into the hot pools. Down here you have to keep 'em from losing themselves, and when you fail in that you have to search for them."

A few miles further they gradually began to break from the heavy black forest of alpine spruce and fir which covered the slopes over which they were passing. Now the trees were scattered and grew in strange grotesque forms. No longer were they straight and true. Instead, they became twisted and distorted. Some lay prone on the ground, unable to lift their heads against the fury of the winds that swept the region. Only behind great boulders was the vegetation assuming a normal state of growth. Many of these grizzled giants of the timberline tree world bore branches on but one side, pointing with the wind. Growth on any other side was impossible. Yet here they grew, veterans of a thousand mountain storms, clinging tenaciously to the earth or anchoring their roots around a small boulder. Their battle for existence had deformed their bodies, but in that deformation they had grown strong and had held their place as the advance army of the tree legions which were to follow them.

Bob had caught glimpses of similar timberline country before, and once or twice he had passed through it, but never had he seen it in such magnitude, stretching as it did for unending miles along the crest of the range.

"Timberline," he breathed.

"Right. The most interesting and mysterious of all our mountain country."

"I've only seen it a few times," said Bob.

"You'll see plenty of it here," the other replied. "A good bit of this park is above timberline and you have to go through it every time you cross the range. Every pass we have is above timberline."

On they went until they were far above the line of trees, and nothing but great wind-swept barrens rolled on either side of the road. There was no sign of man in this region. No buildings were visible, no telephone wires, nothing but the highway which wound on and on across the bleak expanse to show that this was not virgin wilderness.

"Old Indian trail," McDonald said, pointing to a well-worn path. "This was Ute and Arapaho country. They used these trails in crossing the divide and the white men took over the trails when they came. It's interesting to know that, for quite a distance, this road follows the old trail."

"Is that how it got its name?"

"Trail Ridge, yes."

There was something dramatic about this, Bob thought. As he looked off across the rolling barrens the vision of an Indian march came to him. Dog and horse travois were there, moving in a steady line westward. Suddenly the picture faded and, after poising momentarily on the horizon, the procession dropped down the other side—over the Great Divide. In its place stood the highway, mounting with graceful curves until it too dropped over the crest of the range. The horse and dog travois were gone, no longer was moccasined tread of Arapaho and Ute felt along the streams or on the ridges. All this had passed and in its place stood a million dollar highway which led high-powered motor cars over long forgotten trails and hunting grounds.

So engrossed was he in these thoughts that Bob awoke with a start to find himself in the center of a blinding snowstorm. A short time before the sun had been shining brightly, but now the white flakes were pelting downward, making it impossible to see more than fifty feet ahead of the car. He turned to his companion in surprise.

"We get flurries like this up here very often," Mc-Donald explained. "As a rule they don't last long, but you can never tell. Offhand, I'd say that this will be over in twenty or thirty minutes, but no one but fools and tenderfeet prophesy weather in the mountains. Shall we go on?"

"You're the doctor."

"Okay, but let's put on the chains. We'll need them anyway, because it's tough going from here on."

Ten minutes later they started on again and Bob understood why his friend had suggested chains. They were passing through a series of cuts which the snow-plow had made through deep drifts. In these cuts the sun had had no opportunity to dry the road and it would have been impossible to negotiate them without the aid of chains.

By this time he could see the great paradox of the mountains. At the foot of the range it was spring and in the lower valleys of the foothills the ranchers were planting crops. Here men were fighting to open the road and they were traveling through snow canyons which sometimes reached the top of the car. Where the wind struck the slopes the road was clear, but in sheltered spots the snow accumulated in great drifts that were the fear of the tourists and the curse of engineers who opened the roads.

"This is the highest point we reach, Bob," his friend said as he swerved the car suddenly to avoid hitting a large piece of snow which had tumbled down from the white wall that hemmed them in.

"What altitude?"

"Just about 12,182 feet."

Bob whistled. "Highest I've ever been in my life."

Courtesy National Park Service

ABOVE TIMBERLINE ON THE TRAIL RIDGE ROAD

"How do you feel?"

"Fine."

"You'd know you were up in the air though if you got out and exercised. You'll get used to it."

"But I feel okay."

"Yes, you do as long as you're sitting in a car. But if you moved around very fast you'd be dizzy for a little while. I'm not going to give you a chance, however, because I want to get a look at the plow and head back. This stuff's getting thick."

"Nice place to spend the night," grinned Bob as he looked over the bleak expanse.

"Pretty desolate right here. You can't see much, but we have a mighty good name for this. We call it Tundra Curves."

Within a short time they rounded a bend in the road and heard the dull, labored sound of machinery. The snow was too thick for them to see far but Bob knew that a little way ahead of them men and heavy equipment were battling the elements to open a mountain pass. Slowly McDonald moved the car forward through the heavily falling snow. Suddenly he stopped and shut off the motor. A short distance beyond, a large bulk could be seen. It breathed with slow laborious sound as it fought the stubborn snowwall ahead. Men shouted orders through the white blanket. Suddenly operations ceased, a terse order was barked out followed by a dull explosion, then activity began. Bob knew that they had set off a charge of dynamite ahead of the steel monster in order to loosen the snow for another drive. Presently a white figure came toward them and stopped beside the car.

"Hi, Mac," he greeted. "Well, we're gettin' there."

"Mr. Ross, this is Bob Flame, the new Chief Ranger."

The two men shook hands warmly.

"Ross," explained McDonald, "is the engineer in charge of opening this road."

"I don't envy him the job," laughed Bob.

"Say, this is child's play. You should have been here before this road was built and we had to open the Fall River Road every year. Now that was somethin'. Didn't have a Snowgo then. Had to use steam shovels. Drifts thirty feet deep. Shovels couldn't reach to the top to get rid of the snow. In those days we . . ."

There was a metallic grating and the big machine ahead of them became silent.

"Blast 'em," roared the engineer. "They sheared it again. See you later Flame," he turned and strode back toward his work, barking orders as he went.

McDonald laughed and began backing the car out of the canyon. "Hard as nails," he said, "but his heart's as big as the whole outdoors. Many's the night he's sat up till morning watching over one of his men who had gotten hurt. He'd cuss him every time he woke up, but he'd tend him like a baby."

Backing to a level, wind-blown spot he turned around and headed down the road. Three times before reaching timberline they were obliged to use the shovel which McDonald took from the back of the car. In spite of the fact that little snow had actually fallen during the past hour, wind had collected the particles and piled them firmly in stubborn little drifts across the road. After each encounter Bob climbed back into the car breathing heavily.

"Boy," he said after they had removed the chains and were on the clear highway once more, "I believe we *are* up in the air. My head's as light as a feather." The other laughed. "Told you so. But you'll get used to that. You're a lot higher up than you've ever been before."

"I should think that lots of cars would get stuck, not knowing the danger of these small drifts. Surely everyone doesn't carry shovels."

"They do get stuck. Of course we all go equipped, but lots of people have the idea this is the same kind of snow they get in Denver and they have a lot of grief. I'll bet that before the road opens for good someone will get caught up here. There's a sign down at the entrance telling them that the road is impassable and that they can't get through, but they always know more than we do about it. So they come up, get stuck and we have to pull 'em out. Usually all the thanks we get is a good cussing for letting them go when we did our best to keep 'em off."

Bob laughed. "Same the world over, aren't they?"

"Sure are. A great institution—the American traveling public—but you love 'em anyway, God bless 'em."

As they neared the floor of the valley McDonald made a sudden left turn off the main highway and headed down into a beautiful little park.

"Going to take you down into Horseshoe Park," he explained. "We're going to have a C.C.C. camp there in a little while and you'd at least better know where it's going to be."

"When do they come in?"

"Middle of the week. You ought to spend some time concentrating on the stuff that's on your desk. Tells as much about it as we know about it."

Again they turned off the road, following an old lane into the timber and on a tiny mountain meadow, seemingly isolated from the rest of the world. Deer grazed on the brush or wandered listlessly about in the open. Nothing disturbed the peace and serenity of this little valley.

"It won't be like this in another week," McDonald mused. "There'll be trucks and men and tents and equipment, and everything will be confusion."

When they were on the road once more Bob's friend said: "We're doing all we can to buy up private property within the park boundaries—property of people who came in and homesteaded or bought before the park was established. See that area?" He pointed to a level plot of ground fifty yards off the road.

"What about it?"

"Thanks for the compliment. Two years ago a big resort stood there."

"Really?"

"Sure. We bought up the property, tore down the buildings, landscaped it and brought it back as nearly as possible to its natural state. I can see a big change every year. There used to be a mass of wire fences right here in Horseshoe Park, but they're all gone now and it looks pretty much as it did when the first settlers came. After all, that's the policy of the park service

—to keep everything in its natural state—and houses and barns and fences are a long way from how Nature made this country."

"Must be terribly expensive."

"It is, and it's not going to be done over night, but little by little we'll buy up the land and restore it to its original condition. Once it's that way it will be preserved for coming generations."

They returned to the Utility Area and drove into the group of trim brown cabins.

"I haven't said anything about living conditions yet, Bob," his companion said pulling up before one of the houses. "Of course it's up to you. You can have a cabin of your own if you want it or you can live with me. There's plenty of room and we can save rent. Take your choice."

Bob looked at McDonald seriously. After all, friend that he was, he was the Assistant Superintendent and a superior. He did not know how the situation would work out and he said so.

McDonald grinned. "That won't make any difference. We're a democratic lot down here and I'll be tickled to death to have you with me. The winter evenings *are* long."

"Check!" grinned Bob. "There's no argument. I'm in with you."

They shook hands and began carrying Bob's duffle into the little brown cabin which was to be his home during his stay in Rocky Mountain.

CHAPTER V

THE SIZE OF THE JOB

B OB was at the office early next morning, for he realized the size of the job that lay before him. He was taking over the protection of a park in which he had been less than twenty-four hours. The season was approaching with its host of complicated preparations. Not only was there the regular amount of work to be accomplished, but soon a camp of two hundred C.C.C. workers would be in their midst. He was going through a pile of correspondence and instructions when the Superintendent entered the office. He had not seen him since that night at Yellowstone.

"On the job already, I see," greeted the man, shaking hands with Bob and sitting down on the edge of his desk. "Well, you have a lot to do. This is going to be a hectic summer if I know anything about it."

The chief ranger looked at the pile of work on his desk. "Looks as if I'll have enough to keep me busy a little while," he grinned. "By the way, what's been done about the appointment of temporary rangers for this summer?"

At that moment McDonald entered the room. "Just bringing them to you, Bob. Hope you didn't mind our picking your staff for you this summer, but the appointments had to be in Washington, so we sent them

last week. Here's the line-up." He handed him a
large flat envelope filled with papers.

After the men had left, Bob studied the applications
of the appointees. Seven men had seen service before,
while eight were new. A fairly balanced force. He
decided that McDonald had made a good selection,
but he knew from past experience that a man's qualifications always look better on paper than they actually
are.

McDonald had supplied him with a list of important
subjects with which he should become familiar, and
by the end of the day he had informed himself roughly
on these principal points. He returned to the office that
evening, however, and it was after midnight when he
last locked the door and drove to Utility.

The following morning he phoned the three rangers
on that side of the divide and arranged a conference
for the afternoon. Mark Lee, who was stationed at
Grand Lake forty miles away, was unable to attend,
for many miles of snow-choked road separated him
from headquarters and the trip was impossible except
on skis.

At two o'clock Jack Anderson arrived from Wild
Basin, then George Frost from Utility and finally
Judd Hughes from Horseshoe Park. McDonald in-
troduced the men to Bob and then left them with him.

As they came in to meet their new chief he studied
them. Anderson, a graduate of a forestry school, was
tall. Bob liked his drawling speech and easy manner
and at once decided that nothing could upset this lad
who claimed the most isolated station in the park. Bob
smiled when Frost breezed into the room. He was

perhaps forty-five, chunky and with a good-natured
grin which immediately won affection. He had heard
of Frost. McDonald had told him the previous day
that he was the one to whom a former director had
referred as "the best darned ranger in the service."
Hughes was about the same age as Frost, perhaps
slightly older. There was something about the quiet
air of this little man as he sat before him puffing on his
pipe, that made Bob instinctively feel he could be de-
pended upon. It was he who had spent most of his
life in these mountains and he knew them as a mother
knows the face of her child. Hughes had played a part
in every important mountain rescue for many years,
because of his steel nerve and his knowledge of the
region. His bronzed complexion spoke of days in the
open—on foot, in the saddle or on skis in the alpine
snow fields. "Too bad Hughes didn't have a college
education," McDonald had said. "He's mighty interested in natural history, writes a little and is a pretty
fair archaeologist for just having picked the stuff up
and drawn his own conclusions."

As Bob looked at the three men before him his mind
drifted back to the large force of permanent rangers
in Yellowstone. Here were three, with a fourth "over
the hump" miles away. Four men to protect this park
against its enemies—fire and man; to keep four hundred square miles of rugged mountains and canyons
and lakes unspoiled. A hundred square miles to each
man. Although small, this area was visited by more
persons than Yellowstone each year. And four men
to protect it! Suddenly a wave of pity swept over him
as he saw the magnitude of their job. Then the pity

turned to admiration and respect, for they had done that job in the past and they would continue to do it in the future.

He shut the doors of his office and sat down. "Well," he said, "here you are, and here I am."

The men smiled.

"You probably know that this job of being chief ranger is a new one on me, and I'm just as green as any temporary that ever came into this park. It doesn't seem quite right for me to take charge of you because there are so many things I'm going to have to learn from you. Is there anything any of you want to say?"

There was no reply from the men.

"You're going to have to carry on about as you did before until I get on to the ropes," Bob continued. "I'd like to know just briefly what you've been doing so I can get a line on things. Anderson, suppose we start with you. What's your program been for the last week?"

Anderson cleared his throat. "Well," he drawled, "guess I've been doing about the same as always at this time of year. Where the snow wasn't too deep I've been clearing trails. Made a patrol to Thunder Lake Thursday. I have a little campground over there and I've been sort of cleaning that up getting ready for the season."

"You have the wild Basin District, don't you?"

"Yes."

"Hughes, what's been your program?"

The man took his pipe out of his mouth. "Well," he said, "I've been doin' about the same as Jack. I

went to Lawn Lake one day last week for snow measurements. Been doin' a little trail clearin' and takin'
care of my fish."

"Your fish?"

"Yes. I have a rearing pond in my district and it
takes a lot of time keeping the intake clear in this
high water."

"All right, Frost. What are your confessions?"

Frost grinned. "I haven't done a gosh darned thing.
I'm out at Utility waiting for something to happen.
Of course I've made my patrols, and I've kept pretty
close tab on the roads and I've been getting the stuff
ready for fish planting as soon as the trails open. Oh
yea, I went with McDonald one day last week to get
snow depths."

"What about the fish planting down here, Frost,"
Bob asked with interest. "When do you do it and
how?"

"Well, we usually wait till the trails are open and
we get some temporary rangers. Take 'em up in milk
cans on pack horses as far as we can an' then we use
the back cans where we can't use horses."

Bob had heard McDonald tell of the difficult task
of taking small fish to the high lakes for planting in
the spring and fall, and he knew it was one of the
annual jobs which was dreaded by the men. The back
cans of fish and water weighed sixty pounds apiece—
and more, and it was a gruelling task to clamber up
rocky slopes with these precious loads.

"Is there a federal hatchery here?" he asked.

"No, just a state one. All the fish put in here are

state property and that's why we have to require a license."

"Well," Bob said at length, "we'll get lined up on the fish planting a little later. I'd like to watch it. And, Anderson, I want to get into that country of yours as soon as I can. I hear it's beautiful."

"None better," drawled the other with as much enthusiasm as his characteristic slow speech would permit. "Fewer people get into it than any district in the park and it's the prettiest we have."

Hughes grunted disdainfully. "Wait'll you see mine. The Mummy Range has 'em all skinned."

"Why gosh darn you," yelped Frost. "I've got some country myself."

Bob laughed. "Well, I hope to see as much of it as possible before the season starts."

The meeting broke up shortly after this. When the rest had gone Hughes returned. "Mr. Flame," he said earnestly, "if you want to see any of this country I'll be glad to take you over it. I've been here a long time—longer than most of 'em, I guess. I know you're busy here at the office but if you want to go any Sunday just say the word and I'll have a couple of horses ready."

"Thanks Hughes," replied Bob warmly. "I do want to see it by trail just as soon as I can get away, but there's no need of you taking your Sundays to show it to me."

"Sunday's like any other day to me. I'll probably be out prowling around anyway and you might as well go with me."

The following morning McDonald brought another man into the office.

"Bob," he said, "I want you to know our park naturalist, Don Brent. He's been hibernating for the last two days and you haven't seen him."

As the two men shook hands McDonald continued: "Bob was pretty well acquainted with the naturalist in Yellowstone. He got along with him, so I guess you can make out with him."

The chief ranger laughed. "I guess we'll be able to hit it off, Brent. I've found that the naturalist departments have a pretty good bunch of eggs in them."

"Thanks," replied Brent. "That's more than a lot of people will admit."

"Oh, they'll learn. Give 'em time."

"The bunch here is fine that way," said the naturalist slowly, "but there's always a tendency for some people to have a hangover from the old moth-eaten idea that we wear black bow ties and spend our time chasing bugs."

Bob smiled. He knew what Brent meant, for he had heard several men in the naturalist forces of the various parks express the same idea.

"Takes time to sell something like that," he said. "You've probably been in the service longer than I have, Brent, but since I came in I can notice a big change in the attitude toward your work. If they'll cut out the clowning and take a little while to find out what it's all about, some of them will get their eyes open."

Brent looked at him sharply before he spoke. Then he said: "Something tells me we're going to hit it off,

Flame. By the way, I'm going to take a turn around through Horseshoe Park and back. Want to come along?"

Bob considered a moment. "Yes. I haven't been out for two days and I've got to learn something about this place. Besides, I'd like to take a look into some of the entrance stations. Do you have a key?"

Brent nodded. "Master key opens all of them."

It was not long before Bob was glad he had accepted the invitation. Brent proved to be an excellent guide and explained many things which had puzzled him. It soon became apparent that the naturalist had no special business that morning in Horseshoe Park or anywhere else, and that he was voluntarily devoting his time to showing Bob some of the region which he had not visited. After they had inspected the last entrance station Brent said: "I hope you don't think I'm just trying to make an impression on you, but I know exactly how you feel. When I came down here I'd have given a lot to have had someone show me around. Instead everyone was busy and I had to find my own way, so it took me quite a while to get on to things."

"Lord, no," laughed Bob, slapping the other on the back. "I'm green as they come and mighty glad to see all I can."

"Good! Can you spare another hour?"

Bob looked at his watch. "Sure. That will make it just lunch time. Where now?"

"I'd like to take you up to Bear Lake. It's one of the most visited spots in the park and I always enjoy the run up there."

They swung through the valleys and headed up a splendid oiled road toward the base of the range.

"They call this park a primer in glaciation," Brent remarked after they had progressed a few miles. He pointed to the long knifelike ridge along the base of which they were traveling. "And you can see why. That's the best example of a moraine that I've ever seen, and I've seen a lot of them."

Bob marveled at the ridge. He was not a geologist but it took little imagination to see the great ice mass as it had moved down from the mountains, crushing and gouging its way until it had completely remolded the topography.

"Of course you know that old story about the glacier," Brent continued. "It's a classic in geology—the one about where the glaciers have gone?"

"Don't believe I ever heard it."

"Well, it seems that a lady was much interested in the glacial boulders that were strewn over an area and she asked the guide how they got there. He informed her that the glaciers brought them down. She studied the situation for a minute and then asked 'But where are the glaciers now?' In desperation the guide replied, 'They've gone back after more rocks!' "

Bob chuckled.

"That story is as old as Longs Peak but it's always good for a laugh in a geology talk."

"How many glaciers do we have here?" asked the chief ranger at length.

"About five. Of course they're small but they have movement and that's one of the tests. You'll have to go up with us next fall when we take the measurements.

After the season each year, before the snows set in, we take accurate measurements to see how much they've melted back during the summer."

"I'd like to," Bob answered. Then: "You know, you fellows have interesting work."

Brent nodded. "Sure we do. I guess in the long run it's worth all the razzing we get."

By this time they were rapidly approaching the range. The Trail Ridge Highway had gone along the ridges and had offered wide sweeping panoramas while this road ran directly toward the great wall of mountains.

Bob looked up at the jagged granite masses that towered above him.

"I'll never get used to them," he said simply.

"I hope you never do," Brent said meaningly. "When you get used to them, they become commonplace and they are no longer good for a thrill. When these peaks don't make the prickles run up and down your spine every time you look at them, there's something wrong somewhere."

He parked the car at the large circular area which marked the termination of the road. "Let's walk up to the lake," he suggested, getting out. "It's only a hundred yards and you'll want to see the station anyway."

They walked to the shore of the quiet little mountain lake which nestled at the foot of Halletts Peak. A silence such as Bob had never known permeated the place. It was the silence of the wilderness, broken only by the sounds of nature. Waves lapped eagerly at the rocks, a jay cried savagely as he fluttered through the branches of a pine searching for cones. From somewhere a squirrel chattered his unwelcome. It was a silence filled with sounds of harmony. And over all hard, cold granite peaks looked down—peaks terrifying in their grandeur.

"Enjoy it while you can," Brent said softly, "because in a month it won't be like this. It'll be swarming with people and, in spite of all we can do, there'll be papers and tin cans about. It's a popular place and a noisy one in summer. You see, the road ends here and a great many trails begin—trails that lead into the back country. Then, too, there's a lodge at this point."

"Glacial?" Bob asked.

"Yea. Every lake in the park, except the beaver ponds, is just a big granite bowl scooped out by the ice and then filled with water. We have some of the most beautiful lakes in the world here. Wait till you see some of the higher ones at timberline. They're great!"

They spent a short time inspecting the ranger station and then started back. For a long time Bob was silent. Then he said, "You're sold on it, aren't you?"

Brent smiled. "I love it," he said, "and you'll find that everyone down here is the same way. I was transferred from Yosemite and up until then I thought that park was the most beautiful. But I'm sincere when I say that Rocky Mountain is the most beautiful park I've ever seen, and I've seen most of them. It would break my heart if I had to go anywhere else."

"It's the best I've ever seen," Bob sighed. "Every hour here the spell of it grows stronger."

Brent rolled up the window of the car. "Getting

ROCKY MOUNTAIN PERMANENT AND TEMPORARY RANGERS

TEMPORARY RANGERS PACKING FISH TO THE HIGHER LAKES

chilly," he remarked casually. For the past hour Bob had felt the cold chill of the high country but he had said nothing up to this time.

"You just beginning to notice it?" he grinned. "I've been frozen all day."

The naturalist squinted at the sky. "Well, I'm not a tenderfoot and I hope I'm not a fool," he said, "but it looks mighty much as if we're going to get a snow."

"Wind's in the east."

"Right direction. When it's in the west it usually just blows little squalls off the range, but when it's from the east you want to hold on to your hat."

"I didn't imagine we'd get storms this late in the year."

"Sure. I've seen some real ones in May."

Brent's prediction proved true and before they had finished lunch the flakes began sifting downward. They did not come as they had during Bob's trip over Trail Ridge, but with a slow earnestness which he had seen so often during heavy storms in Yellowstone.

"Guess we're in for one all right," Brent said as they entered the office.

McDonald, coming out of Wentworth's office, overheard the remark. "Yes," he smiled, "and we're in for more than snow tomorrow."

"Why?" Bob asked. "Anything wrong?"

"Nothing wrong, but if we get what it looks like we're going to get there'll be a sick bunch of army men when they pull in. We just got a wire that the advance crew and supply trucks will arrive about noon to set up camp."

Brent chuckled. "Oh, oh!"

"When do the gallant two hundred arrive?" asked the chief ranger.

"The wire said they'd be here forty-eight hours after the first bunch comes in. And here's why the snow isn't going to be especially welcome, outside of the fact that it'll be hard to establish camp. Do you know where most of the boys we're getting are from?"

Bob shook his head.

"Texas," laughed McDonald. "Texas where it's nice and warm and it never snows. I pity some of those lads because probably ninety per cent of them never saw snow before in their lives."

CHAPTER VI

THE CONSERVATION ARMY TAKES OVER

THE following morning Bob awoke to a white world. The snow had continued throughout the night and as he looked from his window there seemed to be little evidence of its subsiding.

The pines and firs about the cabin were slender white pyramids, and their branches sagged heavily under the mass which they supported. The air was still and no wind had disturbed the steady, silent fall. Smoke drifted lazily up into the morning air from the half dozen cabins of the area. It was a scene which might have been Christmas instead of May. Bob looked toward the range but a thick curtain of flakes shut out his view. So dense was the fall that he could scarcely see across the little valley to the level spot where the shops squatted like toy buildings in a store window. With difficulty he could see that there was already activity there. Trucks were backing out of the sheds or lining up before the gasoline pump for fueling, preparatory to the day's business. A foot of snow might fall unexpectedly on the region, but the work must go on.

He turned toward McDonald's cot, but the man was already sitting upright with an expression of amusement on his handsome tanned face.

"Soon," he said, jabbing his feet at a pair of leather

73

moccasins and slipping into a robe, "the marines will land."

Bob laughed. "And what a reception they're going to get. Imagine lighting in the middle of a snowstorm to set up camp! Wonder how they'll take it."

"Oh, they'll take it, all right. Anyway, there are only about fifteen of them in this advance outfit that's coming in today. The main bunch won't be in till day after tomorrow. I have a hunch we'll be able to pretty well size up the gang by the way they take this snow. If they crab, we're going to have tough sledding with them this summer; but if they accept it as just one of those things, I'm for 'em."

As they dressed the dull thudding of heavy equipment floated across the white expanse of Utility.

"They're out early," McDonald remarked.

Bob went to the window and looked toward the shops. A huge yellow snowplow was clearing the road for the day's activities. The whirling rotary blades were cutting into the white blockade and the fans were forcing the snow out of the funnel in a steady stream. Bob watched the column of snow as it gracefully left the machine, arched for a moment, and then lay in piles along the highway.

"How did that get down here?" he asked curiously. "I thought it was up on the pass."

"Oh, that's the other one. We have two. They come in handy, especially when we get an unexpected snow. We can never tell when one is going to come, but we're always prepared for the worst."

"We'd be pretty helpless without the plows in parks, wouldn't we?" Bob said as he turned from the window.

"I remember the first one I ever saw in Yellowstone."

"Helpless! We'd be paralyzed. When it snows here, it snows. I've seen a four-foot fall in thirty-six hours, and there would have been a lot of actual suffering if we hadn't been equipped to take care of it. A snow like that doesn't amount to anything in the high country when you're traveling on skis, but down here, with families scattered along the roads outside the park, it's serious. Even when that four-foot fall came we couldn't open 'em fast enough and lots of people had to ski to town for supplies."

Superintendent Wentworth reached the office soon after they arrived.

"Merry Christmas," he greeted as he closed the door and slipped out of his huge sheepskin coat. "Nice day for the army to pull in."

"That's just what we've been thinking," Bob replied, "I'm afraid they won't like the first glimpse of their new home."

McDonald turned from the window suddenly. "Say," he exclaimed, looking sharply at the superintendent, "I've got an idea. It'll be a mess trying to put up camp in this. Why not put them up out at the Utility bunkhouse and then they can take their time tomorrow about getting established."

Wentworth considered the proposition for a moment. "I believe that's the answer, Mac. Better phone out and have them build a fire. It'll be like a barn."

"Right," McDonald said, turning on his heel. "I'll take care of it." After a brief telephone conversation he returned. "All okay. They'll be comfortable enough out there."

The morning hours dragged slowly away. It was difficult to concentrate on anything like paper work, for at any minute a fleet of trucks might pull up to the office. Bob glanced through the open door of Wentworth's office and saw the superintendent in a characteristic pose. He had turned his swivel chair away from the desk, lit his pipe and was gazing moodily out of the window where the snow still sifted silently downward. It was a pose which Bob was to see many times during his years in Rocky Mountain. McDonald had told him of it previously and had said that anyone not knowing Wentworth might think that he was spending his time dreaming. "But," McDonald had continued, "I always know when the boss has something on his mind or is waiting for something to break. He always lights that pipe, swings his chair around and looks out of the window."

Noon came and they went to lunch in shifts in order that someone would be on hand when the army arrived. One o'clock came, two, and two-thirty. At three an olive drab car pulled up and came to a stop in front of the building. Two officers climbed out, stretched their stiff muscles for a moment and then came up the steps. Bob noticed the insignia at once. One of the men was a captain and the other a second lieutenant.

Wentworth came out of his office as they entered. "Captain Benton?" he asked, holding out his hand.

"The same. I suppose you're Wentworth. Lieutenant Anderson, Superintendent Wentworth. Gad, that fire feels good." He slipped out of his service coat and held his hands before the fireplace. "Come over and get warm, Fritz, we've got a job when those trucks get in. Well, Mr. Wentworth," he continued, turning to the superintendent. "We've had the devil's own time getting here. Trucks slipped off the road, cars got stuck and we ran out of gas."

The superintendent laughed. "This isn't a very cordial reception, Captain, but we're not responsible for the weather."

The captain shrugged his massive shoulders. "Don't let the weather worry you," he responded cheerfully. "I've soldiered in a lot worse weather than this. We'll make out okay."

"By the way," said Wentworth, "we've made arrangements for your men to sleep in the bunkhouse tonight. They'll be comfortable enough out there, and it's getting pretty late to set up camp, even if there wasn't a snow."

The captain smiled. "That's mighty kind of you, Mr. Wentworth. Fritz," he said, turning to his lieutenant, "there *is* a god that watches over soldiers like us!"

"You and the lieutenant can stay at the hotel in town if you like. You'll find the accommodations comfortable enough, I think."

But Benton shook his head. "Not for us. We'll stay with the men. When it's smooth going it's all right to live apart from them, but when it gets tough I'll take it with 'em. What about you, Fritzy Boy?"

"Right with you, Captain."

Wentworth called McDonald and Bob and introduced them. "You'll see quite a bit of them this summer, Captain. In fact you'll probably see them more than you do me."

They chatted for a moment together and then the captain glanced out of the window. "Well, Lafayette," he chuckled, "I see we've arrived."

Bob saw a huge army truck parked behind the captain's car. The box was covered by an arched brown canvas and in the cab he saw figures in the uniform of the army. There was something about the sight of that truck, waiting there in the snow, that gave him a thrill. On the side, in neat white, appeared the letters U.S.C.C.C.—United States Civilian Conservation Corps. Another truck rolled in and took its place behind the first. Then another and another until a long line of them was parked along the curb. There was an atmosphere of silent efficiency about these great trucks loaded with equipment and supplies. Bob had been too young to join the army during the war, but he remembered seeing long lines of trucks, similar to these, pulling in and out of the cantonments. Now he suddenly realized that another army had been recruited— an army which would fight as valorously as any other army had ever fought, but with different weapons and for a different cause.

Not until this moment did the realization of a conservation army crystallize in his mind. He had read correspondence and the neatly mimeographed instruction sheets in their crisp manila folders, but they had done little toward aiding him to formulate a picture of actuality. Now he was looking out of the window at a long line of businesslike trucks—the advance guard of an army to come. Suddenly he knew that this was big. He sensed the magnitude of this project which was to place thousands of men in the field, armed with picks and shovels and axes. They were fighting not alone for the conservation of forests and streams and wild life. They were fighting for the conservation of American ideals, fighting with a weapon the extent of whose power and influence was not realized even by the men who created it.

But now was not the time for musing. Wentworth was speaking.

"Mac," he said, "suppose you and Bob show Captain Benton the bunkhouse and see that they're comfortably settled."

Within ten minutes the fleet was under way again and the long line was rumbling down the road in the direction of Utility.

"This is mighty nice of you," Benton said after the trucks had been lined up in front of the bunkhouse and necessary equipment and supplies transported into the building. "It *would* have been rather a tough beginning to have to put up canvas in this snow."

"We're glad enough to do it," McDonald replied. "By the way, what time do you want to pull out in the morning? The place is about five miles from here."

"What's the weather going to do?"

McDonald squinted at the sky. The snow had ceased and it was becoming conspicuously lighter in the west. The thick cloud blanket which had hung low over the range had lifted, and the peaks, white with fresh snow, were visible.

"Say!" exclaimed the captain with enthusiasm, not giving the other an opportunity to answer his question.

"That *is* a sight. This assignment may not be so bad after all. Living with that makes up for a lot of things."

McDonald smiled. "We think so here. Why, it's safe to say the storm's over and you'll have a clear sky in a couple of hours. And I'm not a fool either," he added, winking at Bob.

The captain looked at him curiously.

"We have a saying that only fools and tenderfeet predict weather up here," Bob explained.

The captain grinned. "Thanks for the tip, I'll remember it. If it's going to clear I'd like to get this bunch under way as soon after eight as possible. The storm's delayed us and we'll have a lot to do before the main bunch arrives."

"Fine," McDonald said. "We'll be here and take you out."

They were about to climb into the car when a red-faced little sergeant who had been busy supervising the unloading approached them rapidly.

"Hey, ranger," he called, "wait a minute." He came up to them panting. "Say, just how high are we here?"

Bob looked at him and smiled. "About seventy-five hundred, aren't we, Mac?"

The other nodded. "Yes. Why, what's the matter?"

The sergeant sighed and shook his head sadly. "Boy," said he seriously, "I feel it. This blasted altitude gets my wind. They don't expect a guy to do much work up this high do they?"

The other two laughed and McDonald said: "Oh,

you'll get used to that. Wait'll you have to carry a fat woman down a trail on your back. That'll really make you puff. But a few of them will put you in trim."

The man looked at him with wide-eyed astonishment. "No kiddin', ranger, am I liable to have to do that?"

"No kiddin', soldier, you are," McDonald assured him earnestly.

"Oh, gosh," groaned the little sergeant as he turned toward the bunkhouse. "Why'd I ever leave the Islands?"

The following morning the fleet of trucks left Utility in a long line and wound up the road toward Little Horseshoe Park. The snowplow had worked the previous night and the road was clear, but the warm sun was rapidly converting the snow into rivulets which flowed down the highway in ever-increasing streams. Half an hour later they pulled into the isolated mountain valley which was to harbor the conservation army for many months to come. The drivers pulled their trucks up in a line and awaited orders.

Benton and his lieutenant stood beside Bob and McDonald surveying the scene. The little valley was a beautiful spot with its level floor bordered by white-barked aspen, and the Mummy Range lifting itself majestically beyond its rugged slopes, enhanced by the robe of fresh new snow. At that moment, however, the captain was unable to concentrate upon the scenic values of the spot. For several minutes he stood gazing at the eighteen inches of wet soggy snow. Then he said: "This place reminds me of a camp we once had in China. I don't know why, but it does. We set up the tents on a nice level flat that was made for the purpose. In fact, it had been a rice field at one time. Everything was lovely until——" He crushed his cigarette under foot as if attempting to blot out the memory of that encampment. "Everything was fine until a Chink went up and turned on the flood gates."

Everyone laughed.

"Well," he said suddenly, "I've got work to do. Much obliged to you for showing us in. Give us twenty-four hours and you won't know this place. Come on Fritzy, let's move."

He began barking orders. Men poured out of the trucks and immediately there was a scene of apparent confusion. As Bob watched, however, order began to disentangle itself from chaos in response to the captain's sharp commands. Men with shovels began clearing the snow, others unloaded tents and equipment, while trucks were dispatched to the village for supplies. They were still watching the activities when Brent drove up and climbed out of his car with photographic equipment. While the naturalist shot scenes of the work, McDonald and Bob returned to the office. Interesting as it was to watch the establishment of the first C.C.C. camp in any national park, the regular duties must be carried on.

Later that afternoon they drove back to Little Horseshoe. The change was astonishing. Captain Benton, no longer in full uniform, hurried here and there, an apparently tireless machine. He was coatless, his sleeves were rolled up and his shirt was open at the neck. On his head he wore a battered old campaign hat. He saw them and came up.

"Well, how does she look now?"

"Different!"

"Oh, we'll get lined out. Sorry I can't chat with you but I want to get these tents up before dark."

He hurried away to supervise the raising of another of the brown army squad tents. One by one they had gone up in a double row on the spot which had been cleared of snow. Smoke drifted up from the camp ovens as cooks prepared the evening meal. Equipment and supplies had been neatly stacked and covered with heavy tarpaulins.

"I never thought he'd be that far along," Bob admitted as they drove back to town.

"I guess Benton's able to do anything," McDonald replied. "I've heard of him before. Understand he's a slave driver but the men worship him. He's been working under pressure today though. Hadn't counted on the snow, and it set him back several hours. He'll be ready for them just the same."

By ten o'clock the following morning the village of Estes Park found itself completely occupied and taken over by the Conservation Army. Busses and trucks packed the streets, loaded with men fresh from the process camp at Fort Logan. There they had spent several weeks training, eating rough but wholesome food and acquainting themselves with camp life. There had been a weeding out process and only those who were capable had been assigned to duty. These men, most of whom were under twenty-five years of age had enlisted in the Corps for a definite period. They received one dollar a day and a certain amount of their monthly earnings was sent to dependents. But they did not care if the pay was small, or if the work was difficult. They had jobs, they were living in the open, and they were, as one was overheard to say, "having a whale of a time."

It was a howling, carefree lot that the busses carried up the road and into the camp at Little Horseshoe. Many of them had never seen snow and the majority had viewed mountains only from a distance if, indeed, they had seen them at all. The combination of snow and peaks, of streams and forests loosened the wild reckless spirit of youth on a holiday, and even the commanding officers were helpless to quiet them. Not until the busses rolled into the awaiting camp did the noise subside.

Bob stood beside McDonald and watched them unload. Sergeants called off names and the men were quickly formed into groups. Each group was escorted to its proper tent. As the procession passed by him Bob studied the faces of these boys. Every class was represented. There were boys who had never before been off the city streets, and there were boys who had never been on them; boys from farms and ranches; boys who had hitched and boys who had ridden the rods from Maine to California. Bob thought he had never seen such a heterogeneous group as the men who followed the sergeants to their respective quarters. Every race, every color and every creed seemed represented. He wondered what was going on in the minds of these boys as they trudged down the avenue of brown squad tents with their duffle bags slung over their shoulders.

Here was such an army as had never been recruited under the flag of any nation before. It was an army of construction instead of destruction, an army whose

name would live long after the economic forces which
gave it birth were forgotten. Bob's mind drifted
back to the wording of a bronze plaque which com-
memorated the first Director of the Service—"There
will never come an end to the good that he has done."
And it seemed to the man as he stood there watching
that line file past him that the words were equally ap-
plicable to the men of this group.

At that moment Captain Benton came up to them.
"Well," he smiled, "what do you think of them?"

"Looks like they've all come," McDonald remarked.
"I never saw such a mixture of color and race in my
life."

"It is a mixture," replied the captain slowly, "but
it's a good mixture, and a democratic one. I got to
know some of them pretty well at Fort Logan before
they came up. We have college graduates in that outfit and we have boys who have never seen the inside of
a schoolroom. This life is going to teach them both
something, and it's going to be a great leveling experience. It'll bring some of 'em up and some of 'em down.
Good thing to let one half know how the other half
lives occasionally."

"N.P. 1 C.," mused McDonald as he looked over
the brown tents. "National Park Camp One. The
first to be established in a park."

"And," the captain added proudly, "we're going to
make it the best camp in the outfit."

As they drove back to the village that evening Bob
was strangely silent. The things which he had seen
that day affected him greatly, and the pink reflection

of the sun on the peaks had driven him into still deeper silence.

"Why so quiet, old man?" McDonald asked at length. "Anything wrong?"

Bob shook his head. "Nothing wrong, Mac. I've just been thinking over what I've seen today."

"Makes one think, all right. It's a great undertaking."

"It's greater than we think, Mac."

"What do you mean?"

"That's what I've been thinking about," Bob replied. "Up to now we've been looking at this from a purely material angle. We've been thinking it was a great idea to get these boys off the street, to give them jobs and at the same time get something useful out of them. We've been thinking in terms of erosion control and fire lanes and roadside clean-up."

"Well?"

"Well, this thing's bigger than that. That's not what's going to live after these boys go back to their homes. The big thing—the thing that will live and the thing that will be felt for years to come—is what they learn. Listen, for twenty-five years we've been preaching conservation, and how much progress have we made? Mighty little. But think what it's going to mean to the country to have half a million boys go back into circulation who have *lived* conservation for all these months. They've lived it, and every mother's son of them is going to help for the rest of his life. Can you imagine any of those boys, after they've spent a year like this in the hills, who won't be a booster and who won't back up park policies for all he's worth?

That's what I mean when I say we haven't been looking deep enough."

"Gad," McDonald remarked softly, "I never thought of it that way, Bob."

Both men were silent for the remainder of the trip while the pink on the peaks gradually faded and night settled down on the mountain country.

CHAPTER VII

THE "BETTER MAN" OF THE C.C.C.

Two days after the arrival of the C.C.C. the snow had practically disappeared from the lower elevations. The warm days that followed the storm brought assurance that spring was a reality at last. Even McDonald was forced to withdraw his prophesy that a tourist car would have to be pulled out of the drifts on the Trail Ridge Road before summer.

"I back up," he admitted, "but you'll get a taste of it yet. If it's not a late spring storm it will be an early one in the fall. One season or the other you're bound to have trouble up there."

The days followed rapidly one on the other. Bob was kept so occupied familiarizing himself with the area and the routine of the work that he found it hard to realize another season was practically at hand. It seemed to him that there was never sufficient time to do all he wished to do that spring.

It was impossible for him to accompany Frost on the fish packing expeditions, much as he desired to visit the higher lakes of the park. He managed to drive to the end of the road one morning, however, just as a pack train was about to set out. The horses were heavily loaded, with a milk can filled with fish and water swung on each side. Other cans contained cracked ice, for it was necessary for the temperature of the water to be constant throughout the trip. The men carried large flat cans on their backs and, as he looked at them, empty though they now were, he secretly thanked his stars that he was a chief instead of a ranger.

"I wish I could kid myself into thinkin' these gosh darned cans are going to be this light all day," muttered Frost as he adjusted the shoulder straps on his can.

Bob realized that the boys dreaded this detail. These cans, when filled with fish and water, were far from light; and where they were used no trails ran. If trails had run to some of the high lakes the job of fish planting would be comparatively simple. But horses could not go where the men must travel, so when the country became too rough the precious cargo was transferred to back cans and men completed the work.

"It wouldn't be so bad," Frost said, still muttering to himself, "if I'd ever get a crack at these fish, but dog-gone it, in the spring those lakes are frozen and in the summer the dudes keep me busy and by the time they've gone the lakes are frozen again. I'm goin' to buy me a trout farm where I can fish all by myself."

At last the column moved on up the trail and Bob smiled as he watched Frost disappear around a bend beating time on the rump of a sleepy pack horse while he sang "Fishy, fishy in the brook," to the tune of "Onward Christian Soldiers."

Brent rode back to headquarters with Bob and throughout the trip the naturalist amused him with humorous incidents which had occurred during the fish-packing in previous years.

"Once," he said, "they were packing into Gorge Lakes. It's terribly rough over there and it's a good tough scramble, even without a pack, but they were taking in several thousand small fish. Some temporaries were doing the job, and it was a hot day. The temporaries sweated and cussed and climbed. They had ice with them to cool the fish, but that ran out before long and they were still quite a way from the lakes. Well, the further they went the hotter it got, and the more fish turned belly up. By the time they got to the lake every one of the fish had given up the ghost. There they had climbed all that distance and when they got there all they had were a few thousand dead fish and several gallons of water. They were a mad bunch when they pulled in that night."

Bob laughed. "I can imagine."

"Another time," Brent chuckled, "we had a temporary that was pretty cocky. The job went to his head and he was one of those typical wise guys. Well, Mac studied several days, and finally he hit upon something. He gave the fellow a can full of water without any fish in it; told him not to take the lid off—something about the equalization of pressure would harm the fish—until he got to the lake. He sent him on a pretty long trip—forgotten just what lake it was—but anyway when he got there the lake was frozen over solid. Of course Mac knew it would be. But the worst part of it was that the kid, after he couldn't plant the fish, brought that can of water all the way back. He was a pretty sore and pretty meek youngster when he found out he'd been carrying water instead of fish!"

It was not long after this that fifty C.C.C. men were assigned to Bob for insect control work. There were several badly infested areas which were in need of cleaning out before the adult insects emerged from the trees, and this was one of the first jobs which had been planned for the conservation army. Bob had secretly entertained doubts as to the amount of work these boys would do, once they got in the field, so a few days after the insect control work began he paid a visit to each of the areas.

As he came up the trail to where one of the gangs was working he paused unnoticed to look on. Crash followed crash as steel bit into the wood and the trees went down. No sooner had a trunk touched the ground than the boys were upon it, stripping it of branches, cutting it into lengths, and peeling. The branches and bark were promptly piled and burned and, at the signal "Take 'er away" the log chains were tightened about the trunks and tractors snaked them away to the base of the hill where they would be piled for firewood.

"The boys are getting quite a kick out of it, Mr. Flame," one of the foremen told him. "At first they didn't get the drift and they thought this idea of hunting bugs was a crazy one. Then I explained it to 'em. Peeled away the bark of a redtop and showed 'em the work. Showed 'em the tunnels and the larvae an' the adult beetles. Well they savvied what it was all about then. You know, already some of those kids can spot bug trees as far off as you can see 'em, and the other day I caught one of 'em putting some of the adults in a bottle. Asked him what he was doing that for and said he wanted to study 'em."

Bob walked back down the trail. All through the woods there was a sound of sawing and chopping. Smoke curled up from the burning piles of brush that harbored millions of forest enemies. Tractors sputtered and coughed as they snaked the logs down the hill and returned for more. Shouts of "Timberrrrr" rang out as the trees quivered, poised for a moment in mid-air, and then with a graceful sweep crashed downward.

The chief ranger grinned to himself. "Timberrrrr," he mused. "Hitting it like old-timers. Sound as if they'd been raised in the woods, and half of them have never been off the city streets. We'll make foresters out of that bunch yet." Any doubts which he had had were dispelled by what he saw that day. He had seen boys become men overnight. How different they were from the noisy carefree group which the busses had brought into camp. He was thoroughly satisfied with the results. The C.C.C. had swung to action and was digging in.

As much as possible Bob spent his time away from the office. He knew that he should familiarize himself with the park by personal contact as well as by paper knowledge of operations. Every Sunday found him in the saddle with Hughes, riding the trails. They covered the lower valleys which were the winter range of the elk and deer herds; they threaded canyons along rushing streams; they traveled the bleak windswept areas above timberline. Never was Bob sorry that he had selected Hughes as the man to guide him over the mountains and through the forests of this park. As McDonald had said, he knew every inch of the country intimately. He loved it and he never tired of revealing its enchanting valleys and lakes and peaks to those who would admire it with him. The more Bob was with Hughes the more he appreciated the man's knowledge of the region. Often he would abruptly cut off a trail and plunge down a steep slope to another trail below. There was never an explanation for these sudden departures, but never once did they fail to pick up a trail below the one upon which they had been traveling. Once they were caught in a terrific thunderstorm above timberline. Lightning played about the rocky terrain and danced from one peak to the other. Bob had heard of the danger which accompanied such a display when above timberline, and he looked anxiously at Hughes.

The other calmly dismounted and began leading his horse down a rough slope toward the shelter of a gully. "No use making yourself any higher than necessary," he remarked calmly as a bolt of lightning crashed a hundred yards behind them. "That stuff likes horses better than men," he continued cheerfully. "I remember once . . ."

"Never mind," grinned Bob. "Where are we going?"

Hughes pointed to a small shelter at the foot of the gully. "Built it once when I was up here watching sheep," he explained.

Twice after that they encountered storms, and each

time he led Bob to a shelter which was safely tucked away under a ridge.

"You have 'em everyplace, don't you?" Bob asked one day.

Hughes shrugged his shoulders. "After you've been in these hills as long as I have you'll know the quickest way to get out of a storm, too."

The more he saw of the isolated sections of the park the more Bob recalled what McDonald had said that first day about the high country being the final chapter of the book. As they traveled over the high trails, silent and deserted, and as they penetrated into the more inaccessible portions of the area, Bob felt a growing respect and awe for this mountain wilderness. He had never seen peaks rise in such sheer grandeur, nor had he ever experienced the vastness of deep canyons and the sweeping expanses above timberline until now.

Little by little he became familiar with the landmarks. He studied maps, and often, when they were in an unfamiliar region, Hughes would turn him loose and, far from a trail, allow him to find his way back. Occasionally he became confused; but he had spent sufficient time in the wilderness during the past few years to take notice unconsciously of his landmarks, and he could usually lead Hughes unerringly back to the starting point. The situation was incongruous—the idea of Hughes teaching him the country, when he was supposed to be in charge. One day he said so.

Hughes thought a moment. "No," he said slowly, "that's not strange. I was raised in these hills and I know 'em pretty well. And I've got enough sense to know that the parks have changed a lot from what they used to be."

"Meaning what?" Bob asked curiously.

"Why in the old days," Hughes went on, "the job was mostly protection. We roughnecks could do that job as well as the next fella. I mean we could track a poacher and fight a fire and hunt lost ones. But now, since more and more people are comin' into the hills, it's a different story. It's a job for trained an' educated men like you. I've been here longer than most of 'em, but I'm not begrudgin' anybody their job. You can handle your job a lot better than I could, and I figure I got a little the edge on you when it comes to knowin' the mountains. So we work together, see? Just so long as I've got a cabin and enough grub an' smokin' tobacco, I'll stick around. I'm not aimin' to leave this country again till I have to."

The speech touched Bob. There was loyalty in it and there was pathos.

"How long have you lived in this country, Judd?" he asked.

"Born here."

"You've been away from it, of course?"

Hughes nodded. "Yea. I was in the navy once an' then the army. I've spent time in the Philippines and Hawaii and China. I was with Pershing when he was in Mexico and I spent fourteen months in France."

Bob gasped. "Why, I had no idea you'd been that far, Judd."

Hughes grinned good-naturedly. "A lot of 'em don't know it. Oh, I've been around. But no matter where I am, I always have a hankerin' to get back here. The more you see of other places the more you appreciate the peace and quiet and bigness that this country's got."

Bob always remembered this conversation with Hughes, and the longer he stayed in Rocky Mountain the more it impressed him with its simple truth. Here was a man who had been born in the hills and who, after seeing the Orient, the South Seas, Mexico and Europe, was satisfied to return to the mountains he loved so well and spend the remainder of his days with them.

There came a Sunday when Bob felt he should not devote any more leisure time to seeing the country. Tourists were beginning to drift in on week-ends from the valley towns and, inasmuch as no temporaries had arrived, his place was in close contact with the highways. He was passing the entrance to Little Horseshoe when the thought came to him that it had been several days since he had seen Captain Benton. Accordingly he turned his car down the narrow road and pulled up before the headquarters tent. He found Benton alone, sitting disconsolately at his desk. As Bob entered he looked up.

"Did it ever occur to you," he asked moodily, "that we have absolutely no way of maintaining discipline?"

Bob sat down on a bench and looked at him quizzically.

"In the army," he continued, "we can put a man in the guardhouse, but this isn't the army."

"What's wrong?"

"Well, the boys usually have Saturday night to do as they please, and most of them go into the village."

A C.C.C. CAMP

NATIONAL DIRECTOR OF C.C.C., "BOB FECHNER," TALKING TO
A GROUP OF BOYS IN CAMP

Bob nodded.

"They went in last night. One of them got too much to drink and started a row."

"I hadn't heard."

"Well, he did, and from reports I guess he cleaned up on three or four before they could get him back to camp. All morning I've been racking my brain trying to figure some way to keep the boys under control —some penalty that can be inflicted in case of misconduct. We can't put them in a guardhouse and we can't cut their pay. There are only two things that can be done, and that's prevention rather than cure. We can reason with them and we can threaten discharge."

"From what I've seen of the boys," Bob replied, "I've a hunch you can reason with them. After all, they know why they're here and as a rule they're appreciative."

The captain got up and nodded. "That's the only conclusion I've reached." He opened the flap of his tent and called to one of the boys who was sitting outside. "Say, lad, will you go down and ask Tyron to come up here?"

Within a few minutes a short squatty individual entered the tent. It would not have been necessary for the captain to tell Bob that he had been in a fight. One eye was swollen shut. There was a long piece of tape over his cheek and a nasty cut on his lip.

For a moment the captain looked at him.

"You're a sight," he said at last. "Why didn't you duck?"

The boy before him grunted sullenly.

"I think," mused the captain, "that it might be a

good idea if we gave boxing lessons here at camp. What do you think, Chief?"

Bob was about to reply when the boy burst out: "Well, you sent for me. What do you want?"

"Sit down, Tyron, I want to talk to you."

The other sat down and defiantly lighted a cigarette.

"I hear you were drunk last night."

There was no reply.

"I said," the captain repeated in an even tone, "that I heard you were drunk last night."

"Well, what of it?" growled the other. "Sure I was drunk. What you goin' to do about it?"

"Tough, aren't you?"

"Yea, I'm tough."

"If you were in the army," the captain said quietly, "I'd know just what to do."

"But we aren't in the army," sneered the other. "I know. You're up a tree because you can't put us in the guardhouse and you ain't got any club to hold over our heads."

"You're absolutely correct, Tyron," Benton replied cheerfully. "I *am* up a tree. I'd hoped to be able to reason with you, because I don't want to discharge you. I've looked up your history, and you have a father and mother who are depending on you to help them."

The boy remained silent.

"Isn't that so?"

"Yea."

"And it would knock the props out from under them to have you discharged, wouldn't it?"

For a moment it seemed that the captain had won. Then the boy got up and faced him.

"Listen," he said, "don't pull that sob stuff on me. I'll get drunk when I want to and I'll fight when I want to, and you get that straight."

The captain also rose from his chair. "Oh, no you won't," he said evenly.

"And why won't I?"

"Because I'm going to take all the fight out of you, Tyron. You seem to prefer force to reason, so we'll try force." He walked rapidly to the door of the tent. "Oh, lad," he called, "I want you to round up everyone in camp and get them out in front of the mess hall. We're going to have a boxing match."

Ten minutes later a crowd had assembled. The captain, Bob and Tyron walked out of the tent and toward the group. As Benton adjusted his gloves he addressed the men.

"Most of you know," he said, "that Tyron here was drunk last night and that he got pretty rough. I've just been trying to reason with him and he has informed me that he'll fight at any time he feels like it. You all know that drinking is prohibited and he's also said that he'll get drunk whenever he wants to. It's occurred to me that you boys might like a little excitement this morning, so I've called you out." He stripped off his coat and shirt. "Now I haven't anything against Tyron at all," he continued, "but he's just one of these tough guys who admits it."

The crowd grinned knowingly. In the few days they had known their commanding officer they had learned to respect him. Most of them realized the situation and they knew that Benton was taking a very subtle method of maintaining discipline. They knew Tyron as a bully and a braggart and they crowded about the two curiously.

Someone dashed out of the camp kitchen with a dishpan and a large spoon.

"Two minute rounds," he shouted, "and no jabbing in the clinches." With this he struck the dishpan with the spoon.

There was never any doubt as to the outcome. Benton was outweighed by fifty pounds, but he made up for this in skill. He danced in and out, smashing blow after blow upon Tyron's face. The other attempted to cover up, but it was useless. He rushed the captain time after time, but these bull-like tactics were side-stepped and met with stiff jabs to the chin. At the end of ten minutes the boy was weaving groggily in the center of the circle. His hands were down and his knees were trembling.

"Knockout, knockout!" roared the crowd, but the captain removed his gloves and led Tyron to a nearby hydrant. He pushed his head under it and then took him to the tent. Bob followed.

When the boy had sufficiently recovered, he looked at the captain and a sheepish grin spread over his face.

"Say," he said, mopping his face with a towel, "you're all right. Guess I got you kind of wrong."

Benton smiled and patted him on the shoulder.

"I'm going to depend on you, Tyron, to help me run this camp," he said. "I'm going to need a lot of suggestions, and when you feel that some improvements can be made, let me know. By the way, how's the food?"

Tyron looked at him curiously, then he grinned again. "It's swell—only——"

"Only what?"

"Well, Captain, I like hot chocolate."

Benton smiled. "What about giving the boys their choice of coffee or hot chocolate on Sunday nights?"

Tyron beamed. "Great." He started toward the door and then he paused. "Say, Captain . . ."

"Yes."

"How about you and me gettin' together sometime where nobody can see us? I wanna learn how to duck."

CHAPTER VIII

THE PARK SPRINGS TO LIFE

THE morning of June 15th dawned bright and clear. New snow glistened on every peak and the air was fragrant with the odor of spring. There was something symbolic in the vivid freshness of that morning to Bob Flame as he drove to the office. His uniform was pressed, his stiff brimmed Stetson was cleaned and his boots were highly polished. This would be a memorable day for him, for June 15th marked the arrival of the temporary rangers. His rangers—the words sounded strange to him and he repeated them several times with secret satisfaction.

For a week the permanent men had been busy in preparation for the arrival of the temporaries who would assist them during the summer months. As always there had been much speculation regarding this man or that, for it was no easy task to select fifteen men from a photograph and a list of qualifications which each man himself had prepared. McDonald had smiled to himself as he had glanced over the applications and selected the staff before Bob's arrival. One youngster had written that he had once cooked a meal before an open fire and he felt sure he would measure up to the standard. Another had volunteered his services because of his ability to amuse the tourists on a saxophone, while still another wrote that his interest in the out-of-doors fully qualified him for the position. One by one the applications had been examined, and one by one the applicants had been discarded as unable to meet the rigid requirements. At last eight applications had been selected, eight letters sent and eight men were added to the list of those who would wear the forest green uniform for the first time that season. The other seven men had seen service before and had desired to return.

Entrance stations had been carefully checked to see that they contained the proper equipment. Gun seals and windshield stickers had been taken from their place of winter storage and placed in the little buildings which guarded the boundary, ready for use on the day when the park officially opened. Rocky Mountain was open throughout the entire year but, although there had been many visitors during the past few weeks, travel was not officially checked until the morning of the 16th. From that time on until September 20th the gates would be manned throughout the day. Then there would be a brief rest until they were reopened during the season of fall hunting, which was permitted in certain sections outside the park limits.

All of the important details had been performed by the permanent rangers, but many a task which could be postponed was left until the temporary men arrived. The attitude was aptly expressed in Frost's "gosh darn it, let those kids chop this wood. It'll do 'em good. They're the ones that burn it." And so the chopping of wood, or the thorough cleaning of cabins, or the final clearing of trails was put off with good-natured winks and chuckles.

"I'd like to see Fred's face when he sees that pile of wood," grinned Hughes. "How that boy loves a woodpile!"

"Yea," Frost had agreed, "an' I got a skillet that Carl left dirty last fall. I'm going to present it to him."

At nine o'clock that morning Bob sat at his deck waiting for something to happen. He had cleared it for work, for there were many other things to occupy his attention. He carefully checked over the various items on a list which lay before him. His station assignments were made; he had seen to it that Wilson and James were not placed at the same station, as McDonald had suggested; he had given Green the new motorcycle because of seniority; he had prepared a brief talk for the men. He hoped he had remembered everything. Suddenly he became aware that McDonald was standing in the doorway grinning down at him.

"And his boots are shined and his hair is combed and his uniform is pressed," chuckled the man. "What an example you are to American youth!"

"Nerts!" Bob responded as a wave of embarrassment swept over him.

"And do you have your speech all prepared?"

"Say, what is this?"

McDonald chuckled. "Oh, I know. I know exactly how you feel. I remember the first day I took over the outfit. Boy, your boots are dull compared to what mine were."

"I feel funny inside, Mac," Bob grinned back.

"Aw forget it! They're just another bunch of temporaries. You've seen hundreds of 'em before and they're all the same."

"Yea, I know, but these are *mine.*"

"Which, I suppose, makes them better than any you've ever seen," the other grunted. "Well, bear up. What time do they meet?"

"Ten o'clock. A few of them are hanging around the outside now. I'm signing 'em up as fast as they come in."

McDonald looked out of the window. "Here comes the judge!" he exclaimed. "He's been away on business since you came. Want you to meet him because you two will have a lot to do before the summer's over. All cases go before him, you know."

A man in uniform entered, greeted everyone in a jovial tone and then stopped in the doorway, eying McDonald disapprovingly.

"Well," he grunted.

"Well," McDonald responded.

"Just as dumb as ever," grumbled the judge.

"I've always been under the impression," said the other, "that a United States Commissioner should have some degree of dignity and bearing."

"Where'd you ever get such a silly idea?"

McDonald laughed. "Bob," he said, "I want you to meet the craziest and the most undignified commissioner in the service. He's not only undignified, but he's absolutely heartless when anyone's taken before him."

"Beeler's the name," the judge said, as he shook hands with Bob. "I don't think Mac ever knew. All right, big shot, you can go back to work. I want to talk to Flame." Whereupon he sat down and picked up a newspaper.

McDonald chuckled to himself and returned to his desk.

"Well, I see you're here," said the commissioner, without taking his eyes from the sheet.

"I'm here," Bob replied with equal brevity. He liked this man.

"You'll like it," said the other. It seemed that he possessed a faculty of carrying on a conversation and reading at the same time. He turned the pages of the paper, scanned it, paused to take in an article and then continued his search for items of interest. "Nice place. Nice bunch. Work like hell and don't get any credit. But you'll like it anyway." Then in a voice sufficiently loud for McDonald to hear: "This season I want you to clamp down on speeders. The former chief ranger never had the guts to do it. He was a sissy. I want you to bring me in at least one man a week." He ceased his talking for a moment while he gave a particularly interesting bit of news his undivided attention, then he continued in the same tone: "Funny about McDonald—he lacks nerve—afraid of hurting people's feelings. Your temporaries come in yet?"

"They're reporting this morning."

"Every year it's the same," the commissioner mused, laying aside the paper. "They come, you sign 'em up, talk to 'em, tell 'em to behave themselves and then send 'em out with a prayer you never expect to be answered. Say, are you interested in beaver?"

Bob nodded.

"Come out sometime. Have a whole zoo in my front yard. Guess I'll go out and get acquainted with some of the boys. See you later." He arose and glanced casually into McDonald's office. "So long, chicken-hearted."

Without looking up, McDonald reached into the drawer of his desk, drew out a .45 and placed it beside him. The commissioner sauntered out of the door, chuckling as he went. When he had left McDonald came into Bob's office.

"Well," he smiled, "that's the judge. Everybody knows him and there isn't a better loved man in the park. We all confide in him, from the superintendent down. When the world's all wrong and it looks like everything's against you, nine times out of ten the judge can straighten you out."

"What's the gag about being tender-hearted?"

"Oh, that whistle-neck! I'm always riding him because he never shows any mercy when anyone's brought before him for trial. Honestly, he puts the fear of God in 'em, but he's never unfair. I've seen him fine a man and then turn right around and loan him the money to pay the fine—always got the money back, too. He's a square shooter and everyone in the country knows it, but he certainly cracks down on 'em when they've really done something."

During the following months Bob learned that everything that McDonald had said about the judge was true, and more than once he stopped at the little log cabin on the Bear Lake Road to pour his troubles into sympathetic ears. There was something about the man that encouraged confidences and something else about him which made one know no confidence so given ever passed his lips.

One by one the temporaries arrived and, after signing the oath, assembled on the steps of the administration building. Bob was so familiar with the faces of his men through constant reference to their applications that he was able to call each by name. When the last oath had been signed, Wentworth stood before the group and talked to the men in an informal manner.

Try as he might, Bob could not concentrate on what the superintendent was saying. His eyes and mind kept shifting to this staff of rangers of which he was in charge. He must feel, he thought, much as an old hen when she takes stock of her brood. He was proud of this outfit—proud of the serious-faced lads who constituted it. As he looked at them, he wondered what the summer held in store. There would be triumphs for some and disappointments for others. Never since that first summer in Yellowstone had he seen a group of new men but what the vision came to him of Howe lying in the hospital as a result of a motorcycle crackup. Accidents were bound to happen in this business.

To the old men in this outfit who had served during previous seasons the meeting was "old stuff" as they expressed it; but to those wearing the forest green for the first time the words of Superintendent Wentworth were a sermon of inspiration. Bob knew that under these heavy new uniform coats the hearts of youth were beating loudly. He knew what was going on in their minds—the romance, the adventure of this ranger business—and he realized why those hearts were beating.

He remembered how he had slipped into a uniform for the first time at Old Faithful and how evident his pride must have been with his shining silver Badge of the Spread Eagle and his gold collar insignia. Hicks had called him a good-looking scamp. That seemed years ago. Suddenly he realized that it *had* been a long time, for he was now taking his place among the old men of the service. Stripes were accumulating on the left arm of his coat, each representing twelve months, and he no longer experienced the exuberance, the secret satisfaction, which comes when the snappy uniform of the National Park Rangers is worn for the first time. Instead, the uniform held a warm friendly feeling—a feeling which comes with long association. Bob was in the midst of these musings when he heard his name called. Wentworth had finished his talk and now it was Bob's turn.

For several moments he stood silently eying the group. Then he said: "I was just thinking of the thrill I had when I first wore the uniform. I know just how you new men feel because I felt that way once. To begin with, I want to say that you new men are in the same boat that I'm in this season. This is your first year here and it's also mine. We'll have to learn the ropes together."

Bob had prepared a talk, but in his earnestness he forgot to use it. He spoke to them of the traditions which were theirs to uphold. He told them what would be expected of each man throughout the summer. It was the same story which he had heard so many times, but as he talked it gained new meaning even to him. He had found hidden depths in the words of previous years. They held more now than they ever had before. At length he drew a sheet of paper from his pocket.

"It's more or less traditional in every park," he said, "to withhold the station assignments till the last. I don't know why we do it, unless it's because we want to enjoy life as long as possible. Just one word about these assignments. We've given a lot of thought as to where you are going to be placed this summer, and there is going to be no change in any assignment. If you don't like it, it's just too bad, because you're going to stick or else————"

An expectant hush fell over the group as Bob began reading the list. When he had finished he looked up and noted with amusement the mixture of satisfaction and disappointment registered on the faces.

"I'm glad to see you're all so pleased," he smiled cheerfully. "Now report to the ranger in charge of your district. Grand Lake men will also report to Frost and he'll see that you get over there. Good luck. Go out and hit the ball."

He turned on his heel, entered the building and sank into the chair at his desk. "Well, that's over," he sighed as McDonald came in.

"Nice goin', fella," responded the other. "The season's off to a flying start."

"Remember your first season, Mac?"

McDonald made a wry face. "I'll say I do. I was on the Shoshone Lake horse patrol all summer. Do

I remember it? Every time I think of that summer I shudder."

"Why? The Shoshone patrol's a good one."

"Sure it's a good one. But not when you have boils and have to sit on a horse all day long."

Bob laughed.

"I never dreamed," McDonald continued, "that there are so many ways to keep on top of a horse without actually sitting down. Try it sometime. It's a liberal education."

It was remarkable, Bob thought, as he took a turn around the main roads next morning, that such a change could take place over night. The park had suddenly sprung to life. From an apparently listless area, basking lazily in the June sunshine, it had become an efficient machine, functioning with ease and smoothness.

Flags fluttered briskly from the tall poles in front of entrance stations and cars lined the roads, each awaiting its turn to be checked through the gateway. Up and down the highways, the motor patrol carried on its daily routine. Not only did this sudden metamorphosis of the region impress him, but also the manner in which the new men had swung into the harness pleased Bob. Several times during the day he stopped to watch them at the gateways as they checked in the cars with the same efficiency that they might have been expected to show weeks later. It was much like a football team, he concluded, and already they were at mid-season form.

That evening he stayed at the office after hours,

listening to the reports of the gateways as they came in. Fall River, then Bear Lake, then Grand Lake, one after another in rapid succession they came over the wires. Ten minutes after the gates ceased work for the day he looked over the clerk's shoulder and had at his fingertips everything which had passed into the park since morning—cars, people, guns, horses, dogs. Even the weather at every gateway was recorded in its proper column.

After the reports were complete he strolled down to the little rustic museum which was situated near the administration building. He had paid several visits to the place previously, but he had never met the two naturalists who were assisting Brent during the summer season. He found the three talking together behind the desk.

"Thirty people to Sky Pond today, Bob," Brent said after introducing his assistants. "That's a good start on the season."

"The season's starting out too well," the other replied with a grin. "Do you ever have hunches?"

"Sometimes."

"Well, I have one now. I took a ride around today and I couldn't find anything wrong. Everything's working perfectly. I'm sceptical enough to believe that's a bad sign."

"Forget it," scoffed the naturalist. "You're a hard bird to please."

"Maybe, but . . ."

At that moment the telephone jangled loudly. It was the ring to be answered by the administration office.

"Anyone up there?" Brent asked casually.

"They've all gone," Bob said. "You'd better take it."

Accordingly the naturalist took the phone, but after a moment he passed it rapidly to the chief ranger.

"Twin Sisters Lookout reporting," came a voice over the wire. "There's a smoke on Glacier Creek about a half mile below Sprann's."

"Okay," snapped Bob. "Keep your eye on it." Then hanging up the receiver and turning to Brent: "I told you I had a hunch. Phone Frost. Tell him to take the truck and half a dozen men. It's on Glacier Creek, half a mile below Sprann's. I'll meet him there."

He was out of the building before Brent had time to reply. As he tore up the road and past Utility he saw men already running toward the fire house and he knew that Frost was on the job. Within ten minutes of the time the lookout had reported the smoke, Bob pulled his car up alongside the road below Sprann's resort.

Across the creek, a fire was blazing merrily away on a little knoll which was thickly covered with undergrowth. Although the forests of the park were in no great danger, the warm sun of the past few days had dried out the cover sufficiently to warrant prompt action in the case of the smallest blaze. Snatching an axe from the fire box in the rear of his car, Bob leaped across the creek and began clearing the brush which lay in the path of the flames. He was not alone many minutes, however, before the wail of the truck's siren came to him. As soon as Bob heard this he dropped his axe and ran to the road.

"A pump will do it," he shouted, as the red truck slid into position behind his own car.

There was no need to tell Frost what to do. He called instructions to the six men he had brought with him while Bob looked on with amusement. Frost was always the same, whether it was a small fire or a roaring inferno. Two men quickly unbuckled the left pump and carried it to the bank of the stream. Others began laying hose. The connections were made and, at a signal from Frost, the motor was turned over. It caught the first time, sputtered and coughed for a moment, and then settled down to a steady hum. The intake hose in the creek straightened as water was sucked through it. The flat string of hose running from the machine to the blaze suddenly came to life and straightened as water pounded through it. Then with a rush the stream reached the nozzle, doubled the force as it passed through, hurled itself against the fire.

For half an hour water was thrown against the knoll until the fire was not only extinguished, but the entire area was saturated. At last Bob nodded to Frost and the little pump became silent. Their ears rang from the continued staccato explosions.

"I wish they'd quiet those pumps down," grumbled Frost as they set about disconnecting the apparatus and replacing it in the truck. "Every one we get is noisier than the last one."

After the others had left, Bob carefully went over the burned area. Foot by foot he searched until he at last stopped suddenly and picked up an unburned bit of newspaper. Although muddy and water-soaked he was still able to make out some of the printing.

As he returned to town he stopped at Judge Beeler's to telephone every campground and every entrance. To each he gave the same instructions. "Pick up any car from Newton, Iowa. They're wanted for leaving a campfire burning."

After completing his calls he turned to the commissioner with a grin. "May bring you some business tomorrow, Judge."

The other grunted. "Bring 'em in. I haven't had a case for so long I've about forgotten the procedure. If I don't get something before long I'm going to try my wife."

CHAPTER IX

TROUBLES RING UP

THE fire on the first day of the season was but the beginning of a long series of events which strengthened Bob Flame's faith in his "hunches" as he put it. It was a summer filled with exciting and unfortunate circumstances which crowded one upon the other with disheartening rapidity.

During the first three weeks of the season the weather changed from warm to hot, bringing with it a high humidity. In spite of the most rigid regulations, eight fires broke out along the roads and trails. So often were the alarms sent down from the lookouts that the nerves of every man were near the breaking point. Every ring of the telephone seemed to foretell disaster of some kind.

At last, however, the rains came, the dry forests were saturated and the park breathed easily again, for all immediate danger was past. On one of these rainy days, Bob stood in the window of his office, looking out at the downpour with an expression of satisfaction on his face.

"That rain's music to my ears," he remarked, turning toward McDonald. "Another week and I'd have been ready for an institution."

"We've certainly had our share," agreed the other. "Now maybe we'll get a little peace."

Just then the telephone jangled loudly. "At least," Bob grinned, "that isn't a fire." Then as the buzzer sounded in his office, "but maybe somebody's drowned." He took up the receiver and answered. "Hello. Flame talking. What! Where . . . badly? How'd it happen . . . Never mind, I'll be right up."

He replaced the receiver and sat for an instant as if in a daze.

"Now what?" called McDonald.

"It's Wilson." Bob spoke the words mechanically. "Cracked up on that old motorcycle." Then rising from his desk, "Confound those old wrecks. I was afraid of that wheel, but Wilson insisted it was all right."

"How badly is he hurt?"

Bob shook his head. "Don't know yet. His leg's smashed and he's hurt inside. He's at Bear Lake Checking Station. Want to come?"

As the green government car roared up the road Bob's mind went back over the past few years. He remembered the day Howe had cracked up on the Thumb Road. Then it had been Smith and Stacy and Randall—all of them injured in the performance of duty. But they had pulled through and had come back for more the next year.

"Rotten luck," McDonald snapped, as they came within sight of the station. "Martin's here already," he added, noting the doctor's car in front of the building.

Wilson was lying on an army cot. Two white-faced temporary rangers stood near by. An ominous stillness filled the small room—a stillness broken only by the steady dripping of rain from the overhanging pines on to the roof. As the men entered the doctor looked up.

"He got a bad one," he said simply. "Unconscious. I've given him a hypo. We've got to get him to a Denver hospital as soon as possible."

"Bates," Bob snapped at a temporary who was in the room, "call the C.C.C. camp and have them get an ambulance over here as fast as they can. Tell 'em they're going to Denver, and to hell with speed regulations."

One by one the minutes dragged by. At last the doctor spoke: "I'm not so worried about his smash-up as I am about infection. He must have skidded a long way and he was plastered with mud."

The silence of the room stifled him, and Bob walked out of the door, unmindful of the rain. He felt utterly helpless, yet he was overwhelmed by a desire to help that still form which lay inside on the cot.

"How did it happen?" he asked Malley, who had followed him out.

For a moment the lad seemed reluctant to answer. Then he said, "It looked as if he just lost control."

Bob looked at him sharply but the boy avoided his eyes. "Lost control? A man who had ridden as much as Wilson?"

Malley made a hopeless gesture. When he faced Bob there were tears in his eyes.

"Listen," he said, half choking, "I'm his best friend. I've got to tell you something, because he won't ride any more this year."

MOTORCYCLE PATROL

CHECKING CARS IN AN AUTO CAMP

"Tell me what?" asked Bob, putting his hand on the other's shoulder. "What is it?"

"This is between you and me, Chief, and he'll never know I told you?"

"If you like."

"All right—he . . . he couldn't ride."

Bob started. "Couldn't ride—what do you mean? He'd been with the California Motorcycle Police for three years."

Malley shook his head. "He'd only been on a wheel once in his life when he came here."

"But he said . . ."

"I know. He told me all about it. His folks needed money—needed it bad. He told you he could ride and he said he's been with the police because he knew the park needed motorcycle men. It was his only chance to get a job."

Bob stood in utter amazement and looked at the boy before him.

"I'd known him before," Malley went on. "That first day he asked me to bring his wheel up here to the station for him. Made some excuse that he'd caught a ride or something. Then he told me everything. Each night after work we used to go up on an old road and I'd show him all I could about riding."

"You should have told me about this, Malley," Bob said sternly.

The ranger shook his head. "I promised him I wouldn't. Anyway he was getting along so well that I thought he could stick it out for the summer. He didn't want you to know, because he was afraid if you found out you'd fire him."

At that moment the big army ambulance came rumbling down the road and came to a stop in front of the station.   Malley gripped Bob's arm.

"See that he's taken care of," he pleaded.   "Give him the best of everything, and I'll pay for it . . . somehow."

Bob's hand closed over the boy's.   "He'll get the best of everything," he assured him, "and you won't have to pay for it.   The government takes care of that."

Tenderly they lifted Wilson upon a stretcher and placed him inside the ambulance.   An attendant climbed in and took his station beside him, the door closed and the big machine rolled speedily away down the road.

McDonald looked at his watch.   "Seventy miles," he calculated.   "With Red driving they should be there by five o'clock."

The doctor shook his head.   "They'd better be," he said simply.

McDonald said something in reply but Bob did not hear him.   He was thinking of the lad inside the ambulance.   Vaguely he wondered how many more boys he had with whom were living such fearful secrets.   Wearily he turned toward his car.

"Let's go back," he said.   "There's lots to be done and I'm going to Denver tonight."

Days of anxiety followed, as every man in the park awaited word from the hospital.   Each evening Bob drove the seventy miles and returned long after midnight.   The day at last came when they knew that Wilson would pull through.   He would not wear the forest green uniform again that season but he gamely challenged Malley to a motorcycle race down Estes Park road the next spring.

"He'll stick to a perambulator after this," was Bob's sternly pronounced verdict. But he had talked long and earnestly with the convalescent Wilson and knew that, no matter what the provocation for recklessness, he would look before he even leaped a pebble in his path hereafter.

Events kept crowding one upon the other after Wilson's accident. One morning in early August the commissioner sauntered into Bob's office, and sat down and without a word of greeting began to read the paper.

"Good morning, your honor," greeted the chief ranger.

The man did not reply.

"I said, 'good morning, your honor.' "

"I heard you," remarked the other at last, tossing his paper on the desk. "When are you going to send me some business?"

"You're a blood-thirsty cuss, aren't you?" Bob grinned. "Always wanting us to bring in some poor devil so you can soak him."

The judge yawned and stretched. "Things are disgustingly quiet," he complained, ignoring Bob's remark. "Why even Lindy Lou's getting so tame I have to run her off with a stick!"

"Lindy Lou?"

"Yea, my pet deer."

Bob was about to make a reply when the telephone rang and his buzzer sounded. After a brief conversation he hung up and looked at the other man. "Darn you," he grunted, "sometimes I think you're an omen of bad luck."

The judge blinked. "Something going to break this everlasting calm?"

"Yes. They think Bartlet is on his way over from Grand Lake with his car loaded."

The name immediately brought Judge Beeler out of his lethargic posture. Bartlet was a bootlegger who had been suspected of running liquor into the park for several seasons. In spite of all precautions, he had always succeeded in escaping detection at the time, however. On one or two occasions he had been stopped, but at such times he had managed to get rid of his cargo. Often it was known that he had passed through the park undetected for he had the habit of changing cars often and it was difficult to keep up with these frequent shifts.

"I can just see you licking your chops," Bob muttered. "Well, I hope you get a chance at him. Come on, let's see if we can scare up some excitement."

He got up and put on his hat. As he passed out of the door he spoke to the clerk at the front desk. "Phone all entrances to stop a gray coupe with a Denver license. It's a Ford with one man in it. Tell 'em to watch out for him, because he's liable to try to smash through. Have them report to you at once if they nab him. I'm going up the Trail Ridge Road and I'll phone you from the top."

A few minutes later they were humming up the road. Time after time Bob cut the power as a gray car appeared ahead of them, but they reached the top without incident. Immediately upon their arrival Bob phoned the office.

"No reports yet, Mr. Flame," said the clerk.

Bob hung up the receiver of the emergency telephone and scowled at the judge, who was blinking contentedly in the warm sunshine. It appeared that the man had lost all interest in the chase.

"He's given us the slip," grumbled Bob as he climbed back into the car and lit a cigarette.

"I don't think so," the judge mumbled.

"What do you mean?" snapped the other.

"Nothin', except you beat him up here. He isn't in a plane—just a car with four wheels."

Bob's face brightened as he looked at his watch. "Maybe you're right."

"*Maybe* I'm right! You held this wreck wide open all the way up here, and Bartlet isn't fool enough to do any speeding coming up the other side. He knows the patrol would pick him up, and he's in no hurry. By the way, why didn't they nab him when he went through the gate?"

"There was a new man on. Lee happened out of the station just in time to catch a glimpse of the car."

"Then this may be a wild goose chase and he may not even . . ." The judge never finished the sentence, for a gray coupe topped the ridge and, seeing the official car, shot down the road toward Estes Park.

Bob feverishly backed around and headed after him. Down the highway they went, missing other cars by a hair, skidding around corners in a cloud of dust and then on again. It had taken Bob but a few seconds to turn around, but those seconds had been too long for, although he held the throttle to the floorboard, he could not shorten the distance between him and the gray coupe.

They took a sharp corner on two wheels and the judge looked imploringly into Bob's grim face.

"After all," he said, "Bartlet's only a bootlegger—he isn't Al Capone, and as far as I know he's never killed anyone."

"I thought you wanted meat," gritted Bob. "I'm going to make you a nice present of some when I catch him."

The judge settled resignedly back in his seat. "I didn't say I wanted hamburger," he remarked dryly. "And to think—I just let some of my insurance lapse."

In spite of the breakneck speed at which they made the descent, they arrived at the valley floor without accident. The road forked and Bartlet turned right toward Bear Lake.

"They'll get him there," Bob shouted. "You'll hold court today after all."

But Bob was mistaken. The men at the entrance had received the warning, and they had backed an old Ford across the road, leaving only sufficient room for one car at a time to leave and enter. As luck would have it, no car was being checked when Bartlet arrived. Malley saw him coming and ran across the road, taking up his station directly in the path of the onrushing coupe. But Bartlett was not to be stopped and he headed straight for the ranger. It was evident that the bootlegger would willingly run him down in order to make his escape, and Malley sprang aside, not a moment too soon, as the car whizzed by him and disappeared around a bend in the road. He was out of the park and safe for the time being. Bob jumped out of his car and ran toward the phone, but Malley was there before him, snapping out information to the village police in sharp, concise tones.

"I'm sorry I lost my nerve," Malley said after he had completed the call. "But I didn't like the way the front of that car looked."

In spite of his disappointment at losing Bartlet, Bob laughed at the crestfallen look on the face of the temporary.

"I didn't know you *could* move so fast, Malley. You didn't get out of there any too soon at that."

Malley looked at him. "You're telling me?" he asked. "If you only knew it, I didn't move quick enough." He turned around and sorrowfully displayed a long rip in his trousers. "His fender is cracked," explained the boy, "and a jagged piece got my pants. Another inch and it would have been me instead."

Bob and Judge Beeler rode back to the office, the latter grumbling the entire distance for missing an opportunity to hold court that morning. As they pulled up in front of the building they saw Anderson's car parked in front.

"Wonder what Jack's doing over here," Bob mused and they climbed the stone steps.

His question was soon answered for they found Anderson sitting in the outer office with a man beside him. He was a little man, wearing wading boots, and fisherman's clothing in addition to a crestfallen expression. Bob knew at a glance what the charges would be.

"You stay where you are," Anderson ordered, addressing the little man. The other nodded silently and the ranger followed Bob into his office, closing the door after him.

"What's the matter, Jack?" asked the chief ranger.

"Three counts," replied the other, checking them off on his fingers. "Fishing without a license, undersized fish, and he had more than the limit."

Bob whistled. "The judge," he said solemnly, "had a bad night, and I think he ate hard-boiled eggs for breakfast. We just missed getting Bartlet. With that combination he'll slaughter the poor fellow."

"I feel kind of sorry for him myself," Jack admitted. "He's awful meek. But he had three things against him, so I brought him in."

Bob nodded. "All right, go to it, only if you get a chance tell the judge to go easy—tell him I'll set him to lunch. He'll be rough enough at best."

Anderson passed out of the door and Bob busied himself at his desk. Half an hour later he saw the man leave the building and he knew that the trial was over. Evidently the man had had money with him. Soon afterward Anderson came back.

Bob cringed. "Tell me the worst," he said. "How much did he give him?"

"How much do you think?"

"I have a hunch it was enough. From the way he was feeling this morning I wouldn't be surprised at forty dollars and costs."

Anderson grinned and put on his hat. "Bad guess," he said. "One buck and costs. You'd better buy him a lunch."

Bob chuckled to himself and he was still chuckling

when the judge walked in, looked at him and blinked.

"Well, I suppose you feel better now?" asked Bob.

"Uh huh."

The man at the desk laughed outright and the judge picked up the newspaper which he had discarded earlier in the day.

"What are you laughing at?" he grumbled.

"Your bark's worse than your bite, isn't it judge?"

The commissioner blinked again, rubbed his chin and put on his hat.

"Maybe," he said.

"Tell me," Bob asked curiously, "with all your bloodthirsty intentions why didn't you give him more?"

The other shrugged.

"Come on, tell me."

"Well," drawled the judge, "I knew him. Lives in Allens Park. Has seven kids and a sick wife. They've been living on fish all summer."

He started out of the door but Bob called to him. "Come on and go to lunch with me."

The man shook his head. "Can't. Got something else to do." He left the building muttering under his breath, "flour, eggs, bacon, beans, butter . . ."

Bob watched him drive toward town and wondered what mission was so important that it would force the judge to refuse a free meal. He did not see the man half an hour later, however, as he headed toward Allens Park with the back of his car full of supplies. He did not see him because Judge Beeler took a side road to avoid passing the office.

CHAPTER X

"SOMEONE MISSING"

AUGUST brought great crowds of visitors into the park. There had been a wave of intense heat throughout the middle-western states which had held the region in its sweltering grasp for weeks. Those who could came by the thousands to spend as much time as possible in the cool high altitudes of the Rockies. With this influx of tourists there was, by necessity, an increase in the activities of everyone on the park staff. Things began to happen when they were least expected. Speeders were brought in, and fires occurred by the score along the roads, now that the rains had passed. It seemed that someone was continually lost. No sooner was one missing party located than another was reported and the search was on again. So frequently did persons disappear, and so often were the rangers in the hills, that Bob sent out orders that no searching parties would be organized until the person had been missing for at least eighteen hours. This seemed logical to everyone, for the majority of those who were reported had either found their way back or had never been lost at all.

Hughes was in Bob's office one morning following an especially hard two-day search for a missing fisherman who, in the end, had phoned from Denver saying that he had gone there unexpectedly and was remaining a few days more.

"If they'd only tell us," Hughes grumbled. "Here we were wearin' ourselves out over in the Mummy Range huntin' a man who was havin' a swell time in Denver. I never saw such a season. It wouldn't be so bad if a woman would get lost occasionally, but it's always a man. Believe me, I'll be glad when it's over and the snows come."

Bob nodded. "It's been tough, all right, but when you get as many people as we've had this summer in a small area things are bound to happen."

"I suppose that's why there's so much news in New York City," the other observed dryly.

"Sure it is."

"Maybe," Hughes yawned. "Well, I'm going to bed. I haven't had any sleep for almost forty-eight hours."

The phone rang in the outer office and Bob's buzzer sounded. Both men looked at each other.

"That buzzer's been working overtime these last few weeks," Bob said as he picked up the receiver.

Hughes plugged his ears with his fingers. "I'm leaving," he declared. "Somebody's probably lost."

"You stay here. Maybe somebody left you a million."

Bob answered the phone and, after a brief conversation, hung up with a grin.

"Go on to bed. Why do people have to call me to find out what road to take to Grand Lake?"

Hughes slipped out of the door as if he were fearful that another phone call bearing ill news might come if he remained. The day proved to be uneventful, however, and Bob grasped the opportunity to obtain a full night's sleep by turning in at nine o'clock. He was so tired that he did not hear McDonald come in at eleven, but he was unable to sleep through the persistent jangling of the telephone which aroused him shortly after midnight.

After what seemed hours, he at last found the instrument and answered it, still groggy with deep sleep.

"Sorry to trouble you, Mr. Flame," came a voice over the wire. "This is Condon at Glacier Basin Campground."

"What's wrong?"

"I don't know that anything is, but there's a man and woman here whose son has been missing since early tonight."

While Condon was talking, Bob could hear a discordant chatter of voices in the station. It was evident that the man and woman were highly excited, for Condon turned to them and said: "Please be quiet. I'm doing all I can." Then, into the instrument: "It seems that he and another fellow climbed Flattop with the idea of going on to Taylor Peak. The other one got tired and came back, but the one who's missing, Nelson's his name, hadn't had enough. He said he was going to climb Taylor and get back by six o'clock. I hated to get you out of bed at this time of night but they insisted."

"That's all right," Bob said sleepily. It was the same story he had heard twenty times that summer. "Tell them that if he doesn't show up by noon tomorrow we'll send out a party. Make them see that if the kid has any sense he's probably up there asleep beside a fire. I imagine he stayed longer than he had planned and when it got dark he used his head and decided to spend the night there instead of coming down through strange country."

"I have told them that, and they still think something should be done tonight."

"Well, I'm sorry, Condon, but you'll have to make them see how useless it is to search for anyone at night. It's warm outside and he'll get along all right. You'd better go to bed yourself, if they'll let you, because, if he really is lost, we might have to call on you tomorrow. That's bad country up there."

He hung up the receiver and shuffled back to bed. McDonald stirred uncomfortably and then sat up as Bob sank upon his cot.

"I should have known better than to live with you," groaned the man. "How am I expected to get any sleep with your lady friends calling you up at midnight?"

"Nuts," Bob responded as he pulled the blankets over his head. "We've lost another one."

"That's three this week," McDonald calculated sleepily. "He'll probably show up for breakfast in the morning."

"Hope so. I'm thinking seriously of tying strings on everybody who goes out without a guide. Save a lot of trouble." Bob was going to make a rash guess as to the amount of string such a venture would require, but sleep overcame him and he knew no more until the alarm shrilled the following morning.

It was a clear day. The sun flooded the park and

the world would have seemed very good to Bob as he
drove away from Utility that morning had he been
able to get the midnight call out of his mind. Undoubtedly by this time the boy was well down from
the spot where he had spent the night. Still, a vague
anxiety clung to him through breakfast. Strange, he
thought, that such a feeling had not possessed him
with any of the others who had been lost that summer
—and all the others had come through. He was unable to shake off the feeling, however, and as soon as
he arrived at the office he called Condon.

"Heard anything from the missing one?" he asked.

"Not a thing yet," was the reply.

"How are his folks?"

"Crazy. That is they were last night. They seem
quieter this morning because it's light, but they're still
pretty shot."

"Maybe I'd better come up and talk to them."

"You won't have to," Condon responded. "They're
on their way down to see you."

"Okay," said Bob, "I'll be here at the office. What's
your guess?"

"Well, last night I thought he'd show up early this
morning, but now I've got a hunch."

"Funny," Bob muttered half to himself. "So have
I. What are you going to do today?"

"I was going to make a patrol over by Two Rivers."

The chief ranger considered for a moment. "You'd
better stay at home. We might need you. By the way,
did you know the kid?"

"The lost one? Yea. He's been in the campground
a couple of weeks."

"What about him?"

"Oh, he was a husky. Looked to me as if he could take care of himself. Been climbing most of the time since he came."

"All right, Condon. Phone me if you hear anything."

It was not long before a big gray sedan rolled up in front of the office and an elderly couple got out. In spite of their age they walked rapidly up the steps and entered the building. Bob's attitude toward the whole affair changed at a glance. He had hoped that these people would belong to a certain type which he knew well—a type which was given to emotional display if events did not materialize precisely as they had planned, but these were people who were not given to hysteria unless there was sufficient cause.

The man spoke first. "You are Mr. Flame?"

"Yes," Bob replied, "and I imagine you are the parents of the lad who hasn't appeared for breakfast."

"We are," the woman assured him, sinking into a chair. Her eyes were bloodshot and her hands trembled. "Can't you do something?"

"Let's hear all about it," Bob suggested cheerfully. "Then I hope we can be of some help."

"We've been camping up at Glacier Basin for about two weeks," the man began. "Our name is Nelson. We come from Ventura, California, and our son has done considerable climbing both here and in the Sierras. He's a member of a California Mountain Club and he is perfectly capable of taking care of himself under ordinary circumstances. That's why we both feel that he is in trouble."

Bob took up a pencil. "His name is . . . ?"

"Larry. Larry Nelson."

"When did he leave?" asked the other, making a note of the name.

"Yesterday morning. He and a boy camping next to us decided to climb Taylor's Peak. It seems that the other boy got tired when they reached Flat . . . Flat . . ."

"Flattop?"

"Yes, Flattop. He decided to come back but Larry went on. That's like Larry—if he started out to do anything he'd carry it through."

"What time did they separate?"

"About eleven o'clock yesterday morning."

"And the other boy returned yesterday afternoon?"

"Yes, about two o'clock. He said that Larry had gone on but that he would be back in time for dinner."

Bob considered mentally. Suddenly he knew that a tragedy of some kind had occurred on or near Flattop Mountain. If the boy had been unaccustomed to climbing there would have been a chance of his being lost, but they had said that he was an experienced mountaineer. The case was now doubly difficult, for it was far easier to locate a lost man who was physically fit, and who was able to respond to signals, than it was to locate a man who might be faint from pain or loss of blood.

He asked several other questions and learned that the lad was studying engineering, that he was twenty-two years old, that he had carried a small lunch wrapped in a Ventura newspaper and that he smoked and would, therefore, have a supply of matches.

After making these notations Bob arose and smiled. "I think we may be able to help you," he said, patting the woman on the shoulder. "He knew his way around in the hills, and probably as long as he was up on top of the range he thought he might as well climb a few more peaks. It's a long way up there, you know."

Yet as Bob spoke, he knew he was lying. The woman also knew, for she looked at him and said bravely: "Something has happened to my boy. If he said he'd be back he would have unless . . ." Her lips quivered and she did not complete the sentence.

After they had gone back to their camp Bob sat for several minutes, attempting to organize some plan of action. He called Hughes and Frost, informing them briefly of the details. It was arranged that they select half a dozen temporary rangers who could be spared and report at the office within an hour.

Even that hour was not one of idleness for Bob. He was not intimately acquainted with that country, although he had been through it sufficiently to realize that it contained thousands of rock slides, chimneys and ledges which might have proved a death-trap for the boy. Many of these chimneys looked as if they would afford an easy descent from the top, but they were treacherous and some even impossible to negotiate. He was carefully studying a large topographic map when Hughes entered the office.

"It's a good thing I got caught up on my sleep," the man greeted. "I might have known something would break. What's up?"

Bob turned a serious face toward the ranger. "Another one."

"We'll probably get up there, hunt for him all day and then when we get back we'll find out that he's been in camp for hours," grunted Hughes.

"I don't believe so," Bob replied, shaking his head. "I have a hunch that we've got a job on our hands this time. Did you get some temporaries?"

Hughes nodded. "They'll be waiting for us at Utility."

At that moment Frost blustered into the office. "Gosh darn!" he exploded. "Won't they ever quit losin' themselves?"

"Sit down," Bob said, "and I'll tell you about it."

Frost did not smoke, but Hughes lit his pipe and sat calmly puffing on it while Bob related the events of the past twelve hours. "So," he concluded, "I feel the kid's in trouble."

Hughes nodded. "Looks that way. If he's as good as they say he is he'd be back before now."

"I wish there was some law to keep 'em from wanderin' off alone," Frost snorted. "Why even we don't go through that country without someone along, if we can help it. And we know it like a book."

"I know," Bob said, rising and looking out of the window, "but you'd never get by with it. As soon as you'd put a regulation like that into effect people would begin to insist on their natural rights. They'd never realize that we were trying to do them a favor."

"Not to mention ourselves," Hughes put in quietly.

"Right. Not to mention ourselves."

"Same way with the East Face of Longs Peak,"

Hughes went on. "It's one of the most dangerous climbs in the park, but they insist on doing it. Just because somebody else did it, everybody has an idea they have to. I've taken three off that face after they made a misstep, and they weren't pretty things to look at."

"Been lucky this year, though," commented Frost, "not a one so far."

"Year isn't over yet," replied Hughes dryly.

Bob turned from the window. "Well, let's get down to business. You two know that country better than I do. There will be eight of you on the job and unless I'm needed I'll stay here."

"Any ideas?" Frost asked.

"Not especially. I've been studying this map and drawing on my memory. It seems to me that if he climbed Taylor Peak he wouldn't go clear back to the Flattop Trail when he started home. He'd more than likely cut down one of the gorges, possibly along the side of Taylor Glacier."

Hughes nodded. "That's logical. Chances are if he started down at all he's in one of those chimneys. He might have turned his ankle or broken a leg before he ever got to the peak."

"I'd suggest," Bob said, studying the map again, "that one of you take three men and go up the Flattop Trail as far over toward Taylor as you can before dark. The other one take three more men and look over the gorges from the foot of the range."

They spent a little more time making plans for the search and then drove to Utility where the six temporaries were awaiting their arrival with impatience.

Bob accompanied them this far and watched preparations for departure.

Ropes were carefully coiled, emergency rations were drawn from the storehouse and pack straps were thoroughly adjusted. Each man carried a revolver, for this was the quickest and easiest method of communication in such country.

"If you find anything, report to me at once," Bob instructed as they climbed into the cars. "If you don't find anything, we'll have to start a real search tomorrow. Let's hope you'll find the kid coming down the trail."

They left at eleven o'clock, and at one the parents of the lost boy called at the office.

"We have eight men up there now," Bob informed them, "and if they don't find anything I promise you we'll double that number tomorrow."

The older man looked at him. "I would like to go up there myself," he said.

Bob shook his head. "It's no place for one of your age," he said kindly. "It's hard country even for those who are used to it. You will be of more assistance to us by staying here so that we can reach you in case we need to get more information."

The afternoon dragged on and no word of any kind was received. Night fell on the mountain country and still no word. At nine o'clock Bob's phone rang. It was Condon at Glacier Basin.

"Mr. Flame," he said excitedly, "something's happened. Mrs. Nelson has disappeared."

"What's that?" Bob snapped. "Tell me about it —quick."

"Well, about eight o'clock," the ranger began, "Mr. Nelson came over here to the station to hear if we'd heard anything. He stayed about fifteen minutes and then left. Said he had to go back to his wife. He's here again now. Says when he got back to camp the car was gone and so was his wife."

Thoughts flashed through Bob's mind in rapid succession. A host of possibilities presented themselves, but only one of them seemed logical at the moment. A woman like that, whose son had been lost, would do anything which she imagined would assist in the search. He recalled vividly the strange look of determination on her face when he had seen her that afternoon. At the time he had thought little of it, but now—yes, that was the answer!

"Get a car quick," he instructed Condon, "and comb the road between there and Bear Lake. She's probably started out herself to hunt him. You'll find the car parked at the beginning of some trail and you'll find her on that trail. Be quick. Don't let her wander away."

Half an hour later the phone rang again. Bob was upon the instrument before it had ceased. Hughes' voice came over the wire. It sounded tired and far away.

"Not a trace," he reported. "We found where the kid had eaten his lunch about a mile toward Taylor from the Flattop Trail. You said it was wrapped in a Ventura newspaper, didn't you?"

"Yes."

"Well, that's it, but we didn't find anything else."

"Did you see a woman toward the lower end of the trail?"

"A woman! Is someone else lost now?"

"His mother has disappeared. Probably went to hunt him. Been gone about an hour and Condon is after her. Probably parked the car somewhere and started up some trail. She evidently snapped under the strain."

Bob heard Hughes groan.

"You'll find Condon's car some place along the road. You'd better go up the trail a little way and help him. He'll probably have to carry her back."

It was not long after this conversation before Condon called. They had found the woman, and Bob was right. They had come upon her crawling on her hands and knees up a rocky trail, weeping and moaning for her son.

Bob realized that further search that night was useless, but he spent several hours telephoning and organizing a larger party which would start at daylight the following morning.

When he at last turned out the light his sleep was filled with dreams. He saw a man lying somewhere up on the range, weak from exhaustion. A searching party passed within a few yards of him but he was too weak to cry out. When at last that picture faded, another of equal vividness took its place—a picture of an elderly woman crawling painfully over the rocks and boulders. Her shoes were worn through, her clothing was in rags and her hands were bleeding, but she went on and on through the night, searching for her boy.

CHAPTER XI

SEARCH

As a cold dawn broke over the range, men began to assemble at Bear Lake. They were not in uniform. Instead of forest green they wore the garb of the mountain climbers. Heavy shoes had replaced polished field boots and rough clothing was substituted for whipcord. Most of the men carried packs, some had ropes and many wore guns. Hughes was there, and Frost and Anderson. The rest, with the exception of Bob, were temporary rangers who had spent more than one season in the park and who were thoroughly familiar with the country.

As the last of the searchers arrived, Bob called them about him.

"You all know why we're here," he said. "There's a man up on the range and it's our job to find him. He's been missing for thirty-six hours and if he's still alive he'll probably be too weak to make much noise. There are thousands of places where he might be and we're going to look at every one of them."

He paused and studied the serious faces of the men before him.

"Everything points to the fact that he isn't lost. He's either badly hurt or dead. You men know this country better than I do, and this is no time for one who doesn't know it to head a group. We're going to split up into four parties of four men each. Hughes will head one and I'll go with him. We'll go up the Flattop Trail and then toward Taylor Peak. Frost will take another group to Andrews Glacier, up the side of the ice, and meet us on top. Anderson will take his group and hunt through Chaos Canyon, and then if he doesn't find anything there he'll spend the rest of the day in Glacier Gorge. It's barely possible the boy may have wandered in there. Malley, you've been here long enough so that you know the country pretty well. You'll hunt along the base and sides of Taylor Glacier. Lee is coming up the other side of the range from Grand Lake and he'll meet us on top about noon. Is that all clear?"

The men nodded.

"Look everywhere," Bob continued, "especially in the chimneys. He might have tried to come down one of them. If he wasn't too badly hurt, it's logical that he would crawl under some rocky ledge for shelter. If anyone finds him, fire three shots in rapid succession. Everyone will meet here tonight at seven o'clock. Now go to it—and be careful."

The various parties split up under their respective leaders and each took a different trail, but every route headed directly into the great rocky range which loomed in menacing silence above them. Somewhere in that rugged wilderness of granite lay a man, and if it was humanly possible they would find him.

Hupp and Tabor were the two temporaries who accompanied Bob and Hughes. Both men knew the country perfectly and it was not the first search of this kind which they had been on. Up they went toward the level summit of Flattop Mountain. Their pace, to the casual observer, was not one which might be expected under such a condition. It was a slow easy swing which covered the ground with the minimum of exertion. For the first mile the trail was well traveled, but they soon left this and struck the rough path leading to the summit.

In spite of the slow, steady pace, Bob's lungs burned. He had thought that he was in good condition, but he was no match for Hughes. The trail seemed endless as they mounted higher and higher. Through old forest burns they went, through the ranks of twisted and distorted timberline trees, and on until the bare windswept expanses of the peaks were all about them.

They spoke but little, for breath was too precious to waste in words. It was not until they were well up on the rocky slope with the forest spreading like a great black carpet below them, that they stopped to rest and hold conference.

"As nearly as I can make out," Hughes said, looking about him, "Nelson left the other kid somewhere around here and struck out for Taylor Peak. We found where he'd eaten lunch right in a dead line between here and Taylor. We know that he got that far at least. We went over everything yesterday, but there's always the chance of missing something in this country. Now I've got a suggestion, if Bob here . . ."

"Go ahead, Judd," said the other quickly. "You're in charge of this party."

"All right then. I want Hupp to go straight toward Taylor and climb it."

The temporary looked at him curiously.

"I want to know," Hughes explained, "if Nelson ever got to the top. If he did he probably put his name on the register. If he didn't get on top—well, that's something else again. Anytime you want to start, Hupp, go to it. Don't waste any time hunting, just go. We three will spread out and follow along the crest and see you later."

After a few minutes rest Hupp started toward the peak and the others followed at a slower pace. The ranger's figure became smaller and smaller in the distance until he could not longer be distinguished moving in and out among the boulders. The three men on the mountain moved forward slowly, searching in every likely looking crevice and behind every boulder which was large enough to conceal a man. It seemed to Bob that it was a hopeless task. There was an unending world of boulders for miles along the rugged crest of the range, and behind any one of these the body of Nelson might be lying. There was but one thing to do, however, and that was to continue the search hour after hour. Progress was difficult, and the men often slipped from the rocks, taking hard falls, only to climb to their feet and start on again.

Once Bob paused at the brink of Chaos Canyon and swept the great chasm with his glasses. How aptly named was this gorge, he thought, filled with giant blocks of cold gray granite as large as an ordinary house. They were piled in confusion, making travel so difficult that few persons had traversed the canyon from one end to the other. After careful search he was able to distinguish tiny moving specks far below where members of Anderson's party were laboriously combing the rough slopes. After watching them for a short time he continued on along the rim of the gorge. Their progress was so slow that it seemed negligible in such a country. Always the landscape appeared to remain the same, so vast was the sweeping area over which they were traveling. At last, however, Bob realized that the topography was actually changing, for the rough shoulders of Taylor Peak became larger and larger as they progressed.

It was after noon when they met Hupp coming back, hopping from the top of one rock to the other, or disappearing for several minutes as he made his way around an exceptionally large one.

"Any news?" Hughes shouted, as soon as he could make himself heard.

"He didn't climb it," Hupp shouted back.

Bob worked his way over toward Hughes. "What do you make of it?" he called.

"We don't know much more than we did. He either didn't sign the register or he didn't climb the peak, and that's that. I was hoping his name would be up there."

"Could he have mistaken some other Peak for Taylor?"

"Might have, but I doubt it. Not if he was as good as they say. No, I still have a feeling that he's this side of the peak."

Toward the middle of the afternoon Malley's party met them. "Darned if we found anything," the leader greeted. "Did you?"

"Not a thing," Hughes replied. "Wonder where Lee is. He should have been here before this."

Bob had been watching some distant objects with his glasses. "I think I see him now," he said. "There's a group coming along the edge."

"Well, if they came up the East Inlet, we've covered the whole top of the ridge as far as the boy would have been liable to go," Hughes said, looking far off toward the approaching party.

An hour of suspense followed before the two parties contacted each other—an hour which seemed interminable to Bob.

"Which way did you come?" was the first question asked.

"East Inlet," Lee replied. "Figured that was best."

"Didn't find anything, I suppose?" Hughes asked.

The other shook his head. "Not a sign. We met a couple of fishermen who've been in that country for the last three days, and they haven't seen or heard anything."

One of the temporaries shaded his eyes against the sun. "There's a bunch coming up from Andrew's Glacier," he exclaimed.

"It's Frost," Bob said, looking through his glasses. "They're still hunting, so that's out. What's to be done, Judd?" He looked at Hughes who was quietly smoking his pipe in the shade of a big rock.

The man glanced at the sun and calculated for a moment. "Three o'clock. We've got four hours of light left. Wait till Frost gets here and then I'd suggest we split up again and go back by way of the canyons. One outfit take Chaos and the other Tyndal Gorge."

Lee nodded his approval of the scheme. Bob recalled his view of Chaos Canyon that morning and he had no desire to make the descent that way, yet he knew that he would.

"Think I'd better go back the North Inlet," Lee said after a time. "And we'd better be moving, too, unless we want to get caught in Big Meadows after dark."

Bob, who had been silent for several minutes, spoke. "We've got to keep on with this hunt until all hope of finding him is past," he said. "I've been wondering if it wouldn't save time to establish a fly camp up in the timber. At least we wouldn't have this long climb every day to get up here before we began the search."

"Good idea," Hughes exclaimed.

"All right then, Lee. As soon as you reach an emergency telephone, get in touch with the storehouse and order equipment and supplies for ten men for three days. Get a truck rolling with it tonight. Have them leave it at the end of the trail. You get horses from Grand Lake and pick it up in the morning. Bring a packer and cook with you and make camp at the edge of the timber on the East Inlet. Understand?"

Lee nodded. "Sounds good to me," he said. "I don't relish this climb every morning."

The searchers from Grand Lake started down the trail with ten miles to cover before dark, while Hughes and his party spread out again and walked slowly toward Frost's oncoming group. They met within half an hour, but there was nothing new to report.

"Gosh darned ice," Frost sputtered. "I slipped and sat down." He ruefully displayed a great rip in the seat of his trousers. "That's stuff's cold, too."

They explained the plan to him and, after a short rest, the parties separated and headed down the treacherous canyons which led to Bear Lake. To Bob, who was unaccustomed to such country, the descent seemed particularly hazardous, but Hughes jumped from one rock to another, squeezed through cracks and lowered himself by his hands over ledges until it seemed that he was more animal than man. Yet, after what seemed hours of dangerous leaps and slides, he led them unerringly down into a little fringe of timber and to the shore of a wildly beautiful lake at timberline.

"No name," he explained to Bob as they rested a moment beside the water. "Few people have ever seen it. Shame too, it's so pretty."

Bob turned and looked back at the great wall of rock down which they had come. He was deeply grateful that the dangers of the laborious descent were over. The wall was cut deeply with chimneys and large vertical cracks, and covered with giant boulders which seemed delicately balanced on the very edge of the cliffs. Occasionally a rock would break free from the mass and go bouncing down the slope with a sickening hollow sound.

"Bad place," Hughes commented. "Rocks are always jumping around. I almost got mine there once. You were with me that time, weren't you, Tabor?"

The temporary nodded. "Yea, lightning fire, wasn't it?"

"A thousand places where a man might lie unnoticed," Bob mused as he looked at the wall. "Like hunting for a needle in a haystack."

Hughes agreed. "The worst place in the world to lose a man. He might be any place. Too many boulders and cracks and ledges. It'll only be luck if we ever run across him."

As they went down through the trees Hughes told Bob of another who had been lost during the early days. "Sort of pathetic," he said. "He'd done a lot of pokin' around in these hills. Spent all his summers out here. He was stayin' in Grand Lake the year they established the national park and he started across the range on foot to attend the ceremonies at Estes. He never got there. They looked for days and finally gave up. Found him last year. He'd broken his leg and had crawled in under a ledge for shelter and died there. No one ever knew until the engineers were surveyin' for a trail and found him."

It was long after dark when they at last reached the parking area but the other three groups were still waiting for them.

"Anything to report?" Bob asked.

They all shook their heads. "We didn't have any luck at all," Malley told him. "And I'll swear he isn't around Taylor Glacier."

"It's a cinch he's not in Glacier Gorge or Chaos Canyon," Anderson put in. "We scoured both places."

"We came down Chaos," Hughes told him, "but you can't say he isn't there. You can't say for sure that he isn't in any of the places we've looked today. In that kind of country we might pass within three feet of him and never see him."

"Well, I'll say that if he's anywhere around Tyndal Gorge I'd like to know where," Frost put in. "What do we do now?"

Everyone turned toward Bob.

"Sleep," he answered wearily. "We'll have it to do all over again tomorrow. Bring half a dozen boys, fresh ones if you have 'em, and meet here at the same time in the morning. Come prepared to spend at least two days up there. We'll sleep at a fly camp tomorrow night."

The program on the following day differed but little from that which had gone before. After hours of exhausting search through the rugged gorges and over windswept slopes, the men filed slowly into camp that night to sink by the fire, disheartened by their failure. After a hot meal Bob held a conference with the leaders of the various groups.

"I'm stumped," Hughes admitted, shaking his head, "but I'm darned certain he isn't in one of the canyons —no, I don't mean that, I mean that I don't think it'll do much good to look any more in the canyons. I still have a feeling that he's somewhere up here on top."

Frost nodded. "Me, too."

Bob sat in silence for several minutes. Then he said: "I have only one suggestion. I'd like to get fifty C.C.C. boys and spread them out twenty-five feet apart and go back and forth over this area. If that doesn't do any good, I'm beaten."

"That's an idea," Hughes exclaimed, "just so we don't lose some of them, too."

"I've thought of that," Bob replied, "but we'll have to risk it. And we'll have to get word to them at once. We want them here by sunrise."

The men looked at one another. It seemed a physical impossibility for any one of them to travel further that day. At last, however, Hughes got slowly to his feet and started to adjust a headlamp which he pulled from his pack. Bob watched him with admiration. Suddenly Frost saw what he was doing and sprang to his feet.

"Hey! Wait a minute," he yelped, reaching for his own light. "I'm going, you're not."

"Sit down, you old buzzard," grunted Hughes. "You stub your toe and get lost and then we'd have to hunt *you*."

"Why gosh darn . . ."

Bob turned to Hughes. "Hadn't you better get a couple of hours sleep?" he asked.

The man shook his head. "I'm all right. Should be to a phone by midnight."

"Aw, now listen," Frost protested, still fumbling with his light, "if he can go I guess I can, too."

"No kiddin', George," Hughes said seriously, "you'd better get some sleep yourself. The chief's goin' to need you tomorrow, because as soon as I bring that bunch in I'm goin' to crawl into the blankets and die."

Bob nodded. "He's right. No use of both of you wearing yourselves out."

Ten minutes later Hughes passed from the circle of

light and into the darkness beyond. Those around the fire watched his headlamp bobbing along the boulder-strewn crest of the ridge until it disappeared in the distance. Then one by one they sought their blankets and dropped into a heavy sleep.

Before daylight the following morning a steaming kettle of coffee and piles of flapjacks called the men from their beds. Breakfast was not long over when C.C.C. boys began to arrive. It was evident that the commanding officer had sent the best that he had, for they were all husky fellows, hard and brown from months of work in the timber. In spite of the exhausting journey which he had made, Hughes walked into camp among the first. He plainly showed the effect of his exertions, however. His eyes were bloodshot and his face was flushed.

"Here they are," he said as Bob came up. "Fifty of 'em. Count 'em and don't lose any. I'm . . . tired." He stretched out on a pile of blankets.

Bob brought him a steaming cup of coffee which he gulped down. After he had finished he grinned. "I shouldn't have drunk that."

"Why?"

"Might keep me awake." He sank back on the blankets and within a few seconds was asleep. Bob pulled the covers over him and drew the men to a far side of the camp.

Briefly he explained the situation, warning them to keep within sight of one another and to be careful of turned ankles. "Now," he said, "I want you to spread out about twenty-five feet apart. We'll head for that ridge over there and when we've reached it we'll take another strip and come back. It's going to be a tough day but it's our last chance of finding him."

Slowly, systematically, the long line moved back and forth across the rough, uneven summit of the range. There was no grumbling, even when Bob ordered but half an hour's rest at noon. They opened the sacks of emergency rations, drank hastily from seepage among the rocks and started on again.

As the hours passed even Bob began to lose hope. By four o'clock they had covered every foot of the ground without result. At four-thirty Frost caught up with him.

"Better call it off," he suggested. "The boys are dead and we've done everything we can do."

In his heart Bob knew Frost was right. He knew that they would never find the lost boy. When they returned to the fly camp Hughes voiced the same opinion.

"I don't think it's any use," he said. "We'd have found him before now. This is the fourth day, and we've combed the country. I've been on a lot of man hunts, but this has been the most thorough one I've ever seen."

His failure to locate the missing boy was a bitter disappointment to Bob. It was his first big job in Rocky Mountain and, although he had done everything that was humanly possible, he felt personally responsible for the unsuccessful outcome.

"Don't feel that way about it, Bob," Wentworth said to him several days later. "Even the boy's folks know you did everything you could to locate him.

They've gone back home resigned to the situation. Now forget it."

It was many weeks, however, before Bob could look upon the range without a feeling that he had been beaten. One day he said as much to McDonald.

The man nodded understandingly. "Listen, Bob," he said. "It's just one of the secrets which that bunch of granite holds. One of the many. You're going to have to get used to the range beating you. It's bigger than you are—it's bigger than any man, and it'll whip you a hundred times before you're through. You can't buck it and you might as well learn to take advantage of its moods."

Many times during his stay in Rocky Mountain Bob thought of what McDonald had told him that day, and in the end he himself came to realize that it was useless pounding out one's life and energy on that grim, silent range. Far better, he learned, to bow to it and to understand it, for, as McDonald had said, it was bigger than any man.

CHAPTER XII

SNOWBOUND ON TRAIL RIDGE

SEPTEMBER came at last and with it the usual exodus of park visitors. Those who had taken late vacations were due back at the office, schools were beginning, and so, immediately after Labor Day, the mountain area became all but deserted.

Bob found it difficult to realize that the summer was actually at an end. It had been one filled with problems and difficulties, but it had passed and now the park faced autumn with its accompanying tasks which must be completed before the snows set in.

Gradually the aspens were turning. From small isolated patches of gold on the slopes there grew a sea of color as these trees, like the willow and alder, responded to the crisp nights when frost crept down from the peaks. The color had started high, feeling its way downward until gradually every ravine and gorge was ablaze with yellows and reds.

"Funny," Bob muttered as he and McDonald drove toward Bear Lake one afternoon.

"What's funny?"

"That bunch of quakers. I've been watching the color for a week and every morning the colored portion's gotten bigger."

"Great sight in the fall," McDonald commented, stopping the car on a high vantage point and looking across the great masses of yellow aspen. "I've always wondered why more people don't take their vacations in the fall. They don't know what they miss."

"Well, when you take your vacation in Rocky Mountain," grinned Bob, "you can come in the fall."

"Bet your neck I will," the other maintained stoutly. "Fact is, I think I'll spend my honeymoon here."

Bob made a wry face. "Won't that be fun?" he grunted. "Come home for a nice honeymoon."

"You lack sentiment," McDonald observed.

"Skip it," the other replied, shoving the car into gear and stepping on the gas. "One of these days I've got to start thinking about putting rations in the snowshoe cabins."

Several days later Bob awoke to find the sky overcast. He had been in the west long enough to know when there was snow in the sky, and he turned to McDonald's cot in alarm.

"Say," he barked, "is this weather crazy?"

"Why?"

"Well, that looks like snow to me. Listen, man, there are a lot of things to do before winter comes— don't we have any fall in this country?"

McDonald laughed. "Keep your shirt on—or rather, put it on," he added, observing that Bob was still in his pajamas. "We'll have a month or six weeks of good weather yet. These flurries never amount to much. God always sends 'em to drive the tourists out of the park so we can get some rest before winter."

"Very thoughtful," admitted Bob as he squinted at the sky, "but I still don't like the looks of it."

"Oh, it's going to snow," yawned McDonald, getting out of bed and running his hands through his hair, "but it'll be over in a day or so. At that it might close Trail Ridge for a while. You'd better keep your eye on it and if it gets too thick have 'em block the road. You don't want anyone caught up there."

Before breakfast was over the snow had begun. By ten o'clock Bob had decided that it was time for the barricades to go up and he phoned Hughes on the east side as well as Lee on the west.

"We're taking no chances of anyone getting stuck up there," he told them.

It snowed for the greater part of the day. By late afternoon the clouds began to lift and a wind had sprung up. Before closing time Hughes came in stamping his feet.

"Boy," he exclaimed, "it's blowing up there!"

"Where have you been?" Bob demanded.

"I went up Trail Ridge as far as I could to see what it was doing."

"Bad?"

"Plenty. The wind's blowing a gale and it's drifting fast. Road'll be closed for three days at least, unless we put the plows on it."

"Nobody up there was there?" Bob asked anxiously.

Hughes shook his head. "Not as far as I went. The road crews pulled in last week and as far as I know there's nobody between here and Grand Lake."

"Good thing," the other commented as a cloud of wind-driven snow swished against the window pane. "These storms come in a hurry, don't they?"

"Sure do, but I smelled it last night. Sun'll come

out tomorrow, though, and unless we get a couple of days of cold weather this snow'll be gone in no time."

Toward evening it grew colder and even at lower altitudes the wind whipped the snow across roads in stubborn little drifts which made driving difficult. Going home after dinner that night Bob experienced a vague sense of uneasiness. The thought had occurred to him that there was still the possibility of some car being marooned on the road in spite of the precautions. He knew that long stretch above timberline would be a trap for any car on such a night. All evening he fought to dispel such thoughts.

"Forget it," McDonald grunted. "The road's blocked and nobody'd try to make it."

"But they might have been up there before we blockaded the road," Bob insisted.

McDonald considered. "Possible," he admitted, "but I doubt it."

"It would be just my luck to have some one kick off up there," muttered the man after he had walked the length of the room for the twentieth time.

"For the love of Pete, sit down," McDonald grinned good-naturedly. "You'll have me doing it, too."

Bob sat down and tried to read but his "hunch" persisted. At last he threw his book on the table and went to bed, hoping that by the following morning such thoughts would have vanished.

He was disappointed, however, for the idea hung over him like a cloud. After breakfast he called Hughes.

"We're going to take a trip," he announced.

"Where?"

"I've had a hunch ever since last night that some-one's up on the road, and we're going to find out."

He thought he heard Hughes groan, but the ranger replied, "All right, when do we start?"

"I'll get Frost to take us up as far as he can and then come back and pick us up this afternoon. Meet you in half an hour."

An hour after they left Horseshoe Park Ranger Station, Frost looked dubiously at a high drift ahead of him and shook his head.

"Gosh darned if she'll make it," he announced. "This crate'll go about any place, but I'd have to put skis on her to get through that one. You walk from here."

"Okay," Bob agreed cheerfully. "Meet us here at four o'clock."

He and Hughes climbed stiffly out of the car and started up the road on foot. It was not difficult traveling, for wind had blown the road clear for the greater portion of the distance, and drifts which would have spelled disaster to a car were packed sufficiently hard to allow the men to walk over them with no difficulty. At length they reached timberline. Here, as they passed over the crest of a ridge, the wind, unchecked by miles of country which offered no resistance, struck them full in the face.

"Did I say something about this stuff melting today?" Hughes shouted as he pulled down the fur tabs of his cap to protect his cheeks against the sharp wind.

"You said something like that," Bob shouted back, "but I didn't believe you."

Progress was slower now, and harder, but they

struggled on across the barren snow-dotted expanse. They could see a mile ahead and no cars were in sight, but that portion of the road upon which lay the heaviest drifts was still out of sight, beyond a rocky shoulder. When at last they reached it and were able to look far across to where the highway wound up the slope at Tundra Curves, Bob gave a shout and pointed. There, resting motionless on the snow-choked road, were three dark shapes—cars marooned in the drifts above timberline.

"Guess your hunch was right," Hughes admitted, crouching in the protection of a granite boulder. "I wasn't sold on the idea of this pleasure trip up here, but it's a good thing we came."

"I don't have 'em often," Bob replied, "but when I do have a hunch there's usually something back of it. Come on."

They did not keep to the road now. Instead they started off across the slopes, walking over drifts and around the rocks but heading always for a little group of cars. It was an hour before they were near enough to see people moving about, and from this distance it was evident that the wind had been relentless for it had heaped the snow over one side of the machines until they were nearly covered.

Bob's greatest fear was that some members of the party had frozen, but he was relieved on that score by one of the men who ran to meet them.

"Nope," announced the man, "nobody's hurt, but brother, how that wind can howl up here!"

As soon as Bob had learned that no one was in a serious condition he addressed the group severely.

"How did you happen to be up here? Didn't you see the blockades?"

"There weren't any blockades up when I started over," explained the driver of the first car.

The other two drivers looked at him sheepishly.

"They were up when we came over," one of them admitted, "but we thought we could make it. We got up here and saw this car stuck and we couldn't even turn around."

"How long have you been here?" Hughes asked the first man.

The man calculated. "Since about ten yesterday morning. Over twenty-four hours."

"Hungry?"

A chorus of voices answered the question and people began climbing out of the cars.

"Well, it'll be some time before you eat," Bob announced grimly. "We've got to get you down, and these women can't walk."

One of the girls groaned. "Mister," she said, "I'd sell my hair for a sandwich."

Bob could not refrain from smiling as he looked at her. It was evident that she had opened her suitcase and was wearing everything she could get on. Over her dress she wore a pair of woolen pajamas and her legs were wrapped in burlap sacks.

"Tell you what," Bob said at length. "A mile back up the road at Fall River Pass there's a shelter cabin. You'll find a stove and some wood there. You'd better all go back and wait. You can at least keep warm, and it may be hours before we can get a plow through to you."

One of the men looked at his car, half buried in the drift.

"I guess," he said dryly, "it'll be all right to leave the keys in it."

"I guess," replied Bob with a grin, "that it will."

After a short rest Bob and Hughes started back on their long journey to where Frost would be waiting for them in the car. They had gone but a little way when one of the men shouted after them.

"Have 'em bring some gas up, too. We ran out keeping the motors going."

Bob waved an acknowledgment to the request.

"And bring me a sandwich," shrilled the girl who was wrapped in burlap.

Again Bob waved and they set off down the slope. The wind had not abated, but it was at their backs now and traveling was less difficult. In spite of this, both men were dog tired when they at last reached the waiting car.

"Anybody up there?" Frost asked cheerfully as they climbed inside.

"Three cars and eight people. We'll have to get the plow and it'll probably be an all-night job."

Ten minutes after they reached Utility the place was in a bustle of preparation. The big snowplow was gassed, a truck was equipped with straw and blankets, and lunches were ordered from a hotel.

The plow was on its way by six o'clock, running with its blades high, for there was no need of taking the time to cut through the drifts at the lower elevations. Hours were precious, for at best they could not hope to bring in the party before midnight.

"We can't do any thing for some time," Bob said to Hughes as they ate dinner. "We'd better grab off a couple of hours sleep before we start back. The plow won't hit the drifts for quite a while."

Hughes agreed to this, but at nine o'clock they were on their way again in the car. The big plow had made excellent progress up the highway and it was eating into the drifts a hundred yards from the cars when they arrived.

It was a weird sight which greeted them as they came up to the big throbbing monster. Her spot lights were playing on the drifts ahead and the shower of pulverized snow sparkled as it streamed from the funnels. The heavy pounding of the plow had always thrilled Bob, and tonight as she cut her way through the darkness on this strange mission of rescue, his heart seemed in tune with her humming knives and he was proud to be associated with her and with her crew.

There was little need to spend time at the plow, for it would be necessary to pull the cars out one by one before the crew could pass, and this procedure would take at least an hour. A mile up the road eight hungry people were hovering around a stove, listening to the wind howl about the building and trusting that help would arrive shortly.

With this thought in mind, Bob and Hughes adjusted their headlamps and, placing the lunches inside the packs which they had brought along, trudged off up the road. They were soon out of range of the lights from the plow, but the slender beams from their headlamps cut into the whirling mass of windblown snow and kept them on the highway.

It was a tedious trip, for the old exhaustion of the afternoon had come over them again, and the wind was sweeping over the timberline country at a terrific rate. Bob thought that he had never seen such wind.

"Doesn't this wind ever stop?" he panted as they rested for a moment, thrown on their stomachs in the shelter of a high road embankment.

Hughes shoved up his cap and put his head close to Bob's.

"This is just a gentle little zephyr," he shouted. "Wait'll this winter and I'll show you some real wind in this country."

Bob wanted to reply but there seemed little use wasting breath in competition with the wind. They went on again, sometimes bending low against the gale which beat against them. At last they dropped down into the depression where the tiny shelter cabin was located.

Not a sound came from within, but as soon as they pushed open the door there was a rush of confusion. The only light was thrown by the old wood stove, but even with this Bob could make out the weird sight of men and women huddled about it for warmth. Their faces looked tired and the lines of fatigue were accentuated by the flickering light.

"They're here!" someone shouted, and all the occupants of the cabin rushed toward the two men in the doorway. Immediately they were bombarded with a hundred questions. "Is there anything to eat?" "When can we leave?" "Will it be long?" "Are the cars out?" "Did you bring any gas?" "Can't we start back now?" It seemed impossible to Bob that eight persons could cause so much noise.

At length the excitement died down sufficiently to permit him to speak. When it did he answered their questions in a few words.

"We won't start back for a couple of hours yet because the plow is only as far as the cars. In the meantime you'd better eat."

They needed no urging and it seemed that all thought of anything else vanished from their minds as they fell upon the cold lunches and ate ravenously. When the last sandwich had disappeared the entire group seemed elevated in spirits and was content to sit about the fire and await the arrival of the plow.

"Wait," chortled the girl in burlap, "that's all we've done for two days. I'm getting used to it now. In fact, I'm beginning to feel quite at home here. Hope this building stands for a long time."

"Why?" Bob asked curiously.

"So in fifty years I can come back here with my family and say 'That's where grandma was snowbound in the early days.' "

It was nearly twelve o'clock when the dull throbbing of the snowplow drifted down to the little cabin on the pass. Many of the men and women were asleep, but Bob and Hughes slipped out of doors and stood listening to the sounds of the motor. The wind had died down, the stars were out and nothing broke the velvet stillness of the mountain night except the faint rumble of the approaching plow and the occasional murmur of voices inside the building.

The people inside were contented now. Bob wondered how cheerful they would be had he not played his hunch that morning. He and Hughes had walked fifteen miles, and six men had been battling drifts for the greater part of the night in order to bring these people to safety.

When they were at last on the way back Hughes yawned sleepily. "Well," he murmured, "just another event in the exciting life of a ranger."

"Yea."

"I'll make a bet with you."

"What?"

"I'll bet you we don't even get a letter of thanks for what's been done today."

Bob smiled wearily. "I was just thinking the same thing an hour ago," he said. "They'll remember the night they spent, and they'll tell what a narrow escape they had, but that's all. Those boys on the plow had a lot worse time than they did."

"I know, but it's always the same. Once I spent all night huntin' a woman's kid that had wandered off and gotten herself lost. Found her about three o'clock in the morning. After they left the park the woman almost floored me by writin' a letter of thanks. One of the few I ever received."

"Quit your gripin'," Bob grinned good-naturedly. "That's what we're here for and that's where the taxpayers' money goes. It doesn't make any difference if it *was* their own fault for getting into such a scrape."

"I suppose so," Hughes muttered sleepily. "Wake me up when we get there."

CHAPTER XIII

RESCUE

BOB sat at his desk and smiled sympathetically at Hughes. The man had yawned three times in rapid succession and was making no pretense of concealing his fatigue. It was the afternoon following the rescue of the marooned party, and everyone who had been on that detail felt the need of rest.

"Good thing tomorrow's Sunday," groaned the ranger. "I'm goin' to bed at seven tonight and sleep till Monday morning."

Bob futilely attempted to suppress a yawn. "Cut it. You've got me doing it, too. But I'm with you to the last ditch on that idea. Nothing short of a fire is going to make me lose my beauty sleep tonight."

"So glad you feel that way," murmured the other gratefully. "Thought maybe you wanted me to get up early and take a nice long walk with you before breakfast."

The other made a face. "Even the mention of walking makes my feet hurt." Then he said seriously, "Next week we're going to have to start stocking cabins. That snow really scared me."

"Might be a good idea," Hughes admitted. "Huntin' season'll be here before we know it and then we'll have our hands full."

"Think I'll go along when you stock those in the

north end. I haven't seen much of that country yet."

Hughes considered for a moment. "I've been thinking—why don't we make a three-day pack trip out of it? We'd have to stock the North Fork Cabin from this end anyway, and that would be a separate trip no matter how you figure it. But we could stock Cabin Thirteen and make a swell three-day trip through that country. What about it?"

Bob was just replying when his buzzer sounded for a phone call. "Sure I'll go," he said. "Wait a minute. Hello . . ." He paused and spoke aside to Hughes. "Denver calling, wonder what's up. Hello . . . yes . . ."

There followed a lengthy conversation and when he hung up, Bob looked at the other questioningly. "Did anyone get in touch with you about climbing the East Face yesterday?"

Hughes shook his head. "You were with me all day. Why, did somebody do it?"

"That call was from a man by the name of Hancock in Denver. Claims his son and another fellow started up here to climb the East Face. Were to have been back this morning but they haven't shown up yet."

"Leave 'em alone and they'll come home," Hughes grinned. "And will they be draggin' their tails behind them after *that* trip?"

"That's what I told him. If they had any trouble one of them could have probably gotten back for help. But can you imagine anyone doing a stunt like that on such a day?"

"Sure, I can imagine anything. There's always someone who's got to be the first to do something.

There was the first one to climb the East Face and then the first one to climb it in the rain and then the first one to climb it in the winter. I suppose there's going to be a first one to climb it walking on his hands."

"That Face doesn't tempt me at all," Bob said, shaking his head.

"Me either. I've been up that way once, but never again. I could never figure out just why I should risk my neck going up the Peak the hardest way. As I figure it out, the object of climbing the thing is to get on top. If people could see what they look like when they make a misstep up there, there'd be a lot fewer deaths on the Peak."

"Well," Bob replied, rising and putting on his hat, "as long as there are people they'll climb it, or try to at least, from the most dangerous side; and as long as there are rangers it'll be their job to pick up the pieces. In the meantime I'm going to eat an early dinner, go home and take a bath and go to bed. See you Monday."

"Okay, Chief. Get some rest."

McDonald had had the same idea, for by the time Bob reached the little cabin at Utility, his friend had a warm fire going and was lounging in an easy chair reading a book.

"Look comfortable," Bob commented as he slipped out of his coat.

"Am. Say, what are you doing tonight?"

"Staying right here, and wild horses can't move me."

The other lit a cigarette and nodded agreeably.

"I was hoping you'd have an idea like that. You

know this will be the first evening we've been at home together in a month?"

"You're getting so domestic, darling," Bob cooed, as he ducked to miss a pillow which McDonald had aimed at him. "I'm taking a bath, how's the water?"

"Hot."

Fifteen minutes later Bob emerged from the steaming room. Slipping into a robe he stretched out on the davenport with a book. For an hour he managed to stay awake, then he shook his head and stood up.

"Sorry to break up the party but I'm dead. I'm going to get some sleep. Did you ever stay up all night getting people out of snowdrifts?"

McDonald laughed. "Sure."

"And what did you do the next night?"

"Slept."

"That's the answer. You now have a picture of a model young man retiring at a reasonable hour for once in his life."

"Sweet dreams," McDonald called after him. "I'll wake you up if there's a fire."

"Let her burn and shut up. I'm asleep already."

At eleven o'clock the telephone began ringing so persistently that Bob could not ignore it. He crawled from his warm blankets and made his way sleepily to the instrument. The words "Denver calling, hold the line please," brought him partially out of the sleep-drugged condition in which he had awakened. He suddenly remembered Hancock and his companion, and he knew that this phone call was to inform him they had not yet returned. He scowled, hoping fervently that it was not so, yet knowing instinctively that it was.

The voice which came over the wires confirmed his fears. After a short conversation Bob hung up the receiver and awakened McDonald.

"Come in the other room. I want to talk to you," he said.

"Oh go to sleep and quit prowling around," mumbled the other. "It isn't morning yet."

Bob persisted, however, and at last his friend stood in front of the stove, blinking in the bright light.

"What's the idea?" he complained. "I thought you were sleepy."

"Listen, Mac. I'm scared to death that a couple of kids are stuck up on the East Face."

McDonald squinted and sank into a chair. "Go on," he said, "shoot the works."

Bob related to him the story of the phone call that afternoon. "What do you think I'd better do?"

The man drummed the arm of the chair with his fingers for several seconds before answering. Then he replied: "It's got all the symptoms. That's just how one of these little parties begins. It would be a mess to make that trip for nothing, but it would be a worse mess if we left someone up there. You have to do a lot of chasing phantoms and hunches in this business." He paused, lost in thought for a moment. "All you know is that two kids intended to climb the peak and didn't get back."

Bob nodded.

"Kind of slim information."

"They're probably on a party and didn't even think of letting anyone know they're back."

"Why don't you call . . ."

The phone interrupted him.

"Bet they're home," Bob grunted as he went to answer it. There was evident relief in his voice.

Listening, however, McDonald knew that the call did not bring such welcome news. When the chief ranger returned he did not sit down. Instead he began dressing.

"It was Charlie Hampton," he explained at length, referring to the proprietor of the Rustic Lodge at the beginning of the Longs Peak Trail. This man usually kept close track of everyone going up or coming down the trail, especially at this season of the year, and more than once had he given invaluable service in checking on climbers.

"Funny," McDonald mused, "I was just going to suggest you call him. What did he have to offer?"

"They went up all right. Stopped at the Rustic early yesterday morning. They had sleeping bags which they were going to leave at timberline. Planned to climb the peak yesterday, sleep at timberline and then come down this morning."

"Sure they haven't come down? Maybe they didn't stop."

Bob shook his head. "Left the car there."

"Well," McDonald muttered resignedly, "that about settles it."

"Afraid so."

The other man went into a clothes closet and presently emerged with his arms full of heavy clothing.

Bob looked at him and then went on lacing his boots. "Now what?" he asked quietly.

"I'm going with you. You'll need all the help you can get."

The chief ranger made no comment, although he was overjoyed to know that McDonald was going along. This was the first rescue job on the peak and he felt the need of advice. Going to the phone, he called the three rangers on the east side, explaining the situation to them and giving simple instructions. They were to meet at the Rustic and be ready to hit the trail two hours before sunrise. By getting such an early start he hoped to be well above timberline by the time it was sufficiently light to carry on the work. He would attend to the equipment himself. After talking to his men he called Hampton and requested that five horses be saddled and waiting for them.

Grimly he and McDonald set about collecting the equipment. Ropes were carefully coiled, life belts were examined and picks as well as crampons were placed in the car. It had not been necessary to use the last two articles all summer, but Bob knew that in all probability they would be essential in crossing the ice fields at the foot of the Face, especially at this season. The two men worked continuously and by half past two they were ready to leave Utility.

"I'll drive," McDonald said. "It'll take us half an hour to get up there and you need the sleep. Grab it while you can."

Bob readily consented to this plan and he was asleep before the car had gotten through the government gate. He woke with a start to find himself in front of the Rustic veranda. They were the first to arrive and they went into the lobby where Charlie had a roar-

ing fire and hot coffee awaiting them.   As they drank
from the huge cups the proprietor related all he knew
of the incident.

"They got here before daylight.   Husky lads, both
of them.   I'd just gotten the fires going and they
waited and drank some coffee.   There was no arguing
them out of goin' up the east way.   But I'll say they
were equipped for it.   Had ropes an' picks an' crampons.   One of them climbed it last summer.   They left
the car down by the corrals and planned to get back
this morning.   To tell the truth, gentlemen, they plum
slipped my mind until tonight when I went out to the
corral to see the wrangler.   Then there set the car all
lonesome like and, I tell you, I got scared.   Waited till
about eleven o'clock and then I called you."

Bob nodded.   "Glad you did, Charlie.   We were
just about to call you."

"You'll find trouble up there," prophesied the old
man.   "I've seen a lot of them in my day and when
they're as late as this they never come down under
their own power."

"One thing," McDonald commented, "the weather
has warmed up enough so that if they're just stuck on
some ledge they haven't frozen."

Charlie Hampton nodded.   He knew every foot of
the peak, for he had lived over twenty years at its base.
"They won't have frozen," he agreed.   "You'll find
they've either fallen or they're stuck."

The roar of a car interrupted the conversation.   A
door slammed and Frost stamped in.

"Gosh darn," he sputtered characteristically, "I
knew we wouldn't get through the season without this.

An' all the temporaries gone, too. This would be a nice job for them."

Shortly afterward Anderson arrived from Wild Basin followed immediately by Hughes. As soon as the entire party was assembled the waiting horses were led out of the corral and, after the equipment was made fast to the saddles, the party began its long, tedious ascent.

There was little conversation as the horses picked their way up the dark trail. No sound disturbed the early stillness except the clattering of steel shoes against rocks and the steady wheezing of the animals as they carried the men upward.

On went the silent party through the heavy stands of lodgepole which closed about them like a black blanket as the close-growing trees flanked the base of the peak. Gradually the lodgepole forest gave way to stands of spruce and fir, and finally, as gray dawn was dissolving the blackness over Twin Sisters Mountain, they emerged into the timberline country. Bob thought he had never seen the area so weird or unreal as it appeared that morning in the elusive half-light which lay on the boundary line between night and day. The light silver-gray trunks, twisted and distorted by winds, stood scattered about the barrens—grizzled monuments to the centuries of warfare with the elements.

In the hush of dawn there was no wind, but soon after daybreak it came, moaning ominously through the forest below them and finally sweeping across the wide unbroken expanse of timberline country. The party wound its way in single file over the great glacial moraines, stopping only long enough to allow their horses to blow, then on again toward the base of the great perpendicular East Face which towered above them now like some menacing gray form, terrible in its grandeur, as lights began to play about its top, lights reflected from the blood-red clouds of sunrise. At length they left the main trail which led to the right across Boulder Field and through the Keyhole to lose itself in the ledges and slopes of the last half mile of the West Route. The horses took the left trail which led down past Peacock Pool and into the huge glacial cirque where Chasm Lake nestled at the base of the East Face. A small cabin, built to shelter climbers from storms, stood at the base of the shelf upon which the lake was situated. Here the trail ended and the men tied their horses. They rested for fifteen minutes, hurriedly boiled coffee and gathered the equipment preparatory to the hard climb which lay ahead of them.

As they sipped their coffee they made plans. "Here's another time," Bob said, "when the rest of you know more about it than I do. I should think, though, that we'd better look along the base of the regular route first. If we can't find anything there, look the Face over pretty carefully with glasses. Maybe they're stuck as Charlie said."

McDonald nodded his agreement to this plan. "It would take a lot of guts to hang on up there for this long if they are stuck," he commented, looking at the flat surface with its vertical cracks and chimneys.

"The death-trap of the Rockies," Anderson mused.

Frost looked at him and scowled. "Sign needs repainting," he mumbled, jerking his head toward a large board sign near the cabin.

"I don't know why we ever put it up there," Hughes sighed. "They never read it."

The sign was headed "Warning" and definitely stated that the Service advised against climbing the peak from this side.

"Well," Bob replied, "all we can do is warn them, and then when they don't pay any attention to it we go out and bring them in. Let's go."

They set out, laboring up the steep rock wall which rose two hundred feet to the lake. At last they gained the summit. Across the water, snowbanks and ice fields sloped down from the sides of the Face. In order to reach this it was necessary to traverse the rough jagged shoreline for half a mile. Bob and Hughes brought up the rear and the others were several yards ahead when the latter stopped short.

"What's the matter?" Bob asked, as the man unslung his pack and reached inside.

Hughes did not reply. Instead he pulled out a pair of field glasses and stared intently at the ice field across the lake. At length he lowered his glasses.

"See anything of interest over there?" he asked. "Just below that big boulder that sticks out at the top of the ice."

"You mean that rock?"

Hughes handed over the glasses without comment. Bob looked through them for a moment and shuddered. The mangled, helpless form of a man lay stretched in a horribly unnatural position on the white surface.

"God," he muttered; then, pulling himself together, he called to the others.

"That's the first one of 'em," Frost exclaimed. "Boy what a place he picked! Well, let's get him." There was no trace of sentiment or emotion in the man's voice and he whistled a little tune as he started off over the rocks.

Bob looked at him in amazement but Hughes nudged him with his elbow and the group started on rapidly around the shore. When he had an opportunity, Hughes explained his action.

"You thought Frost was pretty crude," he breathed in a low voice. "He didn't mean it that way. It's simply that if you let trips like this one get under your skin you can't stand it and you'll never be able to go on the next one. You have to act exactly as if—well, as if you weren't dealing with a human being. Things like this get the best of 'em, and Frost dreads 'em worse than anyone. It takes plenty of stuff to make a trip like this when you know what's ahead. You don't understand yet—but I do."

It took an hour to cross that half mile to the ice— an hour which called for the utmost in the form of physical endurance. As they came closer to the ice they could see occasional rocks break from the sheer face and come tumbling into the chasm, striking with a sharp metallic sound. Bob had heard of the dangers from these rocks as they came hurtling through space, but he had never experienced the dread of them before. Once McDonald had told him of them, saying, "One thing in their favor is they come so fast you'd never know what hit you." At that moment, however, Bob found little consolation in the thought.

When they at last arrived Hughes was ahead. He immediately began to adjust his crampons to the soles of his boots. Only with these steel cleats was it possible to negotiate that treacherous ice field.

"Wait a minute," Frost exclaimed, "I'm going to do that, you're not!"

But Hughes paid no attention. Instead, he coiled as much rope as he could handle about his shoulders, took his pick and began slowly working himself out on the ice. Again Frost complained that he was the one who should go. This time Hughes looked down and replied: "You stay where you are. I'll go up and let him over the ice with a rope."

Bob knew why Hughes had gone without orders and he respected him for it. There had been no drawing straws to see who would go. This was the most dangerous work in the world, crossing the glaring ice field, and Hughes had gone without giving anyone an opportunity to so much as volunteer. There was nothing spectacular, or remotely resembling an attempt at show in the man. He threw himself into danger, not because he did not know fear, but because he knew that Frost hated it.

Breathlessly they watched him move across the sheet. Every motion he made was for a purpose. Rocks whizzed through the air and dropped about him, but he kept on. Once his crampons failed to grip the ice and he slipped, but with the quick movement of a skilled mountaineer he dug his pick deep as he fell and hung on. There was a terrifying moment when he swung like a pendulum on the ice, but at last he righted himself and went ahead. When he reached the steeper part of the ascent he became even more cautious. Inch by inch, he worked his way up and across, cutting steps with his pick as he went. It took him an hour to reach the boy. He stopped for only a moment and then went higher until he mounted the large boulder at the upper edge of the ice. Here he paused to sit down and wave a greeting to the men who watched him from below. He was about to get up when another rock slipped from a ledge above him and came downward with a hissing sound. Hughes looked up and then flattened himself against a boulder. The rock smashed into the ice not five feet from where he lay.

"Gosh darned rocks," Frost groaned. "If he gets hurt I'll choke him for not letting me go."

Hughes went to work again. He secured the rope to the boulder and then, grasping it firmly, began letting himself down over the ice toward the unconcious form of the boy. Upon reaching it, he tied the free end of the rope about the waist and climbed back to the boulder. By maneuvering his position he was able to set the inert body in motion. It was not a serene sight, Bob thought, as he watched Hughes let the badly injured boy down over the ice, but it was the only possible means of rescue.

Their eyes followed the battered figure in horrified fascination as it slipped and skidded over the surface toward them. At last it slid smoothly down the slope and lay at their feet. They stepped quickly forward and started first aid for the injured boy. From time to time they turned their anxious attention to Hughes who was untying the rope from the boulder.

"Why the devil's he doing that?" Frost scowled. "He's crazy. Tell him to use the rope to come down on himself. Hey! He'll kill himself coming down there without it."

Bob shouted for him to use the rope in the descent, but it was no use. He deliberately coiled the slack and flung it toward them.

"What on earth is he doing that for?" McDonald groaned. "That's the first time I haven't known Hughes to use his head." Then, without realizing that Hughes had already thrown the rope, he cupped his hands and shouted. "Go back, you fool. Use the rope."

Bob saw the man wave to them and begin to descend. This time, however, he picked a different route, nearer the edge of the ice.

"I don't know what difference it makes," Frost complained. "Maybe he'd rather crack his thick head on the rocks than he would go in the lake. Wait'll I get my hands on him!"

For endless minutes the little group of men shuddered as Hughes came down inch by inch. At last, however, he reached the rocks in safety and walked toward them.

"Of all the idiots . . ." Frost sputtered, but Bob stopped him. Somehow he felt that Hughes had a good reason for not using the rope. The man did not toy with death without cause.

"Why didn't you use the rope?" he asked, as the other reached them and sat down.

"We're goin' to need that rope," he replied quietly.
"What for?"

"I located the other kid. He's stuck on a narrow ledge a couple of hundred feet from the top. I saw him when that rock came. He's alive but we'll have to climb the peak and pull him up."

As they toiled back to the horses, carrying their burden over the rocky slopes on an emergency stretcher, Bob felt that he had never known such a man as Hughes. Risking his life, yet using his head— facing death yet knowing it every moment, simply because . . . the words came back to him . . . because "we're goin' to need that rope."

CHAPTER XIV

BACK INTO THE WILDERNESS

I T WAS with considerable difficulty that Hughes persuaded Bob and McDonald to leave them and to
take the now conscious boy down the trail on a horse.
His argument was a logical one. There was a limit
to the number of men who could continue the rescue
work and three could carry on as well as five. It was
essential that the injured climber be taken out as soon
as possible.

"Somebody's got to go," he urged, "and the three of
us can get that bird up there and bring him down."

It was a difficult task, fastening the suffering boy
easily and yet securely on Bob's horse, but it was at
last accomplished and the two men started carefully
off down the trail.

The others, carrying ropes and packs, began their
long climb to a point on the peak where they could
negotiate a rescue.

Bob and McDonald said little as they trudged down
the trail, leading the burdened horse after them. There
seemed a vacancy in any words which might come to
their lips, for the minds of both were filled with the
events which had taken place during the last few
hours. Bob was tired. His strenuous exertion of two
nights before and today's work, with little or no sleep,
had made his head groggy and every muscle in his body

ache. He thought of Hughes who still had a good six hours of rock work before he could rest.

"I don't see how he can take it," the man muttered, half to himself.

"Who?"

"Hughes. I'm dead and he's still at it."

McDonald nodded. "I've often wondered how they hold up. It's a bunch to be proud of, Bob. We may not have the four snappiest looking rangers in the Service, but they're real men—none better, and . . ." He paused.

"What?"

"I was just thinking about education," he replied. "All the new men coming into the Service must be college graduates. I wonder sometimes if that's going to help them so much in certain cases. Take this morning for example. Would it have made Hughes more efficient up there on the ice when he was getting that helpless boy to have had a college education?"

Bob smiled grimly. "A Ph.D. degree wouldn't have helped him much," he admitted.

They phoned from the nearest emergency box and by the time they reached the end of the trail at the Rustic a car was waiting to take the injured climber to the hospital. There was nothing Bob or McDonald could do toward assisting Hughes and his companions, and so, after a cup of hot coffee which Charlie forced upon them, they drove to headquarters.

Late that afternoon Frost came to the office to report the details of the rescue. It had, according to him, been entirely successful and they had gotten down the trail in good time.

"The kid was scared and cold and half starved," he said, "but we got him on a horse and down the trail. He's in bed at Charlie's now. Did you phone Denver?" Bob nodded. "The kid you rescued is Hancock. His father's probably up at the Rustic now. The lad went down to the hospital hours ago. Did you have any trouble at all?"

"Naw. They just lowered me over with a life-belt. I sent the kid up and then they hauled me out. Nothing to it."

Bob knew that Frost had not told the whole story. He realized that his superficial description of the rescue was far from adequate, and he also knew that he must go to someone else if he was to learn of any of the heroic part which Frost might have played. He subsequently learned it from Hughes who described in glowing terms how the man had been lowered into the chasm, dangled over a thousand foot cliff and had reached the narrow shelf to rescue the half conscious youth.

"And do you think that old cuss blinked an eye when he went over?" he asked. "Not him. All he said was 'Gosh darn it, don't forget to hang on to that rope,' and down he went. Man! That chasm looks big compared to a man hangin' in it from a little piece of rope."

When he had learned all he required to fill out a report of the incident for the Washington files, Bob pushed the papers toward the back of the desk and turned to Hughes.

"Before this little party began we were talking about taking a pack trip. Don't you sort of crave to get

into the back country for a while where there aren't
any rescues or people stuck in snow drifts and where
you can't smell gasoline?"

Hughes' eyes glistened. "Do I?"

"All right. As soon as you can get the rations out
for Cabin Thirteen, and the stuff we'll need for the
trip, we're off. I'm leaving the details to you."

Hughes considered for a moment. "We leave day
after tomorrow at six in the morning," he announced.

At exactly the appointed hour Bob heard a whistle
outside his cabin. Looking out, he saw three loaded
pack animals and two saddle horses. Hughes, in
leather chaps and heavy coat, sat on one of the horses.
His leg was thrown carelessly over the horn and he
was serenely rolling a cigarette. The new white
"mantes" which were drawn evenly over the well-
balanced packs showed bright in the morning light, and
Bob could see the frosty breath of the impatient animals as they stamped and fretted at their bits. It was
enough to make anyone glad, he thought, as he pulled
on an old sweater, buckled his chaps and passed out
of the door.

"The sooner we get away from here the better,"
Bob laughed as he swung into the saddle. "The telephone might ring and I've done nothing but answer
calls of bad news for four months. What time did
you get up to pack these horses?"

" 'Bout four o'clock," Hughes answered as he
started down the road at a brisk trot.

"Why the devil didn't you call me and let me help
you?"

"No use routing you out. Didn't take me long."

There was something about the feel of leather under him and the sound of hoofs and the packs as they "clump clumped" with the rolling movement of the horses that made Bob forget suddenly the grief of the past summer. His spirits soared and he responded to the thrill of being alive and free in the mountain country.

They followed the Fall River Road to near timberline and then turned off the highway to enter the sparsely wooded Chapin Pass. The moment they left the road they were plunged into wilderness. There were no trails, no wires—nothing to remind them of the civilization which they were leaving rapidly behind them. Deer sprang from the edge of the woods to bound across open meadows with long graceful leaps. Jays scolded noisily from the trees at their approach, and elk singly or in groups lifted their heads on distant slopes to stare at the pack train as it wound its way down from the pass. Joyful at three days of freedom from routine, Hughes broke into a song as they rode downward:

> "Oh where didja come from?
> Or didja come at all?
> Didja come from the place
> Called the Hole in the Wall?
> No I didn't, dad burn your soul,
> I come from the place called
> Jackson's Hole."

Bob uttered a whoop. "Where'd you learn that, cowboy?"

"I dunno. Guess I've always known it."

"That's the second time I ever heard it," Bob explained. "The first time was in Wyoming. An old cowpuncher was riding down the road, drunk as a lord, and he was yelling it at the top of his lungs."

At noon they stopped an hour to make coffee and eat a cold lunch. Then on again down Chapin and Hague Creeks. Toward evening they emerged from the timber and entered the wide sweeping valley of the Cache la Poudre. Hughes pulled up his horse and pointed to a tiny building a few hundred yards down the creek.

"Cabin Thirteen," he announced.

Bob thought he had never seen such a small shelter cabin in any park. Usually the cabins were large enough to accommodate three and sometimes four men comfortably, but it seemed that only with difficulty could two crowd into this one.

"Not very pretentious," he remarked as they rode forward.

Hughes shook his head. "Small, and this winter I'll show you how much cold and snow can drift in, but it's a protection from the wind, and believe me that's something in this country."

"How did it get the name?"

"Hangover from the early days, I guess. I've heard somewhere that they used to call the cabins by numbers. Cabins five, eight, ten, thirteen, and so on. Now we have 'em named by where they're located like Lawn Lake or the North Fork or Thunder Lake."

They unpacked and hobbled the horses and then piled the supplies outside the cabin. While Bob dragged wood from the nearby fringe of timber and unrolled the sleeping bags in front of the fire, Hughes prepared the meal.

An hour later Bob rolled back on his sleeping bag and groaned, "Lord, what a feed!"

"Have enough?"

Bob gave him a withering look and then turned stomach down on the bed to watch the purple tints deepen over the Mummies. There was peace here, and quiet. The world of men seemed very remote and far away. There were no telephones to jangle, no automobiles to roar and no people with complaints. A little way beyond, the river rippled over its gravel bed between flanking banks of scrub willow, now yellow and red with autumn colors.

"Cache la Poudre," mused Bob, lighting his pipe and following the long line of willows with his eye. "The Powder Cache. What stories that old stream could tell."

"This whole country's got a history," Hughes agreed as he piled wood on the fire and began to pick up the dishes.

While they scoured the tin plates and cups with water and sand, the ranger told Bob many things about the region which he had never heard before.

"The Never Summers have a lot of interesting stuff connected with them, too," he said, spreading the dish towel over a bush and poking at the fire.

"You mean their origin?"

"Not necessarily, but there *is* some good geology over there. Specimen Mountain's worth pokin' around for a long time, but I was thinkin' of history. Indians called 'em the Never Summers or No Summers because of the snow. Then there are the ghost towns over there."

Bob had heard of the old mining towns of the Never Summer Range which now lay bleak and deserted, but he encouraged his companion to talk. Tonight he felt like listening, and, as darkness engulfed the valley and gradually climbed to the tops of the peaks, Hughes related some of the things he had heard about the early days on the western slope of the range. He told of the Ute legend of Grand Lake which credits the water with possessing evil spirits because of the raft of women and children which capsized there during a battle against the Arapaho. He told of a later and less legendary battle which was fought out with forty-fives on the main street of the quiet little resort town because of a dispute over the location of the county seat. He talked at length of the towns which had flourished during the mining days of the 70's and 80's.

"And so," he concluded at length, "there's Dutchtown and Gaskill and Lulu City, all within a few miles of the main highway, and mighty few people ever dream that they're there."

Bob sighed. "There's always something pathetic about a ghost town to me. It's so much like a person —it was born, it grew, and maybe had hopes and dreams, and then fell by the wayside and was forgotten."

"And there are hundreds of those towns scattered the length of the Rockies," Hughes added.

"Ever been in Cooke, Montana?"

The other shook his head.

"That's another one, but it's better known than most of them. That place boomed for a little while and they almost got a railroad into it, but the railroad

never came and it cost too much to haul the ore out."
He relit his pipe from a burning twig and continued:
"There are a lot of old-timers up there who are still
waiting. Got to know one of them pretty well when
I was in Yellowstone. He went in with the first of
them, and he must have had all kinds of faith because
he put everything he had into a mine. Now he sits in
his shack and smokes and waits because he's sure that
someday the world will find out how rich the rocks are
and a railroad will be built. But he's going to die
waiting someday, just as a lot of others have done."

Gradually conversation lagged and the fire died
down. Still they sat, loath to break the spell of the
mountain night as it closed in upon them. Bob had
spent many nights under the stars, but he could not
remember one in which they had cut through the black
curtain overhead with such brilliance. The sickle of a
new moon lay behind the range, throwing only sufficient
illumination to dimly silhouette the jagged peaks
against a lighter sky.

From a nearby ridge a coyote yipped and then broke
into a wail. Far down the valley another answered
and on an opposite ridge still another repeated the call.
Then in chorus came their voices until there seemed to
be dozens of them. It was like an aurora borealis in
sound as the weird cries faded and then shot up again
from the depths of nowhere.

An owl, beating low over the brush by the river,
spied a rabbit scurrying toward safety. The soft
steady wing motion suddenly changed as the night
prowler dived to sink its wicked claws into the back

of its victim. There was a sharp frightened shriek and then silence again.

At ten o'clock the men crawled into their sleeping bags, but sleep would not come to Bob. The sounds of the wilderness persisted—the sounds which he had learned to love—and he lay awake listening and interpreting them as they came. A porcupine gnawed noisily on the bark of a pine within a few feet of the cabin. From a pond by the river a beaver slapped the water with his flat tail, warning the entire colony of danger, imaginary or real. The wailing of the coyotes continued and, just before Bob dropped off to sleep, he heard very faintly the soft patter of tiny feet on the rough tarpaulin which had been thrown over the supplies. He knew that the little white-footed deer mice with their large bright eyes were exploring the cans and boxes which these strange two-legged creatures had brought with them.

The following morning they were up as the sun sent its warm rays streaming across the frost-covered valley. After breakfast they proceeded to pack the supplies carefully in the heavy ration chests of Cabin Thirteen. These were the rations to be used by the men that winter, on their long ski patrols when all other sources of supply would be cut off.

Canned goods, pancake flour, syrup, butter in brine, raisins, bars of bitter chocolate, cans of sugar and other food stuffs went into the chests, while slabs of bacon and several hams were suspended by a wire from the rafters. Blankets, freshly cleaned, were placed in their section of the chest and a mattress was hung beside the meat.

THUNDER LAKE SHELTER CABIN

CUTTING THROUGH A DRIFT ON THE
ROAD

"Hope I get here before Frost does this winter," Hughes muttered as he examined the label on a can of strawberries with interest.

"Why?"

Hughes did not reply at once. Instead he picked up three cans of the fruit and walked outside the cabin. Curious as to the man's intentions, Bob followed him. Back of the cabin, he dug a hole in the frosty ground with his hunting knife and placed the cans inside. Then he replaced the dirt.

"Are you crazy?" Bob asked casually.

"Nope. Just cautious. Do you like strawberries?"

"I love 'em."

Hughes eyed him for a moment and then without a word went into the cabin and brought out two more cans. Silently he enlarged the hole and added these to his collection.

"What in the devil are you doing?"

"You don't know Frost's passion for strawberries," explained the man, with a sly grin, as he packed the last of the dirt around the cans. "I've seen him come in and eat a whole can at a meal. If that guy gets in first it's too bad, and if he happens to hit a cabin twice in succession on patrols it's terrible. There's just no strawberries left. Last winter it was my luck to follow his patrols the next month, and I didn't have as much as a taste. Nothin' but empty strawberry cans."

Bob chuckled. "I suppose he'll light into me now for not stocking Cabin Thirteen sufficiently with strawberries."

Hughes considered the possibility seriously, then he

nodded. "Probably," he admitted, but he made no attempt to replace the cans in the chest.

They packed the horses, lighter now because of the supplies which had been left in the cabin, and started on. Hughes led the way across the valley, across the river and then headed upstream over the level, willow-studded flats. Bob had not inquired as to their itinerary; in fact he did not care where they went, but now he realized that they were headed along the eastern flank of the Never Summers.

All that day they rode through a world of color. Tongues of yellow and gold shot upward along the dark coniferous slopes where groves of aspen followed the ravines. Various shrubs added their reds and browns to the chromatic symphony while the deep maroon of the Never Summers towered in rugged majesty above them.

Up they went to the Continental Divide and then down again to the headwaters of the Colorado.

"Did you ever think how we have Grand Canyon National Park over a barrel?" Hughes called, as they started down the Colorado River.

"Meaning which?" Bob shouted back.

"Where'd Grand Canyon be without Rocky Mountain? We could dam up this creek and they'd have to close shop down there."

Bob laughed at the friendly rivalry which existed between the personnel of the various parks. "Never thought of it," he admitted. "We'll watch their travel figures and if they begin to creep up on us we'll put 'em out of business."

That evening they entered another wide valley and

pitched camp in the vicinity of a group of decaying cabins.

"Where are we?" Bob asked, as they threw off the packs.

"This is Gaskill, one of the ghost towns I told you about last night. Had quite a rush here about 1880. The town lived about four years and then died out. They even had a road into it and I've heard that they ran a stage a couple of times a week. And now . . ."

"And now," Bob repeated, glancing at the assemblage of roofless and tumbled-down cabins.

While it was still light he made a tour of inspection of the old site. Lights had once burned brightly from these windows which were but square holes in log walls. Hearts must have burned brightly, too, he thought, with the spirit of youth and adventure and the hope that tomorrow would bring wealth. So real was the vision of the old days that he could almost hear the shouting of the men and the crunch of heavy boots upon gravel, and with a little imagination he could see the miners trudging along the trails or toiling at the sluices and cradles by the river. He was silent and thoughtful as he walked slowly back to camp and helped Hughes prepare the evening meal.

Next morning they trotted down the old road which led from the town to Grand Lake, far to the southward. Suddenly they broke from the timber and Bob found himself among a cluster of squat buildings nestling in a beautiful mountain valley.

"Know where you are?" Hughes called, as they rode past the structures, now deserted since the tourist season was at an end.

Bob considered for a moment. "Sure," he exclaimed abruptly. "Phantom Valley Ranch."

"Right. We'll hit the road here and follow it to the top and then come down Windy Gulch."

It seemed strange to Bob, after riding through the wilderness for two days, to come so abruptly upon the Trail Ridge Road. There was little traffic and by early afternoon they were again above timberline. Here Hughes left the highway and took to the thin ribbon of a trail which wound its way over the bleak treeless expanse. At length they left even the trail and headed for one of several gorges which descended from the high country. Hughes selected one of these and they plunged downward on a rough and little used trail into the timber.

This was new country to Bob but as they descended he began to catch sight of familiar landmarks through the trees. It was late when they reached the floor of the valley and they trotted into the gates of Utility long after darkness had fallen.

"Well," Bob sighed as they unpacked the animals and turned them into the corral, "it was a trip."

"It was a trip," agreed Hughes, putting up the last bar of the enclosure.

"What's your program for tomorrow?"

Hughes lit his pipe and considered. "I guess," he drawled, "I'd better throw a few squaw hitches on some rations and take 'em over to the North End Cabin."

CHAPTER XV

GLACIAL MEASUREMENTS WITH THE "BUG CHASERS"

A FEW days after Bob and Hughes returned from the pack trip, Brent came into the office and swung his leg over the desk.

"How's it going?" he asked, lighting a cigarette.

"So so," was the reply. "How is it with the bug chasers?"

Brent grinned. "The bug chasers are taking to the hills tomorrow."

"Where to now?"

"Last spring you said you'd like to go up with us when we took the glacial measurements," Brent reminded him. "We're going up in the morning. Thought you might like to go along."

Bob cocked an eye at the pile of papers on his desk. "I ought to . . ."

"We're only going to measure Tyndall tomorrow," Brent continued, without giving him an opportunity to complete the sentence. "That won't take so long and we thought we might do a little Indian hunting before we came back. Flattop's a great hunting ground, you know."

The chief ranger groaned. "It's too tempting," he said at length. "When do we leave?"

"Meet us at Bear Lake at seven-thirty and bring a lunch."

"Who else is going?"

"Crane," Brent replied, referring to a temporary naturalist who was staying later than usual that season.

At the appointed time next morning Bob pulled into the parking area at Bear Lake. Brent and Crane were already there, adjusting their packs and distributing the load between them. Among the many things which they were carrying were a steel tape, a camera, a pair of field glasses and several notebooks.

As soon as the equipment had been divided they started up the trail which led over Flattop Mountain. Bob had traveled this trail several times during the past few months, and on nearly every occasion he had had a different mission. He had gone over it with Hughes early in the season when he was attempting to familiarize himself with the country, and he had traveled it during those days of fruitless search for the boy who was lost on the range. Now he was going up again, this time for still another reason.

As they mounted higher, Bob thought that he had never seen the aspens so brilliant as they were that morning with the bright October sunshine dancing on their quivering leaves. Here the color was not confined to small groves. They were traveling through an area which, in 1900, had been swept by a terrific forest fire, and over the entire burn the aspens, true to their nature, had come in as the first tree to repopulate the bleak slopes. As far as the eye could reach down the sides of the moraines there was a carpet of the soft golds and yellows of autumn.

Occasionally the men stopped to sit on a log by the

trail and enjoy the ever-increasing grandeur of the view. They were not on schedule and there was no need for them to reach the top at a definite time. The day lay before them.

"Besides," Brent maintained, "if we get back before late afternoon we'll have to spend the time in an office; and who wants to be in an office on a day like this?"

Frequently the naturalists would pause for a quick identification of some bird as it flew from the timber or broke from the ground cover. Once Crane clutched Brent's arm with an exclamation of surprise and pointed. Bob looked in time to see a small bird fly rapidly out of a tree and disappear.

"Myrtle?" Brent asked.

"Not a myrtle," Crane replied, "but I don't know what it was. New one on me."

"Myrtle who?" Bob grinned.

"Her last name's Warbler," Brent explained. "Only it seems her first name isn't Myrtle after all. Crane here is supposed to be an authority on birds and he misses a chance like that. I hire him as an ornithologist and he turns out to be a geologist."

"I'm not an authority on birds," Crane complained, "and you hired me for a geologist."

"That's what we get for picking men sight unseen, Bob," Brent continued, paying no attention to the other's assertion. "They always look better on paper than they are."

Bob laughed, for he knew that Brent was well aware of Crane's ability as a naturalist.

"Seriously, though," he commented, "that's one

thing about you fellows. You're supposed to know a little about everything."

"That's one *trouble* with us," replied Brent seriously. "In a park like this you can't specialize on any one thing and get away with it. You're not dealing with geology or animals or birds alone. You're dealing with all of 'em, and you're supposed to be a specialist in each line."

"A couple of years ago in Yellowstone," Bob said, "a geologist came out from Washington and expected the naturalist there to be a walking encyclopedia on geology. The next week a botanist came and expected him to be able to identify every plant in the park, and before the summer was over a biologist showed up and landed on him for not being able to tell him the name of every bird. They expect the impossible, don't they?"

Brent shrugged. "I suppose that's part of our job," he answered soberly, "but sometimes it looks pretty hopeless."

"It still wasn't a Myrtle Warbler," Crane reminded them with a grin. "Let's go."

When they reached timberline Brent pointed to the slope at the right of the trail. "You've seen that before, haven't you?"

"What?" Bob asked.

"The wall."

Bob carefully scanned the slope and at length was able to make out the line of an old rock wall running up the side of the mountain and disappearing behind a shoulder. It was perhaps two feet high in places and in others, where the rocks had been scattered, it was difficult to see at all.

"No," he said in surprise, "as many times as I've been up here I've never seen that. What is it?"

"Indian wall," Brent answered, starting on again. "We're in Indian country now, but we'll stop and have a look on the way back."

Bob's curiosity was aroused. "What was it for?"

"Probably used in hunting. There are several of them scattered over the high country above timberline. Some people say they were for ceremonial purposes, and some say they were used as route markers, but I can't see it. It's a lot more logical to think of them being used to direct the course of migrating animals."

"So they could shoot them?"

"Yes. There are a good many rock pits out from the wall and I have a hunch that hunters concealed themselves in them and shot the animals as they went past."

Bob wanted to ask more about this strange wall, built by a people long since departed, but Brent and Crane became engrossed in a discussion on glaciers and he knew that when they returned Brent would answer his questions.

At ten o'clock they left the trail that crossed the bare summit of Flattop Mountain and made their way to the left over the boulders until they arrived at the brink of the deep gorge in which was located Tyndall Glacier.

Brent searched for several minutes and at length walked to a small pile of rocks on a promontory which overlooked the chasm and from which an excellent view of the glacier was obtained. Here he took out his camera and carefully made a picture of the ice mass which law below them.

"You see," he explained, "we take a picture from this exact point every year. Over a period of years you get a mighty interesting series of photographs that show recession of the ice. Just looking at the glacier from year to year you wouldn't notice so much change, but you'd be surprised to see what a difference those pictures show just since I came here."

"But," Bob protested, "you say the ice is receding and I thought the ice of a glacier moved forward. Isn't that the test of a glacier?"

Brent nodded. "The ice mass *is* moving forward," he explained, "but the snout is melting back faster than the forward movement. As soon as that happens the glacier begins to disappear. Now, if we should have some exceedingly cool summers and lots of snow in the winter there might come a period when the forward movement would just counterbalance the backward melting. Get it?"

Bob nodded.

"All right. Now let your mind wander a little farther and imagine that the climate changed just a few degrees cooler and the forward movement was greater than the backward melting. What then?"

Bob studied for a moment. "You mean the glacier would begin to move down into the valley again?"

"Sure. We'd have another glacial invasion."

After repacking the equipment, they made their way downward into the cirque which in ages past had borne one tongue of the mighty ice sheet that had overridden the entire valley beyond them. From where he stood Bob looked far down the canyon and on to the parks beyond. It took but little imagination to visualize the picture as it must have been thousands of years before, when ice filled the canyons and valleys —ice which moved with slow irresistible force, plowing, crushing and smoothing until it eventually made radical changes in the topography of the entire region. He glanced at the glacier of today and realized what a tiny remnant this was of the once mighty ice fields.

It took considerable time to make the descent, for the sides of the gorge were covered with loose gravel which moved treacherously at each step. At last, however, they stood on the snout of the ice sheet. Bob examined the great expanse with interest. There were long horizontal cracks which ran across the entire field. Toward the center these cracks curved downward. He understood that the movement of the ice caused these cracks and that the downward curvature was due to the mass moving more rapidly at the center than along the sides.

Suddenly there was the sharp rattle of falling rocks above them and a mass of stones came bounding down over the sheet. Brent looked up quickly and then went back to his work of assisting Crane in unpacking the equipment.

"We're all right out here in the middle," he remarked. "It's when you're on the edges and rocks begin to fall that things get really interesting."

Bob watched the naturalists make preparations for the taking of the measurements. There were, Brent explained, three stations chiseled in the granite boul-

ders at the base of the glacier.   If, by any chance one
of the boulders became submerged by water or was dis-
lodged by the ice it would be a simple matter to cal-
culate its former position from the other two.

"We measure from this station to the nearest ice,"
Brent told him as Crane began walking toward the field
with a fifty-foot tape.   "If the . . ."

He was interrupted by a sharp exclamation from
Crane.   "Say, something's haywire!"

"Why," Brent called.   "What's wrong?"

Crane had stopped unrolling the tape and was con-
sulting a notebook.

"What's wrong?" Brent asked again.

The man looked up with a puzzled expression. "Are
you sure we took these measurements right last year?"

"Sure.   Why?"

"The darned ice is too far from the rock!"

Brent laughed.   "I was wondering when you were
going to tumble.   You're all right.   Go ahead and take
the measurement.   She's melted back about twice as
much as we'd expected, that's all."

After the measurements had been taken and carefully checked, Brent spent a little time figuring in his
notebook.   At length he pushed his Stetson to the back
of his head and whistled softly.   "That's more than
even I looked for, and I knew she'd gone back a lot."

"How much?" Bob asked with interest.

"The park naturalist," Brent replied slowly, looking
at the figures, "has the honor to report to the superintendent, who in turn informs the director, who in
turn advises the Secretary of the Interior, who in turn
announces to the President, that fifty-three feet have

disappeared from the front of Tyndall Glacier since last October."

"My, my," Crane grinned. "What wouldn't some women give for that reducing formula!"

"What's the cause?" Bob asked with a laugh. "Too much exercise?"

"Yea, in a backward direction. An unusually warm summer and a very light snowfall last winter. It's to be expected as long as we continue to have subnormal snowfalls. Well," he said suddenly, changing the subject, "let's eat and then get out of here and hunt Indians."

They selected a huge flat boulder, sheltered from the wind, upon which to stretch out in the warm sunshine and eat heartily after their morning climb. When he had finished his lunch, Bob lay on his stomach, examining the glacier with a pair of field glasses. Suddenly he gave a grunt of surprise.

"What's that old piece of canvas doing over there?" he asked.

Brent continued to eat with disinterest. "If you'll look about ten feet below it you'll see a frying pan," he answered, "and there should be a coffee pot around somewhere."

"I see it," Bob exclaimed, "but what are they?"

"Just the remains of a pack outfit that went off the top years ago. The man's buried up above the glacier and the bones of his mule are scattered through the ice."

Crane chuckled to himself and Brent looked at him disapprovingly. "Don't be disrespectful to the bones of a mule," he rebuked.

Crane continued to chuckle. "I was just thinking," he grinned, "how some geologist is goin' to find those bones at the bottom of a moraine in a couple of thousand years and go crazy over a strange prehistoric jackass that used a coffee pot."

Brent held his nose in disgust. "Your humor," he announced gravely, "is putrid."

After the men had rested for an hour they began the long climb out of the chasm. It was difficult going and Crane's complaint that they slipped backward two steps to every one they advanced was not far wrong. "And you can't get anywhere that way," he said. "Think I'll pull a fast one on gravity and go up backward."

At last they reached the trail and made their way rapidly downward to the series of level sandy benches which appeared just above timberline. Here Brent stopped and turned to Bob.

"Ever hunt Indians?"

"Never."

The naturalist sat down on a rock and lit a cigarette. "We're awfully unethical as far as pure archaeology goes," he said. "Around here we just look and pick up what we find and record where it came from. Of course, if we run into something that looks as if it might turn out to be unusual we usually go slow and see if there's a story in the way it's situated." .

Bob looked puzzled and his companion went on to explain. "You know the real archaeologist takes a lot of notes and a lot of measurements and photographs and all that, in order to be able to tell something about the specimen after he gets it?"

Bob nodded.

"Lots of people have the idea that's a lot of foolishness."

"I always have," admitted the other.

"Well, look at it this way. Several years ago they found a new type of arrow point lodged between the ribs of an extinct species of bison. Just suppose that whoever found it had pulled out the point and taken it home. It wouldn't have meant much—just a new kind of point. But they didn't do that. They got all the information with notes and measurements and photographs. Get the idea?"

Bob looked at him in surprise. "You mean that the point with the animal meant something."

"Sure. It gave archaeologists a clue about the age of the point. Geologists were called in and that find proved to be something mighty important because, from the deposits in which the bison was found, they learned that man was making chipped stone arrow points around the time of the glacial epoch."

"I get it," Bob said gravely.

"Most of the stuff we find here," Brent went on, "is just lying on the surface. It's been washed down from the upper slopes and there's really not much data to be recorded except where it was found. Of course we sometimes find a lot of fragments of pottery in one place and we know pretty definitely that it's an old campsite of some kind. Then we begin to take notes in earnest."

Bob looked up with interest. "Is there really pottery here?"

The other grinned and picked up a small object at

his feet. "Speak of the devil," he said. "This is a piece of pottery. Just lying on top of the sand here. Evidently washed in from somewhere, so there's not much chance of finding any more that belongs with it."

Bob examined the small bit that Brent handed him. It resembled a piece of dried mud, but it was hard and contained sand. There were small indentations on one side which interested him.

"The piece is too small to say for sure," Brent told him, "but those marks were probably made by the thumb nail while the clay was still wet. Might have been for decoration but they were probably put on there for 'non skid' purposes."

"And they mixed sand with the clay?"

"Yes. To temper it."

"Not very ornamental," Bob remarked, looking at the black piece. "I thought Indian pottery was decorated and painted."

"Southwestern stuff is. The pottery we find in this country is very crude and never painted."

Crane was already making his way over the sand flats, crouching now and then to pick up or discard a piece which caught his eye. Bob and Brent joined him and within a short time the level bench began to yield Indian objects.

Brent stooped and picked up a flat disk which had been chipped on the edge.

"What is it?" Bob asked curiously.

"Scraper."

It was not long before Crane found a stone knife and a broken arrow point. Try as he might, however, Bob could locate nothing.

"Cheer up," Brent laughed. "There's a knack to this. Your eyes have to get used to picking out things that don't belong here. After you get on to it you automatically eliminate anything but Indian material."

After an hour on the benches, they began working their way down toward the trail again. Before they had gone too far Bob walked a hundred yards above the trail to examine the old wall which they had seen that morning.

"Strange, isn't it?" he mused, as Brent came up behind him.

"Strange and interesting," was the reply. "See that pit?"

Bob looked and saw, a short distance from the wall, where the stones had been thrown out from the rocky slope making a shallow depression large enough to conceal one man.

"Those are what I was telling you about this morning. I'm pretty well convinced that the walls influenced deer in their migrations to the low country in the fall and that the pits were used as shooting blinds."

At a spring a short distance below timberline they sat down and Brent answered some of the questions which had arisen in Bob's mind.

"We don't know who the first Indians were," he said, in answer to one of the questions. "We know that they were here and then for some reason they left. Possibly they went southwest. After them came the modern Ute and Arapaho."

"I always thought the Arapahos were plains Indians like the Sioux," Bob said, puzzled.

"They were, but they worked their way up into the

mountains to a certain extent. As far as we know they originally came from the Minnesota. They practiced agriculture but they were driven out by invading eastern tribes. They went southwest through the Dakotas where they came in contact with the Mandan and probably learned about the horse from them. Then they came on into Colorado. The horse had made buffalo hunting easier and they gradually ceased agriculture altogether and became a typical plains people."

"And the Utes?"

"We don't know much about them because they were pretty hostile toward the whites. They were more of a mountain people. Didn't use buffalo to any extent. Instead they used sheep and rabbits. Bitter enemies of the Arapaho."

"Maybe," Bob suggested, "if they were both in this country there might have been a fight up on Flattop. That would account for all the arrow points up there."

"Maybe," Brent admitted, "but I'd rather think those points were used for game."

As they went down the trail they talked of Indians and Bob realized that it would take but little coaxing to make him an ardent archaeologist. He learned many things that he had never known before, and the more he heard the more interested he became. As they reached the parking area he asked Brent if he might borrow a key to the museum that evening.

"Now what?" the naturalist asked.

"I just want to look over the Indian exhibit a little more carefully," Bob grinned. "I've been missing a lot of fun."

Brent laughed and handed him the key. "It's bitten you," he said.

"What?"

"The Indian bug. Everyone gets it after they've been here a little while. Well, go to it. There are some books up in my office you might like to look through some time."

CHAPTER XVI

BOB PREPARES FOR POACHERS

As autumn progressed there came a marked change in the animals of the park. Groundsquirrels and marmots, which had been abundant at all altitudes through out the summer, were already safe in their hibernation burrows, where they would remain until spring. Early snows, whipping across the high mountain meadows, signaled the arrival of the migration period for the great herds of elk and deer that had spent the summer peacefully grazing near timberline.

The deer were the first to arrive. They came down through the trees singly or in scattered groups, stopping for days to graze in some choice spot where the grass was still fresh and green, but always heading downward toward the rolling valley meadows of the winter range. After the deer came the elk and gradually, as the mating season approached, the big bulls began their bugling.

This was not new to Bob, for he had seen thousands of elk in the Yellowstone, but the late patrons of those few hotels which remained open during the fall spent hours on the road, watching the big herds move restlessly to and fro, or listening to the clear challenging bugles as the bulls gathered their harems and defied all other males for the supremacy of these groups. When the battles took place there was still another sound as the steel-hard fighting points clashed in combat.

To the late visitors, this wilderness symphony of sound and color appealed as another scene in the drama of the mountains. To the rangers, however, it marked the beginning of a three-week period of constant vigil to protect the animals within the boundaries.

A game reserve surrounded the park but beyond that lay the open area where shooting was permitted for a limited time each year. In order to reach the shooting grounds on the other side of the divide, it was necessary to pass through the restricted area. Hundreds of lawful deer were taken around the park but there was always constant danger of hunters, unsuccessful in obtaining their buck there, drifting into the state reserve and on into the park where the animals were comparatively tame and where they could be shot with but little difficulty.

Two weeks before the hunting season opened outside the reserve Hughes came into the office and sat down. Several times he started to speak to Bob but each time he lapsed into silence.

"Spill it," said the chief ranger at length. "What's on your mind?"

The other looked at him uneasily, as if he was not certain that he should reveal what was on his mind. "Well," he said at length, "you're the boss and you know what you're doin', but don't you think we ought to begin to make some kind of plans for the huntin' season?"

A shadow of a smile played around Bob's lips but his reply was serious.

"Maybe you're right. Have any suggestions?"

The man shrugged. "Nothin' special. I've got a hunch though that we're goin' to have our hands full this year. Money's scarce in the valley an' there's goin' to be a lot of tries at gettin' some fresh meat free."

Bob nodded his agreement. He had not been unmindful of the situation in the towns below the park and he knew all too well that a buck or two would be a welcome addition to the larder of more than one family. He felt a keen sympathy for the families who needed food, but his job was to protect the deer within the park.

"Anything else?" he asked.

"Yes. I got tipped off from a fella in Denver that Bartlet's been braggin' he's goin' to take a lot of meat out this fall. Fact is, I understand that he's already contracted with a butcher in Denver to sell it on the open market."

Bob tapped the desk with his fingers. He remembered Bartlet from that summer and the experience had made him keenly desirous of meeting him again.

"Runs liquor in summer and poaches in winter. Nice guy!"

"Yea," Hughes grumbled. "I've tried for five years to catch him at it but he's always slipped through. Sat up all one night an' darn near froze waitin' for him to come past, an' he went around me in the dark."

"I've a feeling he won't slip through this fall," Bob replied grimly.

Hughes looked at him with interest but if his chief had any ideas his facial expression did not betray the fact. The ranger lapsed into his original slumped position of disgust. He had faith in Bob's ability and he knew that if any plans could be made to capture the poacher he would make them, but for many seasons the best state officers on the job had failed and it would be too much to expect Bob to work miracles his first year.

"What's been the program in the past?" Bob asked. "Kept the gates manned?"

Hughes nodded. "Yea. Stopped every car goin' in or comin' out of the park day or night. When they went in we gave 'em a slip and marked the contents of the car on it. Sealed any guns they had. When they went out they showed that slip an' the car was checked against it."

"Good system," commented the other. "Any patroling done?"

"Some. Two or three of us usually drove around from dark till midnight or after. Sometimes we just parked our cars up on a hill where we could see everything and waited. If a suspicious car showed up, 'specially if they were workin' a spot-light, we'd go down an' investigate."

"Suppose you stirred up something," Bob suggested, "and the car ran away and left you. What then?"

The ranger scowled. "That's the trouble. It happens all the time. Our cars aren't fast enough to run down the average car. Of course, if we can get to a phone and let the station know they can get him at the gate. If we can't, the car usually smashes through and beats it."

"I've kept three temporaries on," Bob said, as if to

dismiss the subject. "They'll be on the gates during the season. You fellows can give them a little relief during the day but outside of that they'll be on twenty-four-hour duty."

"Any new ideas on how things should be handled?" Hughes asked.

The other shook his head. "Not just now. I've one or two notions but I'm not ready to let them out yet. But I still think," he added meaningly, "that Bartlet isn't going to take any deer out this season."

Hughes walked from the office, thoughtfully scratching his chin. He was unable to make out whether Bob had actually made some plans or whether they were to carry on the campaign of protection as they had in former years.

When the man had gone Bob drew a sheaf of papers from his drawer and smiled as he glanced over them. "They should be here today," he said to himself as he consulted the calender. "Wonder if they are?" He reached for the telephone and, after a brief conversation with the storehouse keeper, he drove rapidly to Utility with a satisfied expression on his face.

Once there he carefully counted the stack of boxes which were piled in one corner of the big warehouse. The storehouse keeper watched him with interest.

"Haven't got the bill on 'em," he said half apologetically, "but maybe I can let you have 'em. What's in them boxes if it's any of my business?"

"Surprises for poachers," Bob replied evasively, for as yet he had no intentions of revealing the contents of those large boxes. "The bill'll be along presently and until then just charge me out with ten boxes of surprises."

The little storehouse keeper who, it was said, never let a single bolt across the counter without obtaining the receiver's name in triplicate, moved uneasily. He was curious as to the contents of the boxes.

"They're marked fragile," he suggested.

Bob grinned. "Yea, they are fragile."

"Heavy, too," mused the other.

"They are heavy," agreed Bob seriously.

The storehouse keeper sighed, as if resigning himself to ignorance regarding the shipment. "Well, take 'em along, but mind you, I want your signature."

Bob scribbled his name on the receipt form and backed his car up to the loading platform where he carefully transferred the boxes. Then he drove to the far end of the Utility Area and unloaded them at a vacant building. For several days after this there was considerable speculation among the employees regarding the erection of tall poles in the pasture near the corral and the pounding which was going on inside the vacant building. At length it was impossible to keep the secret longer, for a huge antenna was swung into place and connecting wires run to the building. Even when it became known that a radio set was being installed, the use to which it was to be put did not dawn upon the park employees. The consensus of opinion was that the set was being installed to facilitate communication between the various parks of the system, and Bob was content to let them think what they wished.

At last one afternoon he called the rangers into his

office. "I've been holding out on you," he admitted. "A week ago Judd came in all hot and bothered for fear that I hadn't done anything about the hunting season.   Right, Judd?"

Hughes grinned.   "Yea, but . . ."

"Never mind. The fact is, I've been working on an idea of mine for some time, but I haven't told you about it until I was sure that it was practical and could be applied to our particular problem."

"What is it?" Hughes asked with interest.

"Radio."

"Radio?"

Bob nodded and was amused at the mingled looks of disappointment and amazement on the faces of his men.

"Well, gosh darn!" Frost muttered at length.

"The trouble heretofore," Bob continued, "has been that you couldn't keep in contact with one another when you were patroling with cars. Isn't that right?"

The rangers nodded their agreement.

"I'd have given a lot sometimes," Anderson cut in, "if I could have sent out a call for help to head a man off, but by the time I'd get out of my car and telephone —well, the guy'd be gone."

"My idea is simply this," Bob went on. "We'll equip every car with a two-way radio set. There's already a big set out at Utility. Everybody seems to have gotten the idea that we put that set in to talk to other parks. The fact of the matter is that set will be used largely on poachers. A man will be on the big set and orders will come from him. In other words, the headquarters set will act as a sort of clearing house for cars."

"Just like airplanes!" Anderson exclaimed with enthusiasm.

"Just like airplanes," Bob agreed.

"When can we see it?" Lee asked.

Bob consulted his watch. "We have a test with Yellowstone in just twenty minutes. After that I'll show you how we're going to use it on poachers. Let's go out."

Even the chief ranger exceeded the speed limit as the group drove from the office to Utility where the big set was being tuned up. When they entered the building Hughes yelped with enthusiasm.

"So that's what all the secrecy's been around here," he grinned as they sat down and watched the operator who was busy at the instrument panel.

"Nobody's been allowed in here except the operator," Bob explained, "because if the idea didn't work you wouldn't have the laugh on me."

"Well, does it work?" Frost asked sceptically.

"Sure it does," Bob assured him. "Wait and see." He glanced around the room with pride. It was a completely equipped radio station. Wires, switches and high powered apparatus were everywhere; and in one corner, neatly stacked in a pile, were four portable sets.

The clock on the wall said exactly three when the operator took off his head phones and switched the receiver over to the loud-speaker. There was a loud hum and then, as he adjusted the set, there came a voice, loud and distinct.

"KNJB calling KNJT. KNJB calling KNJT. KNJB calling KNJT. Yellowstone calling Rocky Mountain. Yellowstone calling Rocky Mountain. Yellowstone standing by for Rocky Mountain. Come in. Rocky Mountain."

Immediately the operator switched to the transmitter and began droning a reply. "KNJT back to KNJB. KNJT back to KNJB. Hello, Yellowstone. You're coming in okay. Signal strength about three I would say. Are you getting this, KNJB? KNJT standing by. Come in."

A switch brought the voice again. "KNJB back to KNJT. Yes, you're coming in fine. This is King talking. Is Bob Flame or McDonald in your station? McMannon is here and would like to speak to them."

"KNJT back to KNJB. Bob Flame is here, but McDonald is not. I'm turning the mike over to Flame."

Before Bob knew it he was sitting in the operator's chair, holding a one-way conversation with an invisible person miles away. He did not know whether or not he was being heard but he talked for several minutes and then signed off with the customary "Come in."

Upon shifting the switch McMannon's voice came into the room. Bob stared in amazement at the receiver. There was no distortion to the voice. It was as if his old chief were standing beside him. "Hello, Bob," said the voice. "How's tricks? Seems good to hear your voice again. You sound perfectly natural. We missed you here last summer but I've been hearing good reports on your work down there. Glad you got the same idea about using radio. We've found it very useful up here, especially when our phone lines go out, but you know all about that. We should be able to talk often. Now I have an idea you might like to talk to some of your old friends. Stand by and I'll turn you over to Lake Station." Bob sat spellbound as he heard Yellowstone headquarters calling one of its outlying stations.

"KNJB calling Lake. KNJB calling Lake. KNJB calling Lake. Hello, Lake Station. You've probably been listening in on this conversation. Sedgewick, if you're there you might say a word to Bob Flame down in Rocky Mountain. KNJB standing by for Lake Station."

Bob grinned and something resembling a lump came in his throat as he heard his old friend's voice. It seemed impossible for him to sit in Rocky Mountain and listen to the men whom he had known at Lake Station. He pictured the room in which they were— a room where he had spent so many hours during the long winter evenings. How different it would be at Lake, he reflected. Now there would be no telephone lines to keep in constant repair through the winter months, for the new radio system would greatly facilitate communication throughout the entirety of that vast area.

At length he brought the conversation to a close. He shut off the machine and turned to face the rangers assembled in the room.

"Well," he said, with a trace of eager enthusiasm in his voice, "does it work?"

Frost made his characteristic comment. "Gosh darn," he said.

"It sure works to perfection on a call like that,"

Hughes admitted, "but just how is this two-way stuff going to work out here in the park? This station and the one in Yellowstone are both strong sets. You can't get much power out of a little set that we'd carry around in a car with us."

Bob arose from his seat. "Come on and I'll show you," he said. Then turning to the operator, "Carl, stand by and I'll contact you."

The operator nodded and the five men walked rapidly toward the government garage. There Bob drove out one of the coupes. In the front seat was a portable set. "This was the trial car," he explained as the rangers examined it with interest. "This short antenna is used for points reasonably distant. When we get too far from the station and the signals begin to fade we simply unroll the long one, toss one end over a limb." He pointed to a spool of wire which was attached to the spare tire.

The car would not accommodate all of them but they followed in their own machines stopping each time Bob made the tests. By the time they had progressed eight miles up the Bear Lake road the signals began to come in too faintly for accurate work. Bob unrolled the spool of wire, tied a weight on one end and threw it across the limb of a nearby pine. With the additional antenna, the signals once more came in loud and clear.

"You see," he said, after they had completed the test and the headquarters set had signed off, "it works and it's going to be a great help."

"I'll say it will," Hughes agreed enthusiastically. "It's just like a radio car."

"Better," Bob told him. "Most radio cars don't

have two-way communication, but with these sets we can both send and receive."

It was several days before the regular routine of the hunting season began and one by one the rangers' cars were equipped with radio. Much time was spent by the men in familiarizing themselves with the new equipment and it was not until they became fully aware that the world was able to listen in on their conversations that they confined their speeches to business subjects. Even then at times they forgot that they were not using telephones. Bob happened into the radio shack one afternoon just in time to see the operator doubling up in a fit of hilarity. When he was able to talk he explained the cause of his merriment. "Poor old Frost's been out all afternoon trying to adjust his set," he said. "Every once in a while he forgets himself and tells the set what he thinks. I've been having a picnic listening to him grumble. Listen yourself!" He switched the machine to the loud speaker.

"Hey, Carl," came Frost's voice, "what's this cockeyed gadget down here on the right-hand side? Ouch! Nuts to this idea. These earphones are pounding away like a couple a' cow bells. What the devil's wrong?" Then as if suddenly realizing that others might be listening to his tale of woe, he continued in a more dignified strain. "Car 704 calling KNJT. Come in Carl."

"KNJT back to car 704" was the prompt reply. "Frost, I think your 'cow-bells' are caused by a loose connection. Better come in and I'll fix it for you. KNJT signing off to car 704 and standing by."

Bob chuckled. "Better tell him to remember he's

not alone on the air when he comes in," he grinned, "and to watch what he says."

There was much interest and amusement in the new equipment but the men applied themselves so that on the day before the gates opened for the hunting season they were well versed in the operation of the sets and contacted one another as well as the headquarters station with as much efficiency and dignity as if they had always carried radios in the seats beside them.

CHAPTER XVII

RADIO CARS IN ACTION

TWO days prior to the opening of the hunting season beyond the game reserve the gates of the park were manned. Heavy swinging logs were placed across the road at each entrance and no cars were allowed to pass in or out of the area without first being thoroughly checked. If guns were found on the incoming cars they were promptly sealed, and every firearm in the outgoing machines was handed over for inspection. If the seal was broken it went hard with the owner.

Twenty-four hours each day the men were on duty, checking the cars in and out of the park. There was no favoritism shown. Often familiar autos would appear, carrying persons well known to the men, but at such a time it was difficult to distinguish friends from enemies and each car was treated the same as the last one. Through long night hours red lights burned on the swinging logs and white lights burned in the tiny buildings on the boundary—lights which signified that men were keeping their constant vigil.

The patrol cars were ever-active in and around the area, and there was seldom a time when the sets were not in use, making test calls, requesting information or receiving instructions to investigate suspicious cars within the park lines.

As the hunting season approached the entrances were kept increasingly busy, checking cars and sealing the guns of hunters bound for the open shooting grounds on the other side of the reserve.

"That was an arsenal all right," White grinned as Bob stepped out of his car on one of his frequent rounds of the entrances. "You know, those two birds had seven guns between 'em. Just ask 'em and you'll find out there's no doubt but what they'll bring back a buck apiece. Some people seem to think the more artillery they take along the better their chances are for getting meat."

Bob nodded. "I know it. How's business?"

"Rushing. Only got a couple of hours sleep last night. Seemed that every time I'd begin to doze off some car would bust up and sound the horn so I'd have to get up and let it in. Boy, if you want to get the low-down on who goes riding with who late at night just take this job. Gosh I'm sleepy," finished the lad, attempting to stifle a yawn.

The chief ranger was sorry for the men on the gates during hunting season, for he knew that there was a constant strain and little rest.

"Sorry," he replied, "but I'm afraid you can't look for much sleep on this job."

"After two seasons of it I ought to be getting used to going without sleep," the other replied dryly. "Seriously though, any hope of getting a couple of hours shut-eye this afternoon? Honest, I'm a nervous wreck and I'm losing on the average of ten pounds a day."

Bob smiled as he looked at the heavy ranger before him.

"You can stand to lose it," he retorted. "Maybe though, you'll get some sleep before night. I'm going to try to arrange some relief for all the gates this afternoon."

The other sighed contentedly. "You're just too good to me," he murmured. Then as Bob climbed back into his car, "Bring me some more seals, will you? I'm running low."

The other tossed him a paper sack of the small lead seals which were so essential in temporarily putting guns out of commission. "Everybody's calling for them and I've gotten so I carry a supply with me. Well, good luck. I'll remember the relief."

But the promised relief did not come, for in the early afternoon of that first day the grapevine telegraph, which is always active at such times, brought the news that Bartlet had passed into the park unrecognized.

When the news arrived Bob was sitting in his office. It did not surprise him. He had been waiting for this very thing to happen and he was ready for it. It was what he had planned on and he knew, as everyone who heard the announcement knew, that Bartlet was there for no good reason. Reaching for the telephone, he called the radio station.

"Call all cars," he ordered. "Bartlet is inside the park. He's driving a big black sedan with a Denver license. Tell them to be careful because he isn't taking any chances of being caught and he's threatened to shoot his way out if they corner him. Have the cars contact the gates and don't let any car out that answers that description unless it's been thoroughly searched. Did you get that straight?"

"Right," came the reply.

Within fifteen seconds the powerful transmitter was humming and the operator was flashing the message to the patrol cars, wherever they might be. "KNJT calling all cars. KNJT calling all cars. KNJT calling all cars. Bartlet is now inside the park. Driving a black sedan with Denver license. Be careful, as trouble is expected with him. Notify all stations to search every car carefully which answers this description." Three times he repeated the message, as was the custom, and then he began checking the cars in order to make sure it had been received. "716 did you get that?"

Immediately the reply came. "716 back to KNJT. Yes, everything okay. We'll be on the lookout."

"708 did you get that?"

"708 back. Okay."

"732 did you get that?"

"732 back. Got it."

"704 did you get that?"

"704 back. All right KNJT. We're ready for him."

Bob realized that every moment was potent with the possibility that Bartlet might be picked, yet there were serious doubts in his own mind if the man would begin his work until after darkness fell. More likely he would reconnoiter during the daylight hours and be prepared to strike when there was the least possibility of his whereabouts being discovered. Nevertheless Bob knew that if the car was sighted the radio station would be the first place to receive the news and that he would be better able to keep track of the chase from there. Therefore he drove to the station and spent the afternoon in restless anticipation. He caught his breath each time a car called but nothing outside the regular routine occurred. Each fifteen minutes the operator contacted the patrols and sent out time reports, but nothing was seen or heard of the menacing black sedan.

"He's probably keeping under cover until darkness," Bob grumbled as the long shadows began to creep down from the peaks and the sky behind the range was blazing with the brilliant scarlet of an autumn sunset. "We're going to have a busy time of it tonight unless I'm mistaken."

Before dinner he made a round of the entrance stations. The men were tired from their long unrelieved shifts, but there was no complaining. Instead, the proximity of Bartlet had keyed their nerves until everyone was keen and alert in spite of the fatigue. They realized the situation, and, in addition to the possibilities which every hour brought, they knew that at such a time every man was needed. There might be sleep on the morrow but there would certainly be none that night. Cars came and went, their occupants little realizing the excitement which was going on in the minds of the trim uniformed rangers who met them, or that the stage was set for a man-hunt as soon as darkness closed over the mountain country.

After a hurried meal Bob returned once more to the radio station, resolved to spend the entire night there if necessary. One by one the cars had taken time off while their drivers snatched a bite to eat and then reported back in service again. By eight o'clock every man was on duty, facing the long night hours which might or might not bring the action they sought. For two hours Bob sat beside the operator, impatiently listening to the fifteen-minute checks of the cars as they drove slowly along the roads within the boundaries or parked on some high point where they could overlook large sections of country. As the minutes passed his impatience grew. There was always the same "everything okay" or "nothing to report" in response to queries. According to instructions they never gave their locations and Bob himself had little or no idea of where they were, for there was always the possibility that alien cars might be similarly equipped with radio. At last the inactivity goaded him beyond endurance.

"Call 732 and tell him to come in," he ordered. "I'm going to take a turn around with him."

Obediently the operator switched to transmission. "KNJT calling 732. KNJT calling 732. KNJT calling 732. Come in to the station, 732. Come in to the station."

"732 back to KNJT. 732 back to KNJT. Okay, I'll be right in. I'm not very far from you now."

Within five minutes the lights of a car flashed along the road leading into the Utility Area and shortly Hughes burst into the door. He was wrapped in a heavy sheepskin coat with the collar turned up.

"What's doing?" he asked eagerly. "Any news?"

Bob grinned. "Not a thing. I just got the jitters sitting around the station waiting for something to

A Radio Patrol Car

The Red Fire Truck

happen so I called you in. I want to go out with you for a little while."

"All right," the ranger agreed heartily, "but you'll freeze and you'll be bored to death. Dead tonight. Not a thing doing. I don't believe Bartlet's within a hundred miles of here."

"He's here all right," Bob insisted. "I got it straight. Maybe we'll get a break before long. It's early yet. Get warm and let's get going. I've sat around here so long I feel like a fossil."

The operator looked up and grinned.

"Oh yeah? How'd you like a twelve-hour shift on this baby?"

"No thanks," replied Bob, shaking his head. "I want more action than that."

The two men passed out into the night and soon the car was under way, cruising cautiously without lights up the road, guided only by the sliver of a moon which hung over the range.

"I don't know which is worse," complained Bob as he pulled himself down beneath the dash to light a cigarette, "getting the jitters back there or out here."

"Why?" Hughes asked in surprise.

"Somehow this idea of driving without lights gets on my nerves. Do you actually know where you're going?"

The other chuckled. "Sure. You get used to it once and you can see just as well. If a car's up to anything he'll soon quit it if he sees a pair of lights comin' at him, and he'll have time to make a get-away. This way you can sneak up on 'em and catch 'em red handed."

Bob agreed to himself but he still could not reconcile himself to driving along a winding mountain road without the aid of lights. He knew approximately where they were and he realized that there was a sheer drop of several hundred feet on one side of the highway. This thought did little to cheer him.

At length Hughes parked the car on an observation point and settled back in the seat. Bob knew that from this point they could sweep long expanses of meadow land. In the darkness below them were thousands of deer and elk grazing peacefully or wandering at leisure over the rolling glacial hills and valleys. The chill of night crept into the car and bit into the men in spite of the heavy sheepskin coats which they wore. The moon sank behind the range and the night became blacker than ever. Each fifteen minutes the radio droned out its time check.

"KNJT testing at eleven o'clock."

"KNJT. Eleven-fifteen test."

"Eleven-thirty. KNJT."

Each fifteen-minute period seemed longer than the last. At length Bob said, "That fellow's clock must have stopped."

Hughes grunted sleepily. A faint signal on the radio attracted their attention but it was not sufficiently strong for them to distinguish the words.

"One of the cars calling in," commented Bob.

Hughes started to speak but at that moment the big headquarters set came to life. "Okay, okay," it said in reply to the signal to which they had listened. Then "KNJT calling all cars. KNJT calling all cars. KNJT calling all cars. A black sedan in Beaver

Meadows. A black sedan in Beaver Meadows. Working a spotlight. Working a spotlight. 704 is giving chase. 704 is giving chase. Heading for Highdrive. Heading for Highdrive. Heading for Highdrive. All cars be ready to move at once. All cars be ready to move at once. KNJT standing by."

Hughes switched on his lights and started the motor. All thought of the cold and darkness was forgotten as the moment for which they had been waiting approached. "He'll be showing up in a minute or two," he snapped as he pulled the car squarely into the middle of the road. "Shall we wait for him here?"

Bob nodded. "Looks like our best bet." Then he clutched his companion's arm. "Look!"

For up the road a piercing shaft of light swept around a curve, disappeared for a second and then reappeared. A quarter of a mile behind another shaft cut through the darkness. The radio began to speak again but neither of the men paid any attention. Now it could tell them nothing that they did not know —they who stood directly in the path of the oncoming cars. At length the cars reached a comparatively open stretch of road and they had a good view of the chase as it approached them. It was evident that Frost in 704 was being speedily left behind in his unequal race with the powerful black sedan.

The radio cut in again. This time it was another voice—Frost's voice. He wasted no time on call letters. Instead he began talking.

"Gosh darn," he wailed, "he's leaving me. He's getting away. Head him off somebody before he gets to an entrance. Head him off, head him off, he's leaving me behind."

There was no time to reply. The big car suddenly shot around a curve ahead and came down the road—a great two-eyed monster bearing down with its motor roaring upon the two rangers. Like a flash Bob and Hughes were out of their car with drawn guns facing the oncoming car. There was a sudden screaming of breaks and then, to their utter astonishment, the car swerved, bounced off the road and on to a rock-strewn flat and headed back in the direction from which it had come, reaching the highway behind Frost. Bartlet had eluded the trap but like a flash 732 was after him.

Bob took the wheel while Hughes handled the radio. "732 calling KNJT. 732 calling KNJT. 732 calling KNJT. He's headed back up the Highdrive," rasped the man. "Headed up the Highdrive. Probably making for the Fall River Entrance. KNJT give 708 a call and tell him to block the road at the Horseshoe Bridge. Block the Horseshoe Bridge."

Before headquarters could relay the message there came a weaker signal. "708 calling 732. 708 calling 732. We picked that up, 732. We're waiting for him here at the bridge. We're on the bridge now. If he gets through he'll have to smash us or jump the creek. Keep on his tail, we may need help. Signing off and standing by."

Immediately the big headquarters set began to drone. "KNJT calling all cars. KNJT calling all cars. KNJT calling all cars. Go at once to the bridge in Horseshoe Park. Go to the Horseshoe

Bridge. Go to Horseshoe. Trouble is expected. Go
to Horseshoe. Go to Horseshoe."

Bob grinned in spite of the tense situation, as they
skidded around curve after curve. "Where do you
think we're going, you sap, to Denver on a joy ride to
see a show? Ask him where 716 is."

Hughes transmitted the question and the big set
once more sent out a call. "716 give me your location.
KNJT calling 716 for location."

There was a moment of silence and they knew that
716 was replying with a signal too weak for them to
pick up. Then "Okay, 716. Okay 716. KNJT back
to 732. 716 reports that they are near the Roaring
River Bridge and they're going fast to back 708.
They'll be there in a couple of minutes."

Hughes switched to transmission. "732 calling 704.
732 calling 704. Are you coming behind us Frost?"

"Gosh darn yes," sputtered the man in the car behind them, "but I'm eating all your dust. Either get
out of my road or get that crate out of second. I'm
in a hurry."

Hughes chuckled and Bob set his jaw in grim satisfaction as he pushed the throttle further toward the
floor. With two cars blocking the bridge and two
more behind the sedan there was no hope of escape,
and with less than a mile to go he felt like shouting at
the efficient manner in which the sets had massed the
rangers where they were needed within a few short
minutes.

Down the long grade roared the two cars, every
second bringing them nearer the bridge where he knew
four men would be waiting with guns to receive the

notorious poacher. A sharp turn in the road blocked his vision of the bridge so that he was unable to see the actual capture, but he heard the screaming of brakes as the big sedan skidded half way around to keep from smashing the government cars which barricaded the road.

When Bob arrived on the scene Bartlet was standing full in the glare of the headlights. He was surrounded by rangers and covered so that escape was impossible. From the back of the big car Hughes pulled the carcasses of three does—one evening's work for the poacher. A high-powered rifle equipped with a silencer reposed in the front seat. Had Bartlet not confessed to other similar episodes there was ample evidence here to convict him; but, before Anderson slipped the handcuffs on him and bundled him into a car bound for the commissioner's office, the man had related the entire story of his fall poaching in past years.

Bob appeared against him at the short trial on the following morning. Simple grim facts related by grim men whose duty it was to protect the animals within the park made a strong case against Bartlet. It took the judge but a brief period to sentence him. When it was pronounced even Bob gasped. No leniency had been shown. The judge had given him the maximum sentence which he was empowered to pronounce—six months in the Federal prison and five hundred dollars fine.

After the fine had been paid and Bartlet had begun to serve his time at Fort Leavenworth, Hughes dropped into Bob's office one day.

"It's funny," he mused, "how little they are after they've been taken."

Bob looked at him inquiringly.

"Bartlet, I mean. You know we all thought he was such a big shot while he was runnin' liquor and poachin'. He thought so, too. But now that he's through with it and we've gotten him where we want him, he's just an ordinary person who thought he was bigger than the law."

The other nodded. "He'll have six months to think things over and when he comes out I'll bet he'll have reached the conclusion that those three does were pretty expensive meat."

"Especially since he didn't even get to eat 'em," Hughes added with a grin.

CHAPTER XVIII

BOB DOES SOME FANCY SKIING

THE hunting season past at last and the park sank back once more into ordinary routine. The capture of Bartlet had been the high spot of the season, and compared to that event there had been little excitement for the patrol cars. News of the man's arrest had swept the surrounding country and many a would-be poacher changed his mind and went elsewhere to practice his unlawful killing. If Bartlet, who had been the cleverest poacher in the mountains, had been captured, there was little chance for one of lesser experience to slip inside the boundaries and bring out a deer. Nevertheless, the patrol cars remained active until after the hunting season in the surrounding regions had closed and all fear of shooting within the park was passed.

The brilliant colors, accentuated by the frosty nights, continued throughout the entire month of October. It was the month when the big animals came into their own. Elk bulls bugled their challenges and fought fierce, slashing battles on the rolling meadows of the park. Seldom was there a night when the sound of clashing antlers could not be heard drifting across the still air of the feeding grounds. The great herds of elk were a constant source of wonder to those fortunate ones who spent their autumn vacation in the region. Bob had always felt that the park visitors had a

natural interest in the animals, but it was not until he
had a chance to observe the fall visitors to Rocky
Mountain that he learned how great that interest was.
The resort owners, keen to entertain their guests, were
quick to take advantage of this interest, and each evening saw scores of cars parked along the main highway
where good views of the herds could be obtained. As
Bob mingled with the cars he found that the tourists
had discovered what he already knew—that animals
have personalities.

Such names as "The Gold Dust Twins," "Old
Gray," "One Horn," "Rasputin," "The Dutchess,"
and "Pop-eye" were in common use among the visitors. Many resorts had their favorite elk, and considerable friendly rivalry was shown when the
champions of two hotels staged a fight before the onlookers. After a few evenings on the road Bob was able
to distinguish the various outstanding bulls and to recognize the characteristics which led to their christen-
ings. "Old Gray," for example, was an immense animal with a grayish cast to his coat. "One Horn" was
another large bull who, in spite of the fact that he had
lost an antler earlier in the season, was able to hold his
own with any of the others. "The Dutchess," although
quite evidently misnamed as to sex, was a haughty individual that remained apart from the others and
always held his head ridiculously high when he ran.
"Pop-eye" was a short, heavy-set bull of tremendous
power. For a long time Bob was unable to distinguish
"Rasputin" but at length one of the guests explained
that the bull with the unusually long black beard had
been given that name. "The Gold Dust Twins" were

two twin spike bulls who were always together and who, in addition to closely resembling each other in appearance, always seemed to be doing the same thing. There was something about "elking," as it was called, that warmed Bob toward all the visitors who participated in the sport. To him those who indulged in this evening pastime were friends, not only of the park, but of all for which the park stood. They were fond of the animals—they knew and loved them—and he felt sure that there was not one person in the hundreds who watched the herds as they moved here and there through the meadows that would ever afterward kill an elk, even though the opportunity presented itself.

As the mating season of the elk waned, the deer began their courting and fought with all the savagery and fierceness of their larger relatives. During one of these battles the antlers of two bucks became locked. The fight had evidently begun in the morning, for by evening the two contestants were nearly exhausted. As Bob came up the road he saw a group of visitors standing beside the highway. Catching sight of an animal on the ground he concluded that a car had struck a deer and broken its leg, as had been the case several times that fall. Upon examination, however, he discovered the two bucks with locked antlers. They were lying on the ground, still glaring defiance at each other in spite of the nearness of their audience.

Bob realized that antlers once locked are practically impossible to separate. He procured a saw, therefore, and, with the assistance of several of the onlookers, tied the feet of the animals and sawed the antlers free.

When the bucks were at last separated and the ropes cut, they staggered to their feet, looked at each other for a moment and started fighting again in spite of their lack of equipment. It was not until several men had interposed and pushed the animals away in opposite directions that peace was restored.

"Those fool bucks sure must have a grudge against each other," one man remarked as the crowd dispersed.

Since the tender field mice and other rodents went into winter quarters at higher altitudes the coyotes that fed upon them throughout the summer had begun drifting downward to the winter range of the deer. Here they would remain, lying in wait for old or sickened animals until it was time to again return to the high country. Each night their yipping, wailing choruses could be heard throughout the lower reaches of the park. Their songs floated out on the air like the wailing cries of the wilderness, but every animal understood them and knew that the season of poor hunting would soon arrive.

It came with a fury and suddenness that amazed even those who had predicted an especially hard winter. One morning the mountain country lay bathing luxuriantly in warm sunshine. By noon a faint haze obscured the sun and the mercury began to drop rapidly. At six o'clock the heavens were heavy with storm clouds and a steady fall of snow had begun—snow which, before it ceased two days later had laid a white blanket four feet in depth over the park.

Had they been unprepared, the rangers would have faced a serious problem, but every cabin was stocked and the force was waiting patiently for the winter season to set in. The big snowplows rumbled out of their sheds and, with rotary knives humming, pulverized the snow and sent it soaring from the funnels to be deposited in long mounds beside the road. There was no doubt that this was the snow that would close the country. Previous flurries which had forced road and trail crews to abandon their high camps were but warnings of this, the main assault of the winter storm legions. No longer would cars be of value on some of the roads, and it would be many months before horses could be used on the trails. Now travel through the interior of the park would be confined to skis and snowshoes.

Those roads which the service wanted open were cleared, while those over which they wished no travel were blocked by the snow blanket. The closed roads simplified the administrative duties of the park personnel and narrowed its activities to a few definite localities in which visitors were permitted at this time of year. It also signaled the time when the boundary patrols would become active, for Rocky Mountain contained thousands of fur-bearers that, unless strict patrols were maintained, would fall victim of the fur poachers who were still active in the region and awaiting an opportunity to strike at the untapped riches which the park contained. It was not alone for the protection of mink, marten and beaver that these patrols carried on through the unbroken wilderness. Strict measurements of snow depths were maintained in order to allow the irrigated areas in the low country to make preparations for a wet or dry season, for the snow in the mountains meant life or death to the crops. The conditions of various species of animals were watched with great care by the men on patrol, for occasionally the huge drifts blocked the only entrance to the winter feeding ranges.

A week after the first storm Hughes came into the office and dropped down upon a chair in his customary manner. It was Saturday morning and, barring unforseen events, the majority of the men would be relieved of official duty until Monday.

Bob looked up from his reports as the man entered. He was dressed in rough clothes and wore a pair of heavy ski boots.

"Doing anything this afternoon?" he asked.

The chief ranger shook his head. "Nothing much. Cleaning up the house and writing some letters. Why?"

"Well, the snow's good for telemarkin' and I'm goin' up to Bear Lake an' do some practicing. Thought you might want to come along."

Bob grinned. This was something new. In Yellowstone the ski patrols had been the most strenuous of all the winter work. The men dreaded the long tortuous journeys and even the old-timers looked upon them as a necessary evil which aged men rapidly as it called for the best they had in physical stamina. But now Hughes sat beside him and proposed that they go out and ski for practice. Bob had heard enough of skiing in Rocky Mountain to realize that it called for a technique entirely different from that to which he was accustomed. Here it was a matter not only of floundering hour after hour through the snow when it was soft, but it called for skill as well. In this park there were mountain trails which were steep and winding and, with a crusted surface, it was necessary to have a thorough knowledge of every skiing trick in order to negotiate them. He had never been called upon in all his winter service to make sharp rapid turns on skis, and for several days the idea had haunted him. There seemed to be no good reason for procrastination, however, for he realized that sooner or later he must master the finer points of skiing before he undertook any trips into the high country.

"Okay," he agreed, "I'll go, but you're going to have to show me a lot about this fancy stuff. All I know is just straight plugging and breaking on the boards."

Hughes nodded knowingly. "There's more to real skiing than that, but you've ridden 'em enough so that it won't take you long to pick it up. What kind of riggin' did you get?"

That fall Bob had discarded his Yellowstone ski binding and had purchased the type used by the rangers. It consisted of a toe-clamp such as is used on ice skates and a strap running around the heel. The strap too was equipped with a clamp so that when the binding was properly adjusted it held the foot in a vicelike grip, permitting movement of the foot only in an up and down direction. It was impossible to move the foot sideways without moving the ski, thus giving the rider almost perfect control of the boards. In addition to the rigging, Bob had purchased a pair of heavy ski boots with the heels grooved to retain the binding strap. He described these to Hughes who nodded approvingly.

"That's what you'll want," he said. "When Mc-

Donald came down here he used his Yellowstone rig-gin' on the first trip and we darned near never got him in that night. Remember that, Mac?" he called through the open door to the assistant superintendent.

"What's that?" asked the man, looking up from a pile of blue-prints which he had been studying.

"Remember the first ski trip you took down here?"

A loud groan came from the adjoining room. It was evident that even the memory of that first trip was painful.

"I'll never forget it to my dying day. That was terrible."

By one o'clock Bob and Hughes were driving up the freshly cleared Bear Lake Road with two pairs of skis protruding from the back of the car. As the machine climbed up and up by the highway, piled high on both sides with snow which the plows had deposited in their work of clearing, it was evident that the fall had been much greater at the higher altitudes. By the time they reached the parking space at the lake, six feet of snow lay on the level, while the wind, in unprotected spots, had piled drifts ten to fifteen feet in depth.

Bob was surprised at the number of cars which were already there. It was evident that many others, not only from the village, but from the surrounding valley towns as well, were taking advantage of the week-end and good snow. He had watched with interest the reports of the persons entering the park, but this was his first opportunity to come into actual contact with the winter sports enthusiasts who had discovered that the national park held as many charms in winter as in summer.

There were approximately twenty-five cars parked at the area. The air was filled with the shouts of men and women as they rushed down the slopes on skis or toboggans. Bob noticed to his embarrassment that there were many excellent skiers, especially among the women, and he watched the graceful manner in which they swished down the steep runs, gliding this way and that, missing trees and shrubs by simple pressure of the feet or movement of the body. These people manipulated the long ten-foot skis with as much ease as if they had been ice skates. Suddenly a wave of self-consciousness swept over him, for he realized that he knew nothing of this sort of skiing—he, Bob Flame, who had mushed over thousands of miles of wilderness snows, realized that some of these women could easily put him to shame.

Hughes relieved the situation in a diplomatic manner.

"There's a good hill over on the other side of this ridge," he remarked casually. "Never could figure out why more people didn't go over there, but they always stay on this side. There's better snow and better slopes over there. What say we go over and get the swing of the thing?"

Bob was grateful for this suggestion. He knew that Hughes understood his embarrassment and that he was attempting to do away with it as much as possible. Once behind the ridge Bob felt his self-consciousness rapidly disappear. He felt confident of his ability to manipulate the skis in heavy snow, and he had proved his ability elsewhere to break trail with the best of them. In realizing his weak points, Bob had a distinct advantage over others who were learning to ski for the first time. He undertook his course of education seriously, as he had done several years before at Lake Station in Yellowstone.

Time after time he climbed wearily up a slope, braced himself with his poles while he turned around, and then with a swish he was off down the steep incline. He edged his skis and threw his weight in the exact manner of Hughes, and he was surprised to see how the usually stubborn boards responded to his efforts. He watched his instructor skimming down the hill, weaving back and forth with graceful curves or coming to a sudden stop in a cloud of snow, and he marveled at the perfect balance which the man seemed always able to maintain.

After an hour of concentrated effort he began to feel that the time was well spent. Although his curves were not always as graceful as those of Hughes, and notwithstanding the fact that he often missed his balance to tumble headlong into a drift when he came to the end of a run, he began to sense that by practice he would become proficient enough in time.

His lessons did not cease on that afternoon. Often he and Hughes would slip away from the office an hour before closing time for a few practice runs, and he often went alone to Bear Lake to spend an hour or two behind the friendly shelter of the ridge.

Two weeks after his first lesson he felt that he had made sufficient progress to attempt a trip to one of the nearer snowshoe cabins. Calling Hughes into the office one morning, he proposed a two-day trip to Fern Lake.

"It'll be good for both of us," he explained, "and we should be getting some snow measurements up in that country for this month."

Hughes readily agreed to the proposal. He was never averse to a trip into the hills, which he loved, whether it was in summer by horse or in winter on skis. Early the following morning they set out from Bear Lake, climbing the steep glacial moraine up which the snow-choked trail zigzaged to the summit.

Half way up the slope Hughes stopped, breathing heavily.

"Man!" he panted, "you've got better wind than I have. You must have been holding secret practice."

Bob leaned on his ski poles.

"I'm used to this kind of stuff. It's coming down and getting out of the way of a tree that worries me."

They went on again, sometimes herring-boning up the slope with legs spread wide and the points of the skis at a wide angle, sometimes sidestepping upward, foot by foot, when the hill was too steep. At last the top of the ridge was reached and they set off around the rim, skirting a large area of burned timber, the trunks of which glistened gold in the morning sunshine. Half a mile beyond they plunged into the timber again and began a slow gradual climb to the top of a steep gorge.

"Odessa Gorge," Hughes announced as they paused on the brink and looked far below to a clear level spot in the carpet of firs. "That opening's Odessa Lake and Fern's a mile below—but you've been over this country before."

"Yes," Bob agreed in a voice that was genuinely

troubled, "but never in winter. I'm worried about getting down there."

Hughes shook his head. "It's not nearly as bad as it looks," he said with reassurance. "The gorge looks bad from here, but just follow me and keep right side up. Ready?"

Bob nodded grimly, although he would willingly have given his entire monthly pay check to skip the next few minutes. Hughes started downward, taking the steep slope by a series of broad sweeping curves. Bob waited until he was well on his way and then he too pushed himself over the edge and headed down the glistening white hill. As he went he gained momentum but he was able to retard his progress sufficiently on the curves so that he maintained his balance. Down they swept, two tiny flashing spots in a wilderness of white. Bob felt that he had never known such speed. The trees rushed by as if he had been on a rapidly moving train. The cold air seemed to form a glaze over his eyes, but he could not wipe them, for to loosen his grip on the ski poles would have meant a headlong tumble down the incline. Ahead he would see a rolling drift and then, seemingly at the same instant, he was upon it and over it and heading downward again. He felt that his heart had ceased beating in this mad flight. Almost before he could realize it they were at the lake, but Hughes did not stop. Instead, the momentum which he had gained carried him over the surface at lightning speed and they were off again, heading down the last winding mile to Fern Lake. Bob did not know how he negotiated that trail with its sharp curves. He vaguely realized that he must make the turns and that he must keep his balance, for to lose it would mean being hurled headlong against some of the big trees. Time after time it seemed that he must fall, but he always managed to regain his balance and shoot down the trail after his companion.

At last, after a dozen miraculous escapes, they broke from the timber and glided to a stop on the smooth surface of Fern Lake. Hughes did not look around. Instead he leaned on one ski pole without saying a word. When Bob came up to him the man was deathly pale.

Bob felt that he too must be pale but he managed to stammer, "That was a ride, fella."

Still white, Hughes turned to him. "You can qualify for any down-mountain ski race in the country now."

"Well, I was plenty scared," admitted the other.

"So was I."

Bob looked at him in amazement. "What do you mean?" he asked, puzzled.

"I couldn't stop," replied the other, pointing to his right foot.

Bob looked down. The man's rigging was hanging unused around his boot. One of his ski poles had also snapped in the downward rush.

"You see," he repeated, "I couldn't stop. If I'd stopped I'd have spilled myself all over the landscape so I had to keep ridin' 'em. Don't get proud of yourself and think you were the only one who was scared. I know what it feels like myself."

CHAPTER XIX

A TRIP WITH HUGHES

EVEN the old-timers in the region had never seen a winter of such unprecedented snowfall. After the first big fall there was a brief period when the sun shone with dazzling brilliance from a cloudless sky. Then storm after storm broke over the range, dropping their white burdens until at times it seemed that clear weather would not appear again that winter. High winds whipped the mountain country, driving the fallen snow before them and packing it deeply in the gorges and canyons. These same winds uprooted the lodgepole pines by the thousands and tore roofs from summer dwellings as if they were so much paper.

Through the white wilderness the rangers plunged on their patrols. Skiing was extremely difficult, for in the timber the snow might be soft while in the exposed areas it was wind-crusted and slippery. One never knew what kind of snow the next mile might bring. In spite of the bitter cold and staggering blizzards the little band of men who remained to guard the park carried on. Every cabin on the boundary was visited at definite intervals as the ceaseless patrols for fur poachers continued. Many an elk and deer was rescued from the deep drifts into which he had blundered while the big yellow snow-gos were kept ready in their sheds for any emergency which might arise.

Bob had already taken several short trips with his men, and by February he had become quite as proficient as they in the manipulation of skis. For some time he and Hughes had planned a long trip into the northern section of the park. They had hoped to visit Cabin Thirteen, ski over Mummy Pass and drop into the headwaters of the North Fork from which point they planned to make their way down stream past Lost Lake, the North Fork Shelter Cabin and on to civilization. The weather, however, had seemed to be constantly against them. But one morning Hughes came into the office beaming good-naturedly. The sun was shining and there was every evidence that fair weather might be in the offing for several days.

"Looks like we might get a break," he remarked, looking out of Bob's window at the blue sky and the range which sparkled dazzling white in the morning sun. "What say we tackle that trip tomorrow if it stays clear all day?"

Bob had spent the past week in his office and he was more than willing to get a brief rest from the routine and paper work of his desk. He grinned and replied half eagerly: "Sounds good to me. What's the weather going to be?"

Hughes shrugged. Weather was much the same to him. He had traveled the mountain country in good times and bad and he still felt young enough to battle the worst blizzards which the hills could produce.

"Well, we've both struck rough weather before," he replied casually. "If it *should* change we can al-

ways lay over, but I've got a hunch it's goin' to stay
clear for a spell at least. Lord knows we've had
enough for a little while."

The sky remained cloudless for the remainder of
the day, much to the delight of Hughes, and that night
Bob thoroughly inspected his equipment. Remember-
ing Hughes' experience on the Fern Lake Trail, he
carefully went over every inch of leather and every
rivet of his rigging. For an hour he worked on the
skis themselves, first ironing hot parafin into the soles
of the boards, following this by hot wax. After sat-
isfying himself that they were properly attended to,
he turned his attentions to the contents of his pack. He
would be gone three days, but long ago he had learned
that traveling even in a snowbound wilderness required
little in the way of personal equipment, and that a light
kit was essential. He accordingly cut his pack to the
bare necessities. An extra pair of socks, a small toilet
kit, a headlamp, a pair of dark snow glasses, a topographic map, a waterproof match case and an extra
supply of tobacco comprised his luggage. Blankets
and food would be in the cabins, and every pound
would be a dead weight as they struggled through the
deep snows which they would most certainly encounter before their return.

Early the next morning Frost drove the two men as
far up the road as possible and, after they had assisted
him in shoveling the car out of a deep drift which he
had managed to get into while turning around, they
started off up the snow-choked highway toward Fall
River Pass.

Hughes' prediction that they would have good

weather seemed to hold true. The air was still and the sky was cloudless. As they began the long steady ascent it seemed to Bob that he had never seen such a perfect winter morning.

"Man!" he exclaimed with enthusiasm, as they stopped on a promontory for a brief period to catch their breath, "I haven't felt like this since I left Yellowstone."

"Sort of makes you live again to breathe this air an' feel the blood pumpin'," Hughes nodded. "Many's the time when I've been eatin' tourists' dust in the summer that I've hankered for a morning like this—sort of crisp and clean."

His cheeks were red with health and as Bob looked at him he could not fail to wonder how many men of his age—men who might easily surpass him in accumulated worldly goods and power—could boast of the same energy and love of life as could this humble ranger.

They went on again, and at the end of two hours Hughes led the way off to the right of the road and into the timber. Abruptly he started to slide down a steep hill which brought them eventually into a white wilderness of snow-covered alpine meadows near timberline.

"Looks different, doesn't it?" Hughes asked.

For a moment Bob pondered. Then he remembered that he and his companion had passed over this very spot a few months before while stocking the shelter cabins in the north end of the park. "Chapin Creek?" he asked.

Hughes nodded and started on again. Sometimes

they slipped easily over the wind-crusted snow. At other times, however, they floundered wearily through the soft drifts in the timber. It was exhausting work and once again Bob's mind drifted back to the beginning of his ranger days when he had learned to ski. He vividly recalled his first long patrol with its heartbreaking weariness and the stinging, pounding sensation in his lungs as they fought desperately for sufficient air to permit him to keep his feet. He smiled grimly as he plunged along, now ahead, now behind Hughes, as they took turns breaking trail. By this time he had been in the service long enough to have overcome any feeling of romance connected with this grueling work of patroling. Three year ago there had been a spark of the romantic in it for him, even though he had fallen exhausted time after time in the ski trail. It was deadening and he knew that the monotony of pushing ahead foot by foot through unbroken wilderness would kill any idea of romance in even the most enthusiastic of them sooner or later. Still there was a feeling of exultation—of conquering the wild, which even he could not help experiencing as he looked back over the bleak expanse at the trail which had been broken. It was a trail smashed by brawn through the snow where rangers were penetrating the silence of a land locked by snow and ice. How many such trails threaded the white forests of western parks, he thought —and each trail broken at the expense of tortured muscles and bleeding lungs.

Hughes' voice interrupted his thoughts.

"I'll take it. You must be a horse."

Bob grunted as he stepped aside to let Hughes pass and take up the work of breaking.

"I was just thinking about my first days of skiing. Remember yours?"

The other man shook his head seriously. "No, honestly I don't. I was raised here in the hills, you know, and I don't remember when I learned to ski."

At noon they stopped for a cold lunch and then on again, sometimes making good progress, sometimes traveling less than a mile in an hour as the snow conditions became more and more difficult. The sun dropped behind the range, relieving the torturing glare on their eyes which, had it not been for the dark glasses, would have brought snow-blindness within a short time. But the sinking sun brought with it the biting cold of a mountain night.

"Goin' to be sharp," Hughes predicted.

Bob shivered in spite of the exertion and buttoned the neck of his leather coat.

"Going to be? Seems to me it's cold right now."

"Soon be there," Hughes returned cheerfully.

He was right. Within fifteen minutes they broke from the timber and Bob recognized the tiny log structure on the bank of the creek which they had visited together that fall. How different it was now. Snow had drifted to the eaves and had he not seen it before he might easily have passed it by, so well did it blend into the bleak and desolate background of cold, naked aspen and willow. As they approached, Bob marveled that Hughes had been able to lead him unerringly to that tiny black dot in a white wilderness.

"Everything's jake," called his companion as he

came to a stop in front of the cabin and slipped out of his skis. "Just like I left it last month. Say," he continued as he pulled a shovel from under the eaves and began digging through the drifted snow to where he knew the door was located. "How many time's Frost been over here this winter?"

"Twice," Bob replied, knocking the snow from his skis and sticking them upright in the drift. "Why?"

"Just wondered. Remember we cached those strawberries?"

Bob smiled as he recalled the painstaking care with which the other had hidden the cans of fruit that fall.

"Well," Hughes continued, "it's a good thing I did. When I pulled in here last month, that mug had eaten every strawberry in the place."

While Bob started a blaze in the wide stone fireplace Hughes set off toward the creek, swinging along on his skis with an axe in one hand and two pails in the other. Soon he returned, having cut a hole in the thick ice and dipped out the precious water—precious, for already Bob had learned that the greatest hardship in the high country during the winter is the lack of water. There was snow in abundance but at best it was a poor substitute.

Hughes handed down the full buckets and then slid into the hole and through the door of the cabin. It was a tiny room, not more than ten feet square. The fireplace occupied the greater portion of one wall while a large, heavy food chest stood in a corner. In another corner was a similar chest containing bedding, while a mattress and pair of springs were suspended from the low smoke-blackened rafters. There was no floor in the cabin and they soon lowered the springs to sit upon, as the ground was uncomfortably cold.

As the meal was being prepared the wind began to howl about the small log structure. Bob went to the door and looked out. He was greeted by such a cloud of blinding snow that he beat a hasty retreat back to the fire, wiping the water from his face.

"Getting a blow," he sputtered, as he returned to his seat. "Can't see your hand in front of you."

Hughes nodded and absently poked a gunny sack further into a large crack between the logs. "This place is pretty bad when it blows," he replied. "I've spent some tough nights here. We ought to get a couple of senators or the whole blasted appropriations committee to spend a night here when she's blowin' and heapin' snow. I'll bet we could get some money for another cabin then."

Bob chuckled as he attempted to picture two robust senators crowding into the tiny room. He wondered what they would think and how they would act. Once he would have thought twice before spending a night in such a cabin with the wind piling drifts rapidly over the country, but he had spent many such nights as this in the past few years and he knew that, whatever the weather might be, it would break sooner or later and with a good pair of skis a man could get through any kind of country unless an accident of some kind befell him.

There was little to do after they finished the meal and washed the dishes. They sat in their cramped quarters, smoking and replenishing the fire from time to time. Outside the storm had seemed to increase in fury. The cabin was a low solid structure built of heavy logs, but at times it seemed to quiver before the blasts as they struck at it. In spite of the roaring blaze in the fireplace it was impossible to heat the small room. Snow on the mantel refused to melt. The wind-driven crystals found the tiniest holes and poured through so that by the time they crawled into their blankets there was a thin layer of white over everything in the cabin. Sleep came spasmodically for, in spite of the abundant clothing, the stinging cold came through. Several times during the night they shook the snow from their blankets and crawled out to pile more logs on the embers.

At four o'clock they were up and had the fire blazing again. The wind had subsided but a steady fall of snow had set in, and, when they at last clamped on their skis two hours later in the cold dawn of a winter morning, there was a fresh fall of several inches covering the old trail.

"Looks like we're in for one," Hughes said, turning his face upward to look at the millions of white flakes sifting downward from a leaden sky and striking the earth with a soft hissing sound. "Think we'd better tackle it after all?"

Bob shrugged. "You know this country better than I do. What's it like between here and the North Fork Cabin?"

The other man frowned. "It's level for a few miles. Then we climb and climb and then drop down pretty steadily. Not so bad when you can ski all the way. I'll never forget one trip, though, when we hadn't gotten much snow and the wind had blown what little we had off from above timberline. We had to carry the boards for miles and it was plenty tough. You can't ski on bare ground. Well, what say?"

"Let's tackle it. I've made pit camps before."

Hughes grinned the reckless grin of a man who loves danger. It was evident that he desired to make the trip and that he had been fearful lest Bob should decide against it. "On our way," he called gaily as he gave himself a shove with his poles and went gliding easily down the little incline away from the cabin.

After an hour it became apparent that the snow was there to stay and that there was little hope of its abating that day. It was piling rapidly and as Bob pushed on he estimated that approximately an inch an hour was being added to the already deep blanket. Each hour it became harder and their progress was correspondingly slower, for the new snow was not of a consistency to permit easy sliding.

At length they came to the head of the gently sloping valley up which they had been traveling, and Hughes stopped. "How you comin'?" he asked.

"Right with you," Bob replied, although he would have readily welcomed a half hour rest to relieve the burning sensation in his lungs and the terrific aching of his legs.

Hughes pointed to a steep slope whose top was obscured by the storm. Heavy timber clothed the sides and Bob knew that in that timber the snow would be still softer and deeper than it was in the open.

"We go up that," his friend announced. "Strike timberline on top and then we should have it fairly easy." He consulted his wrist watch. "Better grab a bite here. I think we can get water in that gully if we dig deep enough, an' I don't know of any more till we get down the other side. Probably be late this afternoon."

Standing on one ski to keep from sinking into the snow, Hughes used the other as a shovel and, after excavating a deep hole in the drift, struck a tiny trickle of water. Wetting his ski pole, he placed it carefully in the soft snow. Then back in the water and then in the snow until a mass of the saturated snow clung to the webbing of the pole. Then they took turns sucking out the precious water as they would have from a sponge. The meal consisted of cold ham which they had boiled that morning, raisins and chunks of frozen bread. It was not a meal which possessed appetizing qualities, but it was nourishing and Bob felt greatly rested when they at last shouldered their packs again and began the long tedious climb up the steep slope.

He had had no illusions about this being an easy portion of the trip; and as they plunged into the trees, fighting their way foot by foot upward through the soft snow, Bob became increasingly aware that it was a heart-wearing job. Up they went, first one and then the other breaking away the mass, battling to gain a foothold and then grasping desperately at limbs and brush in an effort to hold what they had so laboriously gained. Stops were more frequent now, for it was impossible to make more than a hundred feet without resting.

At last, after what seemed hours to Bob, they came to a large clearing in a great amphitheater. It was snowing harder than ever now, but from the edge Bob could see that it was the semicircular head of a valley which had been cleared of trees, either by early fires or snowslides during the winters of big snows.

Hughes hesitated before starting across the slope. "Looks all right," he said dubiously, "but somehow I have a feelin' about it."

"What?" Bob asked wearily, for he welcomed the open area with its harder snow.

"Snowslides," Hughes said simply. "Guess it's all right, though. Don't follow too close. Better stay at least fifty yards behind, just in case something does give way."

Bob was tired, but this was a danger which he had never experienced before. In all his skiing he had never encountered the treacherous snowslides of the Rockies, and he was at once on the alert as he pushed out across the open slope, well behind his companion.

CHAPTER XX

HUGHES moved cautiously over the unbroken snow, feeling his way with his ski poles. He was half way across the open space when he gave a warning shout and threw up his hands. Before Bob realized what had happened he saw the entire side of the hill give way. Moving slowly at first, it seemed to pause momentarily and then with horrible rapidity it crumbled and slid downward.

A second later it was over and Bob stood spellbound, looking at the bare, lifeless expanse before him. It was like a giant shell-hole in a mountain of snow. Hughes was nowhere to be seen, and a sickening sensation assailed the man on the edge of the pit as he swept it for some sign. Throwing off the stupor which seemed to root him to the spot, he slipped his pack from his shoulders and plunged downward toward the place where he had last seen his companion. Seconds dragged as he searched desperately through the mass. Suddenly he saw a ski pole stuck in the snow fifty feet below him. He circled it and looked wildly about for some trace of the man with whom he had been traveling but a minute before. Then a slight movement in the snow almost under his feet caught Bob's eye. Bracing his skis against the slope he dug rapidly with his hands. Suddenly he came in contact with something hard. It was an arm. He worked furiously and after what seemed an interminable period he uncovered Hughes' head. Digging this free, he continued his labors and eventually he was able to drag the man out of the white trap and bring him to a sitting position.

Fortunately Hughes was not injured. He was groggy and it took several minutes of frantic work on the part of the chief ranger to revive him, but at last his efforts were rewarded. Hughes opened his eyes, stared at the sky for a moment and then grinned sheepishly.

"What hit me?" he asked weakly.

In spite of the seriousness of the situation Bob laughed. The tension of the past few minutes was relieved.

"You got into a slide."

Hughes vigorously shook his head like a fighter who has just received a hard blow. Then he climbed slowly to his feet.

"Man!" he exclaimed, "that was a close one. Good thing you were here to pull me out. I've been in 'em before but I've always been able to ride 'em out. This one pulled me down too soon."

After they had rested for a few minutes they started on across the expanse again. This time they were doubly cautious, for the experience had left them both badly shaken and they had no desire to repeat it.

At last they arrived at the tongue of timber which projected out into the clearing. Here they stopped again to adjust their riggings before beginning the last portion of the steep climb toward the top of the ridge.

It took them more than an hour of heavy work to

negotiate the ascent. Every few minutes Bob imagined that he could see the top ahead of him, but it invariably proved to be only a small rise in the topography of the main ridge and, upon reaching it they seemed to be no farther toward their goal than before. Finally, however, they topped the ridge and paused to look back at the steep slope up which they had so laboriously come. Ahead the country lay like a great rolling prairie, sloping gently downward to a "U" shaped defile. It had ceased snowing yet Bob could distinguish nothing beyond that defile.

"That's Mummy Pass," Hughes told him. "Good reason why you can't see anything beyond. There just ain't anything to see. From the pass she drops off for a thousand feet straight down to Lost Lake and the headwaters of the North Fork."

"How do we get down after we're through the pass?"

The other shrugged. "There are several chimneys and they're usually free from snow. We'll get down 'em all right."

The brief pause rested them and, cheered by the thought that the worst was over, they made good time down the gentle slope to the pass.

"This is more like it," Bob shouted, as they skimmed over the windblown surface, curving in and out to avoid striking the boulders whose gray heads protruded above the snow.

Hughes nodded his agreement. "Better than comin' up that ridge with your heart in your mouth lookin' for snowslides."

As they approached the pass Hughes veered to the

left. Bob, however, kept a straight course toward the very center of the pass. He could not resist the fine smooth run which the snow at that point was affording and he was unable to understand the other's change in course. Hughes shouted something to him but the whistle of the wind in his ears made the words indistinguishable. As he approached the edge he slowed down, for he had no desire to go over the brink and into the great white gorge which was rapidly opening before him. He retarded his speed sufficiently for ordinary conditions, but at that moment something unexpected occurred and before he realized what had happened he was in the grip of a terrific wind. It was like being tossed about by a powerful unseen force. Bob was thrown to the ground with such vehemence that for a moment he lay there half stunned. He attempted to rise but he was promptly knocked down. Time after time he tried to get to his feet but each attempt met with a similar rebuff.

At last he lay back exhausted, clinging desperately to his ski poles. The skis themselves were caught by the wind and he was swung around like a straw in a gale. He attempted to crawl to the protection of a boulder but he found it utterly impossible to change his position. Gradually he became very cold as the great wind continued to suck up from the gorge and hurl itself through the pass.

Finally he discovered that by pulling himself along inch by inch on his stomach and keeping very low to the ground he could make slight progress. In this manner he reached a small boulder. It was not large enough to afford him protection but it gave him something to hold. There he clung desperately, looking into the very face of the chasm which dropped away not fifteen feet ahead of him. It was well, he concluded half consciously, that he was unable to gain his feet, for he might be battered this way and that until he slid over the edge. But he wondered if his present position was any better. His hands were becoming numb and his face seemed to be without feeling. Unless Hughes arrived shortly it would be impossible for him to remain much longer without becoming badly frozen.

Vaguely at first and then more certainly, Bob felt that something was going on behind him, but he was not able to change his position sufficiently to make out what it was. At length the realization came over him that Hughes was attempting a rescue. As the sounds came nearer he was able to crane his neck enough to make out the figure of his companion crawling along on his stomach and pushing a ski ahead of him.

Gradually the man worked his way nearer until the ski was opposite Bob. Then Hughes shouted, but in spite of the fact that a scant twelve feet separated them the words were too faint to be understood. The continuous roar of the blast drowned them. By means of signs Hughes made it known that Bob was to grasp one end of the ski. He did so, half mechanically, caring little now what happened, for the cold was beginning to have its deadly effect. Once he had hold of the ski he clung to it as desperately as he had to the boulder, and he felt himself being dragged slowly back from the edge. Then he remembered no more.

When he regained consciousness he was lying behind

the protection of a boulder, while Hughes rubbed his hands and cheeks with snow. He lay there for a moment, pitifully weak, and then, as his senses returned, he seemed to gain strength. He attempted to sit up but Hughes shoved him back.

"Take it easy," he said. "Rest a minute."

Bob lay back on the snow and submitted to the rough treatment which Hughes was administering. He was grateful, for he knew that his friend had saved his life and that he had also saved his hands and face from severe freezing by the application of snow.

At length Hughes allowed him to sit up. "How do you feel?" he asked.

The question seemed strange to Bob and it was not until he was upon his feet that he answered: "I'm all right. How did it happen? What did I get into?"

"Updraft," Hughes explained, as they made their way slowly along the left hand side of the gorge. "Some of the passes get it sometimes. I yelled at you as soon as I saw snow driftin' up from below but you didn't hear me."

"I heard you, but I couldn't make out what you were talking about and I wanted to take advantage of the run before I stopped."

Hughes chuckled. "I bet you never run down into a pass again without lookin' it over first."

Bob merely grunted but he knew that his friend had taught him something about winter traveling in the mountains which he was not likely to forget. He thought again of the strange fact that each had saved the other's life within the brief period of a few hours that day.

After they had progressed a short distance along

the rim, Hughes stopped at the head of a steep chimney from which the snow had blown clear.

"This is it," he announced. "It's steep and there's lots of loose rocks, but if you can keep your feet on the ground you're all right."

They slipped out of their skis, tied them together, and then, using their poles as brakes, began the treacherous descent of the gorge. A thousand feet below them lay several small lakes which had blown clear of snow. These, Bob knew, from past studies of the topographic maps, must be the source of the North Fork of the Thompson River. Far below the lakes, in a dense, snow-choked wilderness of fir and spruce, lay the shelter cabin where they hoped to spend the night.

While they made their way slowly downward, Bob had an opportunity to admire the rough, wild country below them. The great gorge was packed with snow which swept suddenly but smoothly down to the dark carpet of trees which bordered the lakes. He wondered if there was a living soul in that region besides his companion and himself. There were animals—bobcats, marten and weasels, hardy creatures who braved the rigors of the higher altitudes, killing and being killed until the spring sunshine made the world bloom again. Probably few of the larger creatures were there, he reflected, for the elk and deer were far down the stream, well within the security of the winter feeding grounds. Suddenly a rock went clattering down an adjacent chimney and Bob looked up with a start.

There, high above him, a great bighorn ram stood on the brink, silhouetted against the sky. The big animal watched the two men curiously as if wondering what might prompt these two-legged creatures to penetrate the wilderness at this time of year.

Bob stopped short and stared in amazement. "What on earth are sheep doing up here?" he asked Hughes.

The other laughed. "Lots of 'em winter up in this country," he replied. "Fact is, a good many of the sheep in the park winter at higher altitudes than they summer."

"But how do they live?" exclaimed the other, still dumbfounded that these lords of the peaks could weather the snowy months at so great a height.

"They get along all right," replied Hughes, as the rock under him began to slip and he jumped for a more substantial one. "It really isn't so tough above timberline in winter. Not as bad as one might think. Lots of times I've been enjoyin' warm sunshine up here when it was stormin' cats an' dogs in the low country. The wind blows the ground an' grass clear in spots an' they can get on the lee of a cliff if the weather gets too rough."

For an hour they proceeded downward, slipping, jumping to safety and balancing themselves to keep from plunging headlong down the slope. At last they reached the end of the chimney. Almost immediately the snow became so deep that they were forced to strap on their skis. The slope was still steep and the crust was sufficient to bear their weight. Down and down they went, swerving this way and that, over knolls and into hollows until at last Hughes stopped in a cloud of snow. Bob wiped his face free of the crystals and looked about him. For the past fifteen minutes he had been traveling at such a terrific rate that he had

had no opportunity to pay attention to the landscape. It had been all he could do to keep his footing and avoid the shrubs and tops of small snow-covered trees. When at last he had the chance to observe his surroundings he found that they were standing on the shore of a fairly large lake whose surface, like those above, was free of snow.

"Lost Lake," Hughes announced. "There's an old cabin down a little ways. Let's slide down there and have a smoke."

He led the way through the heavy timber to a tumbled-down log shack. Inside there were the remains of two bunks as well as several pieces of rusted equipment. An old stove was in one corner of the room and a pair of sagging springs was in the other.

"Not much of a place, but it's helped me out a lot of times," Hughes remarked as he entered the shelter and sat down on the earth floor.

"What is it?"

"Just an old shelter cabin, built a long time ago. Nobody uses it now except a few fishing parties that get up this far in summer. I've stopped here a lot of times though when I got caught. It's a wind break an' that's about all you can say," he concluded, glancing at the caved-in roof and the huge gaps between the logs where the chinking had fallen away.

"How far to the North Fork Cabin?"

"Five or six miles."

Bob looked at his watch. It was already four o'clock and the sun had dropped behind the ridge. A chill was settling over the valley and he became suddenly aware that he was tired.

He sighed audibly. "Wish we were in."

Hughes nodded. "Will be before long. That stretch goes fast. Downhill drag all the way."

The words cheered Bob but he did not know whether or not the old mountain man was speaking them simply to bolster up his spirits. They proved to be correct, however, for immediately upon leaving the lake they began dropping by an easy grade. There were switchbacks in the trail and, being tired as he was, it was difficult for Bob to negotiate them without falling. On several he lost his balance and plunged head first into the drifts. Each time it became harder and harder for him to kick his skis free and climb upon them again.

Finally they reached level country. The river was lined with masses of willow whose tips protruded above the snow. This proved to be another difficulty to Bob for it seemed that the tips of his skis were constantly becoming entangled in them. Light was failing rapidly and Hughes finally stopped and took off his pack.

"Better put on our lamps," he suggested. "Cabin's only half a mile further, but we'll need 'em before we get in."

With the shafts of white light cutting into the growing darkness about them, Bob felt more comfortable. Now he was able to push forward without fear of tripping over something in the half-gloom of the valley. At times it seemed that they would never arrive, and his thoughts went back again to the deadening fatigue of his first long ski patrol, when he and McDonald had been forced to make a pit camp in the Yellowstone wilderness.

Hughes' light seemed to creep farther and farther

away from him until at last it was swallowed up entirely in the darkness as a bend in the trail separated the two men. This did not worry Bob, for it was a simple matter to follow the other's ski tracks. He was about to conclude that his companion had missed the cabin when he smelled the pungent odor of burning pine. Looking up suddenly he saw a light streaming from a cabin window a hundred feet ahead of him.

"Hope you didn't object to bein' left alone," Hughes apologized. "Thought I'd just slide on in an' get things started."

Bob climbed out of his skis and shook his head. "I had a hunch that was what you were up to. Boy! I'm fagged!"

The other grunted sympathetically. "That's no pleasure jaunt over the hump. It's a real trip. But we're in now, an' a few miles downhill tomorrow'll put us on the main road."

Bob contentedly sipped the soup that Hughes handed him.

"How are we going to get back to headquarters?" he asked suddenly. "This trail lands us ten miles from the village, doesn't it?"

His companion nodded wisely.

"Frost'll be waitin' for us. I called him up before we started, just in case I forgot, an' told him to meet us at the road at eleven o'clock."

The chief ranger sighed and continued to sip his soup. "You think of everything, don't you?"

Hughes shook his head soberly. "Nope. I didn't think to salt this soup."

CHAPTER XXI

A NEW TRAIL

THE prediction of the old-timers that the winter would be one of much snow proved correct, and their prophecy of an early spring was equally so. As the weeks passed, crowding one upon the other, the weather at the lower altitudes grew constantly milder. Although the high country still lay in the icy grip of winter, the drifts in the valleys melted farther and farther back. The ground, saturated by the water from melting snow, suddenly seemed alive. The smell of wet earth permeated the lower reaches of the mountain country. Solitary pasque flowers broke through the surface to mock the blue of April skies. Marigolds opened in a glorious burst of white and yellow and followed the retreating drifts, often growing in the icy runoffs of the snowbanks.

As the early spring flowers came into bloom there was another change in the animal life of the park. New birds arrived and ended their long migratory flight. Robins frequented the open meadows while bluebirds with flashes of dazzling color searched out the solitary snags. The deer and elk began their slow trek to the high country, following the drifts as did the flowers. Marmots and groundsquirrels emerged from their hibernating burrows to blink in the bright sunshine, while bears, followed by tiny waddling cubs, lumbered through the damp meadows in search of succulent grasses and bulbs upon which to feed a stomach small and shriveled by a winter of inactivity.

But this increased activity was not alone among the wild creatures of the park. When good weather set in, the engineers began preparations for opening the roads and, as it progressed, the actual consummation of these preparations was seen. Big snowplows moved into the high country. Trucks containing powerful explosives, equipment and supplies, began rumbling out of the Utility Area and up the road toward the snow line. Roadcamps were established and all day long the throbbing motors of the heavy plows could be heard on the highway where they battled the big drifts in an attempt to open the roads and allow them to dry before traffic started. Time after time these human and mechanical snow-fighters were beaten back by late squalls and high winds which swept the mountains, but they battled their way onward, often re-doing the work of days which the storms had obliterated.

While this battle was progressing on the high mountain roads Bob was busy making preparations for the coming season. Applications for temporary ranger work which had been pouring in for months were carefully reviewed and the men for the summer staff selected. Plans for fish planting were made, cabins were cleaned, the stock of wire and lead slugs for sealing guns was replenished, and a thousand small details attended to before the rush of the season was upon them. Two new C.C.C. camps were established within the area, and this took considerable time, as Bob was becoming more and more responsible for the efficient working of these conservation groups within the area.

One morning he and McDonald were talking in the office when the telephone rang. They paused momentarily for the clerk to ring one of their buzzers but she took the message herself and they resumed their conversation. For a minute she was busy at her typewriter. Then she came in and handed Bob a telegram. He read it and chuckled.

"Another one gone wrong," he grinned as he handed the slip to McDonald.

The assistant superintendent took the yellow paper and read aloud:

"You lose stop Jean and I married last night
Howe"

"Remember when I came down here last spring I told you he was on the verge of it?" Bob asked.

The other nodded and smiled. "Suppose now McMannon will be tearing his hair trying to find quarters for them. There never were enough houses up there."

Bob grinned as he reread the telegram. "Guess I'm not much of an influence when it comes to anything like this. I tried to talk him out of it but apparently it was no go."

A week after this conversation Bob returned from a short inspection trip to find a note on his desk. It was signed by the superintendent and requested him to come to his office when he returned. Wondering what the summons could mean, Bob made his way to the other end of the building. As he walked that short distance his mind worked rapidly. He thought of all the things which he might or might not have done that would provoke a call from his superior. Still wonder-

The Ceaseless Vigil

Shadow Mountain Fire Lookout

ing, he entered the room and took a seat beside Wentworth's desk.

The superintendent looked up and there was something in his glance that told Bob this was not an ordinary summons. Something important was in the air. Instead of speaking, the man handed Bob a letter. It was from Washington—brief and to the point—a request that Bob report immediately to the Washington Office on special assignment.

Trying to speak calmly, he asked, "What's it all about?"

The superintendent shook his head. "I haven't an idea. It says a special assignment and that's all I can tell you. That may mean any number of things, from Alaska to Hawaii."

For some time Bob sat without speaking. "What's the answer?" he asked at length.

Wentworth shrugged his shoulders. "That's up to you. You don't have to go if you don't want to, and I don't want to lose you if I can help it. On the other hand, that's a rather selfish way to look at it because it may mean an advancement. Why not take this home and sleep on it? Let me know in the morning."

Bob took the letter and walked slowly out of the office. His head was a confused jumble of thoughts. So upsetting was the news that he was unable to concentrate to any extent upon the work which he had laid out for the day. That afternoon he got into his car and headed up the Trail Ridge Road. Not that he had any duties there, but he wanted to be alone—to think things through. Parking at Many Parks Curve he sat for an hour gazing dreamily out over the great valleys and on to where the square granite head of Longs Peak lifted itself majestically above the other mountains of the Front Range. He had come to love this country of wooded valleys and rugged splendor. He had grown to know its moods and to understand the calm peace of its meadows and the splendid fierceness of its timberline storms. But he had come here to make a decision, not to dream. He had felt the same about Yellowstone, as he had driven to Livingston with Mitchell for the last time. Then he had felt that there could be no place in his affections for another region, but now he had come to feel the same about Rocky Mountain.

At length, with a serious face, he started the motor and headed back toward the valley. He was starting on a new trail which would not end at the office or at Utility Area or at the little log cottage which had sheltered him and his dreams for the past year. This new trail led to Washington and to whatever the new assignment might hold in store for him.

THE END

EXPLANATORY NOTES

Notes are keyed to page and line numbers. For example, 1:1 means page 1, line 1.

1:1. Located behind historic Old Faithful Inn, the Old Faithful Ranger Station, completed in 1930, offers a variety of interpretive programs.

1:24. Although the first of these dog races was run in 1917 from Ashton, Idaho, to Yellowstone National Park, a distance of 55 miles, by the time Yeager's book was written, the races took place in the Ashton area.

3:15. The road through Golden Gate Canyon on the way to Mammoth Hot Springs (U.S. Highway 89) dates from 1885, when it was nothing more than a wooden trestle hugging the canyon wall above Glen Creek. By Yeager's day, the wooden trestle had been replaced by a concrete viaduct. It is called the Golden Gate because of the profusion of yellow lichens on the canyon walls.

4:2-5. Reachable only by trail, Shoshone Lake, the largest backcountry lake in the United States, is three miles east of Yellowstone's Old Faithful area.

4:6-7. Black Sand Basin, a mile east of Old Faithful, is the site of two of Yellowstone's most famous hot springs.

7:18. The term "sagebrushers" apparently originated in Yellowstone as a name for visitors who preferred camping to staying in one of the park's hotels and lodges. Albright and Taylor (see Afterword) devoted a whole chapter in their 1928 book, *Oh, Ranger!* to "Dudes and Sagebrushers."

9:25-29. Park headquarters is at Mammoth Hot Springs, near the northwestern boundary of Yellowstone. It is the site of the original Fort Yellowstone, which was constructed by the Army in 1891. Madison Junction, Norris Geyser Basin and Dead Man's Turn are on the route north from the Old Faithful Ranger Station.

11:24. The Civilian Conservation Corps (C.C.C.), a public works program for unemployed young men (initially between the ages of 18 and 25), was created by President Franklin Roosevelt on March 21, 1933, in response to the Great Depression of the 1930s. Its aim was to relieve unemployment while addressing the need to conserve the natural resources in the nation's parks and public lands. By the time the C.C.C. program ended in 1942, it enjoyed widespread public support and was one of the most popular of Roosevelt's New Deal programs. C.C.C. recruits lived in camps supervised by U.S. Army personnel, and in national parks like Rocky Mountain, they worked under the direction of Park Service staff. They were paid $30 a month, $22 of which was sent home to dependents.

14:20. Park Point is on Lake Yellowstone.

15: 8. Grand Teton National Park, established in February of 1929.

15:9. The "big fire" alluded to, the largest in Yellowstone's recorded history, which burned 18,000 acres, took place in the vicinity of Heart Lake in southern Yellowstone in 1931.

19:2. Livingston, Montana, located on today's Interstate Highway 90, is 90 miles north of the North Entrance to Yellowstone National Park.

22:25. Mammoth Campground, at Mammoth Hot Springs, is located near Yellowstone's North Entrance.

25:18. 10,921-foot Emigrant Peak is clearly visible from U.S. Highway 89 south of Livingston.

25: 29-32. The Yellowstone River north of Gardiner, Montana, flows through Yankee Jim Canyon, a favorite place for whitewater canoeing. Cinnabar, three miles north of Gardiner, was, as the author suggests, the site of the first railroad service to the park and between 1883 and 1903, Yellowstone's primary gateway.

26:1-2: Prominent Electric Peak (10,992-feet) in the Gallatin Range is located in Yellowstone's northwest corner near Mammoth Hot Springs. Its name comes from the electric charge caused by lightning that nearly killed members of the party that made the first ascent in 1872.

26:4. The east entrance, or East Gate, of Yellowstone is 50 miles west of Cody, Wyoming.

27:4. The lack of a listing in the 1927-1928 Fort Collins telephone directory suggests that the Forestry Club is fictitious, though there was a student organization with that name at Agricultural College of Colorado (now Colorado State University). During the late 1920s, many of the school's forestry program graduates, including Yeager's friend John McLaughlin, joined the National Park Service.

30:1. As the text suggests, Jim Bridger (1804-1881), William Sublette (1799-1845) and Ceran St. Vrain (1802-1870) were all involved in the development of America's western fur trade.

30: 28-29. Today's Colorado State University was founded under the Morrill Land Grant Act in 1870 as the Agricultural College of Colorado six years before Colorado achieved statehood, though it did not open its doors to students until 1879. In 1935, it was re-named the Coiorado College of Agricultural and Mechanical Arts (Colorado A&M). It became Colorado State University in 1957. From an early date, CSU offered courses in botany, horticulture, entomology and irrigation engineering. Today, these specialties are housed in the Department of Forest, Rangeland and Watershed Stewardship.

31:27. Thorofare and Lake Station are two of Yellowstone's patrol cabins.

33:23-26. Mariana Modina (1812-1878), who spent his younger days as a trapper, hunter, scout and guide, in 1858 established a stage stop on the Big Thompson River three miles west of present Loveland, a place that became known as Namaqua, or Modina's Crossing. Louis Papa (1848-1935), Modina's stepson, for most of his life ran cattle for local ranchers. Yeager had researched Modina's life for the brief article titled "Facts and Fables About Namaqua," which he wrote for the November 1931 issue of *Nature Notes from Rocky Mountain National Park*.

34:5. 14,259-foot Longs Peak is the highest mountain in northern Colorado's Front Range. It is named in honor of American explorer Stephen H. Long (1784-1864), whose pioneering scientific expedition of 1820 passed by at a distance as Long and his party made their way south along the foothills of the Front Range.

34: 9-10. As Bob Flame explained below, "park," in the parlance of the mountains, means "valley." According to tradition, Kentucky-born Joel Estes (1806-1875) came upon the valley that would bear his name in October of 1859 while on a hunting expedition with one of his sons. Attracted by the possibilities of ranching, Estes returned the following summer and built two cabins and several corrals; but he did not occupy them until 1863, when he moved his family and herd up from today's Platteville on the South Platte, where they had been living since the summer of 1859. The valley was named for Estes by William N. Byers, founding editor of the *Rocky Mountain News*, who took advantage of Joel's hospitality in August of 1864 while on his way to an unsuccessful attempt to climb Longs Peak. After Joel Estes and his family left in April of 1866 to pursue ranching opportunities elsewhere, "Estes's park" (or "valley") became Estes Park.

36:1-2. The road (today's U.S. Highway 34) across the Continental Divide, linking Estes Park and Grand Lake, opened for use in 1932. It was then, and still is the highest continuously paved highway in the world. Trail Ridge Road replaced Fall River Road, completed in 1920, whose steep grades, tight switchback curves and frequent need for repair made automobile and bus travel difficult.

36:9-16. Windham Thomas Wyndham-Quin (1841-1926), the Fourth Earl of Dunraven, an Irish nobleman, first visited Estes Park in December of 1872 on a hunting expedition, and came to own title to a great deal of the valley through means that were, at best, questionable. That his scheme was "nipped... in the bud," however, is not wholly accurate, for Dunraven, through his agent Theodore Whyte, gained legal title to thousands of acres all the across Estes Valley. Dunraven, an avid sportsman, chronicled his later hunting adventures in the Yellowstone region in *The Great Divide: Travels in the Upper Yellowstone in the Summer of 1874* (1876). Dunraven Pass is located on the Grand Loop Road between Tower Falls and Canyon.

37:2. Until 1967 and the opening of the new east side administration building and visitor center at Beaver Meadows (today's Park Headquarters), Rocky Mountain National Park's administrative offices were located at the edge of the village where Moraine Avenue turns west along the Big Thompson River. The building (which still stands on its original site) was completed in October of 1925 on land loaned by the Estes Park Woman's Club. This building replaced the original headquarters building on lower Elkhorn Avenue, also within the village of Estes Park, used between 1915 and 1925. That small, white wood-frame building has been relocated to a site behind the Estes Park Museum.

41:20. Beaver Point (on U.S. Highway 36, the road that leads to what is now the Beaver Meadows entrance of Rocky Mountain National Park) is named for Beaver Brook, which flows out of the park to enter the Big Thompson River nearby.

46:18-21. By the late 19th century, elk had been hunted out of the Estes Park-Rocky Mountain National Park area and had to be re-introduced by bringing two small herds in from the Jackson Hole region of Wyoming in 1913 and 1915.

47:28. The scenic overlook called Many Parks Curve, like Fall River Pass and Tundra Curves mentioned below, is a much-visited site on Trail Ridge Road because of its panoramic views.

48:28-29. Bob Flame is quoting (actually slightly misquoting) from the Organic Act of 1916, which created the National Park Service.

49:32. The West Thumb Geyser Basin, one of the most concentrated in Yellowstone, contains some dozen identified geysers. During Bob Flame's time, it was the site of a general store, photo shop, ranger station, cafeteria, lodge and cabins, almost all of which have since been removed.

51:1. The Mummy Range, a subset of the Front Range, lies north of Trail Ridge Road, largely within Rocky Mountain National Park. Its most prominent peaks include Mount Chapin, Mount Chiquita, Ypsilon Mountain, Fairchild Mountain, Hagues Peak and Mummy Mountain.

53:3-6. There were at least three separate trails used by the Ute and Arapaho to cross the tundra of the Continental Divide.

55:29. RMNP Superintendent Roger Toll began experimenting with dynamite in the spring of 1922 as a way of expediting snow removal.

56:11. The "Snow Go," a rotary-type plow, was purchased in 1931. As noted below, it significantly aided the work of the specially constructed 17-ton steam shovel, which was first used to clear snow on the Fall River Road in 1925.

57:30-31. The first C.C.C. camp (officially Camp N.P. 1-C) in Rocky Mountain National Park was established in Little Horseshoe Park on May 12, 1933. The adjacent flat valley, known as Horseshoe Park, gets its name from the way it was sculpted by a retreating glacier.

58:17-24. Rocky Mountain National Park began purchasing private property, or "inholdings," in late 1931 for the purpose of returning the land to its natural state, and in certain places, increasing the grazing corridors for the park's growing elk herd. The first property purchased was the Horseshoe Inn, the "big resort" referred to here.

63:24-25. Thunder Lake, deep in Wild Basin, and Lawn Lake, above

Horseshoe Park and referred to below, are popular backcountry destinations. Each has a small patrol cabin.

64:26-29. Park Superintendent Roger Toll would not have agreed. "These packs are so comfortable," he explained in his monthly report for June 1922, "that they make carrying fish a pleasure." See the accompanying photograph.

64:31. The Estes Park Fish Hatchery on Fall River Road near the eastern entrance of the park was begun by local citizens in 1907. It was taken over by the state of Colorado in the late 1920s and remained in operation until it was destroyed by the Lawn Lake flood of 1982.

67:29. Bear Lake, below Hallett Peak, is, as suggested, one of the park's most-visited (and congested) places. The lodge referred to below is Bear Lake Lodge, removed by the National Park Service in 1959.

68:30. Naturalist Don Brent was correct. There are five "true" or "living" glaciers in Rocky Mountain National Park. As noted below, taking accurate measurements of their growth was – and remains – a yearly activity.

73:19. The arrival of the first C.C.C. contingent in Estes Park was accompanied by an unexpected spring snowstorm, forcing some of the newly arrived recruits to be initially housed in the Utility Area and in other makeshift dormitories within the national park.

78:4-5. Capt. Benton is using the phrase ("Lafayette, we are here!") usually, and wrongfully, associated with Gen. John J. Pershing's arrival in France with American troops in 1917 during WWI. The words were spoken by Pershing's aide, Col. Charles E. Stanton, during a July 4 ceremony at the tomb of French hero the Marquis de Lafayette, whose intervention in the American Revolution helped turn the tide of war. The remark implied that America had now repaid its debt to France.

83:23. Fort Logan, near Denver, served as the C.C.C.'s administrative headquarters for its Colorado and Wyoming camps east of the Continental Divide.

85:4-5. The allusion is to Stephen T. Mather (1867-1930), who became director of the National Park Service when it was established in 1916. This frequently cited epitaph comes from a congressional eulogy.

85:25-26. The statement is not quite correct. Camp N.P. 1-C was the first C.C.C. camp in a national park west of the Mississippi River.

90:3-4. The Gorge Lakes above Forest Canyon, which include Arrowhead and Doughnut lakes, are, as noted, some of the more remote in Rocky Mountain National Park.

96. (Photograph). Robert Fechner (1876-1939), founding director of the C.C.C., visited the camp in Little Horseshoe Park during the summer of 1934. In May of 1940, a commemorative plaque honoring the recently deceased Fechner was planted near the site of two other C.C.C. camps in Hollowell Park.

112:11-12. This small museum, which sat close to the road below the headquarters building, was opened in June of 1931, the month of Yeager's arrival.

112:17. Sky Pond lies on a shelf above Loch Vale in the Glacier Basin region of Rocky Mountain National Park.

113:6. The fire lookout on Twin Sisters Mountain above the Tahosa Valley predates the national park. It was built by the Forest Service in 1914.

113:8. In using the name "Sprann's" for a resort on Glacier Creek, Yeager is obviously thinking of the rustic hotel built and opened in 1914 by Estes Park pioneer Abner Sprague (1850-1943). The hotel was removed in 1960.

124:7. Al Capone (1899-1947), known as "Scarface," was the boss of organized crime in Chicago during the 1920s and 1930s.

127:17. The mountain village of Allenspark (now spelled as one word) is 15 miles south of Estes Park.

130:22-23. The trail up 12,324-foot Flattop Mountain begins at Bear Lake; 13,153-foot Taylor Peak and its glacier are located some two miles to the south of Flattop.

132:27. The allusion is to Two Rivers Lake near Glacier Gorge.

136:32-137:6. The technical climb of the rugged 3,000-foot East Face of Longs Peak was, and is, the goal of many mountaineers, and has been the site of many accidents, some fatal.

142:2-8. The route in question up Andrews Glacier begins at Loch Vale, ascends the glacier itself, and at its head intersects the trail between Flattop Mountain and Taylor Peak. The route up Chaos Canyon (or Otis Gorge) begins at Bear Lake, passes Lake Haiyaha and intersects with the Flattop-Taylor trail further north between Otis and Hallett peaks. Flame's hypothesis is that the missing hiker used one of these routes in his descent.

142:29. As with a number of other names in Yeager's book, "Hupp" is a deliberate choice. The Hupps were one of Estes Park's pioneer families.

146:6. The North Inlet is where Tonahutu Creek enters Grand Lake on the west side of Rocky Mountain National Park. From there, a long trail leads through an open area named Big Meadows to the western slope of Flattop Mountain.

149: 11-21. The allusion is to the mystery surrounding the Reverend Thornton R. Sampson (1852-1915) from Austin, Texas, a Presbyterian minister and president of the Austin Theological Seminary who disappeared while crossing Flattop Mountain from Grand Lake on his way to attend the dedication of Rocky Mountain National Park on September 4, 1915. His remains were discovered above Odessa Lake by a trail crew on July 8, 1932.

161:28. The Fall River Pass shelter cabin was built in 1924. No longer used, it is located near today's Fall River Visitor Center.

168:4. This patrol cabin is located on the North Fork of the Big

Thompson River, close to the park's northeastern boundary. Cabin 13 was located in the Cache la Poudre valley near the intersection of that river with Hague Creek.

172:8-14 The Rustic Lodge and its proprietor, Charlie Hampton, are a thinly-veiled reference to Hewes-Kirkwood Inn and Charles Edwin Hewes (1870-1947). Hewes-Kirkwood, which dates from 1914, was a popular point of departure for climbs of Longs Peak, and Charlie Hewes was widely known for his hospitality as an innkeeper.

176:13. Peacock Pool is fed by water coming down from Chasm Lake, which lies below the East Face. The original stone shelter cabin at Chasm Lake was built in 1931 and destroyed by an avalanche in 2003.

184:14-15. Beginning in 1933, a college degree was required of permanent rangers. Like MacDonald, many veterans grumbled at the time, wondering about the wisdom and necessity of the new requirement, precisely because it would eliminate men like Hughes from the National Park Service.

187:1-11. At Chapin Pass off Fall River Road, the trail they are taking, as noted below, leads down Chapin and Hague creeks to the valley of the Cache la Poudre River and Cabin 13, which was built about 1917.

189:24. The Never Summer Range rises abruptly from the Kawuneeche Valley on the west side of Rocky Mountain National Park.

189:28. 12,489-foot Specimen Mountain north of Trail Ridge Road at Milner Pass is volcanic in origin.

189:31. The ghost towns, identified below as the mining camps of Dutchtown, Gaskill and Lulu City, are located in the Kawuneeche Valley along the Colorado River. Lulu City and Dutchtown date from 1879; Gaskill from 1880. By Yeager's time, only a few decayed structures and refuse dumps remained.

190: 8-12. The Ute story about Grand Lake and the capsized raft is an established part of local legend.

190:12-15. The contest over whether to locate the seat of Grand County in Hot Sulphur Springs or Grand Lake led to a bloody battle between local partisans on July 4, 1883, leaving two men dead and a third mortally wounded. No one was ever held accountable for these killings.

190:28-32; 191:1. Cooke City, Montana, a few miles northeast of Yellowstone, was the site of considerable mining activity in the 1870s.

196:2. Phantom Valley Ranch, on the Colorado River a few miles south of Lulu City, began life as Camp Wheeler or Squeaky Bob's, after its proprietor Robert L. Wheeler (1865-1945), who began the small resort about 1908. In 1926, its new owner changed the name to Phantom Valley Ranch. The buildings were purchased and razed by the National Park Service in the early 1960s.

196:4. The return trip to the Estes Valley, as noted here, was to be made via Trail Ridge Road and the "thin ribbon of a trail" that leads down Windy Gulch into Upper Beaver Meadows.

196:28-29. Presumably the North Fork Cabin mentioned above.

198:26-29. This fire, begun by careless campers at Bear Lake in 1900, burned for days and stretched to timberline. Its scars were visible for many years afterwards.

200:29-3; 20:1-2. Like Dick Brent, modern archaeologists recognize these rock walls as game drives used by Native Americans for hunting. See also the Afterword.

205:19-32. Yeager is making use here of the story of the horses and possessions of one J. P. Chitwood, which were found on Tyndall Glacier in September of 1921. Chitwood's body had been discovered a year earlier on a cliff above the glacier. Man and horses had been caught in an early winter snowstorm.

233:3. Until it was blocked off and the roadway obliterated in 1934, the High Drive provided direct access to Rocky Mountain National Park. This road left Highway 36 at Beaver Point and extended northwest to Deer Ridge Junction. The route is now a hiking trail.

234:20-21. The reference is to the bridge over the Fall River at the west end of Horseshoe Park.

235:13-14. Car 716 is near Roaring River Bridge on Old Fall River Road heading east toward the barricade in Horseshoe Park.

248:27-31. Fern and Odessa lakes in Odessa Gorge were popular winter skiing destinations. For a number of years, this was the site of the Colorado Mountain Club's winter outings, which made use of the overnight facilities at Fern Lake Lodge.

252:8-11. Mummy Pass lies just south of 12,258-foot Fall Mountain in the Mummy Range, in the extreme northern section of the park. From there, the trail leads past Lost Lake. The route, as before, begins at Chapin Pass and drops down Chapin Creek to the Poudre Valley.

269:9. The lakes of the North Fork are Lake Louise, Lake Husted and Lost Lake. The trail ends at the North Fork ranger cabin.

271:8-26. The location and history of this old cabin are unknown.

275:30. The two new C.C.C. camps were Camp N.P.-4-C, the park's first permanent year-round camp, established on Mill Creek in Hollowell Park in May 1934, and Camp N.P.-3-C, near Phantom Valley Ranch on the west side. N.P.-3-C was actually established in June of 1933.

276. (Photo opposite). The Shadow Mountain fire lookout on 9,923-foot Shadow Mountain near Grand Lake was completed in 1933. Its stone building remained in use until 1968. It was placed on the National Register of Historic Places in 1987 and restored in 1992.

J.H.P.

AFTERWORD

To My Comrades In Forest Green
Who by Their Unselfish Devotion to an Ideal
Are Molding a Dream Into a Reality

– Dedication, *Bob Flame, Ranger* (1934)

F ew figures in American life are more admired than those who wear the distinctive forest-green uniform and stiff-brimmed Stetson of the park ranger. Yet when the National Park Service was established in 1916, a competently trained corps of rangers did not come with the 14 national parks and 21 national monuments entrusted to its care. A ranger service had to be created, together with a broad base of public support for the parks themselves. Stephen T. Mather (1867-1930), the energetic and visionary first director of the National Park Service, and his deputy and successor, Horace M. Albright (1890-1987), found a way to do both. Vigorously promoting the parks so people would enjoy visiting them and become their advocates was an early priority. So too became building and professionalizing the ranger force with whom those visitors interacted. Mather, Albright tells us, "had a special vision of what the rangers should be."[1] Knowledge and skills were, of course, essential. So too was "an ability to relate to the public." But Mather wanted something more. He wanted his rangers to exist in the public mind as individuals who embodied in word and deed the ideals and values of Park Service itself.

Creating this ranger mystique took time – a full two decades and more – and the efforts of many. Park naturalists, always the smallest part of the ranger staff, played a particularly critical role. Because they talked to thousands of tourist-visitors, it was the naturalists, one historian noted, who "probably did more to shape the public impression of rangers than all the rest... contributing much to the image of the ranger as both self-reliant woodsman and expert naturalist."[2] Contributing significantly to this effort was ranger-naturalist Dorr Graves Yeager (1902-1996), who during the 1930s introduced to the world the fictional ranger hero he named Bob Flame. His adventures in Yellowstone National Park, Rocky Mountain National Park and elsewhere were intended to provide not only a realistic portrait of ranger life, but to exemplify what Yeager felt was best and most admirable in those who protect and conserve the nation's parks. Bob Flame made his first appearance in 1935 in the novel that Yeager titled *Bob Flame, Ranger*. He returned again in its sequel, *Bob Flame, Rocky Mountain Ranger* (1936), and twice more in *Bob Flame in Death Valley* (1937) and *Bob Flame Among the Navajo* (1946). While each of these novels has its interests, it is in *Bob Flame, Rocky Mountain Ranger* that we see Bob Flame and Dorr Yeager at their very best.

* * *

Using rangers to patrol and protect national parks was not a new idea. Historians agree that the concept dates back to the time of Harry Yount, a grizzled veteran of the Civil War and Ferdinand Hayden's geological survey who in 1880 was appointed "game-keeper" in Yellowstone, the nation's first national park. Yount's assignment was to watch over Yellowstone's herds of elk, bison, deer, antelope and bighorn sheep in a region he knew intimately from his days as a buffalo hunter before the park's establishment in 1872. In addition to making sure that hunting limits were observed (hunting within the park was then permitted), Yount was at times called upon to act as a guide for visiting officials. Though Harry Yount resigned late the following year (the park was simply too big, he said, for one man to oversee it), he left behind the suggestion that "the game and natural curiosities of the park be protected by officers stationed at different points of the park with the authority to enforce observance of the park maintenance and trails."[3]

Yount's recommendations bore fruit. When the United States Cavalry took over the official management of Yellowstone in 1886, a number of civilian scouts were hired because of their knowledge of woodcraft and their wilderness survival skills. From such individuals and those like them in other parks and the nation's forest reserves a group of men loosely identified as "park rangers" gradually emerged. It was these men, and those recruited to join them, that provided the nucleus of the ranger staff that Mather inherited in 1915, when he agreed to leave corporate life to oversee the creation of the National Park Service. With them came a set of regulations that specified that rangers be between the ages of 21 and 40, of good character and sound physique, and tactful in handling people. They were also required, as Albright later put it, "to possess a common-school education, be able to ride and care for horses, have experience in outdoor life, be a good shot with rifle and pistol, and have some knowledge of trail construction and fighting forest fires."[4]

Mather and Albright worked hard to nurture *esprit de corps* within the Service. Each year, Mather tried to visit as many national parks and monuments as possible to spread his "Park Service gospel," making it a point to wear his uniform rather than a Washington-style business suit to demonstrate his pride as he mingled easily and confidently with local rangers. "His visits to the various parks," Albright said, "were always eagerly anticipated by the rangers, for they were always times of good fellowship. Through these frequent visits his distinctive vision of the national parks and the uniqueness of their personnel permeated the outlook of the whole service."[5] Horace Albright, who between 1919 and 1929 also served as superintendent of Yellowstone, took similar pleasure in spending his evenings in uniform "with visitors around the campfires, explaining the wonders of nature." Like his boss, Stephen Mather, he was delighted to be accepted "as just another ranger."[6] Albright particularly championed the cause of education, insisting that park visitors not only be well treated, but well informed. One of his first acts as superintendent, in fact, was to appoint Milton P. Skinner, a Yellowstone veteran well versed in the area's flora, fauna and hydrothermal features, to be the park's first year-round naturalist – an entirely new position in the Park Service – and give him responsibility for developing a museum and expanding the park's schedule of educational programs.

Albright also wanted to improve the capability of his entire ranger staff. In the early 1920s, he began making a special effort to recruit college students as summer seasonals ("ninety-day

wonders" they were called) in the hope that some could be
persuaded to join the Park Service upon graduation. One of the
collegians Albright hired on for the summer of 1924 was 23-
year-old Dorr Yeager, a student at Iowa's Grinnell College,
beginning a relationship between Yeager and the Park Service
that would last for more than 30 years.

Despite the fact that his roots were Midwestern, Yeager's
path to Yellowstone and the National Park Service, though
hardly planned or anticipated, was in many respects a
predictable one given his previous summers in the West, at
Yellowstone and in Colorado, and the combination of interests
that emerged during his adolescent and college years. Born in
Gilman, Iowa, in a second-floor bedroom of the house where
his mother had spent her own childhood, Yeager was named in
honor of the country doctor and maternal grandfather who
delivered him (Dr. Dorr Graves). His stay in Gilman, a railroad
town between Marshalltown and Grinnell, lasted only a week.
As soon as Dorr and his mother could travel, he was taken to
Grinnell, where his father, Harry Irving Yeager (1879-1973), a
watchmaker, owned a jewelry store on Fourth Avenue in the
downtown business district, within easy walking distance of
the family home on High Street. The influence of Harry and
Ethel Yeager (1873-1969) on their son's upbringing and
education was significant. Dorr would dedicate his first animal
novel about a grizzly called *Scarface* (1935) to both: "To a
Mother who has encouraged my writing since childhood" and
"To a Father Who First Initiated Me to the Out-of-doors."[7]

Grinnell was the home of Grinnell College, the first institution of higher education west of the Mississippi River, and like
most college towns, a genteel place of well-cared-for homes
and tree-lined residential streets, to which the stately brick
buildings of the campus added a look of stability and dignity.
Surrounded by small and prosperous farms and anchored by
north-south and east-west railroads, Grinnell was the largest
community in Poweshiek County. By the time Yeager reached
adolescence, it boasted 5,300 permanent residents, two movie
theaters and thanks to the college, enough additional ongoing
activity, including athletic contests, to make growing up there
tolerable, even interesting.

Yeager attended the local schools, including Grinnell High School, where his classmates included the sons and daughters of Grinnell College faculty members. One of them, Richard M. Steiner (1901-1975), the son of Dr. Edward A. Steiner (1866-1956), professor of applied Christianity, became Dorr Yeager's life-long friend. Though a year his senior, Steiner was a willing participant in the best-remembered event of Yeager's youth, when apparently as a summer lark the two boarded a cattle car and rode hobo-style as far as Chicago, a 300-mile escapade that for Dorr, ended with a case of cattle encephalitis that cost him a number of weeks of missed school. Another summer during Yeager's teens yielded happier results. The Steiners invited Dorr and his mother to their Colorado vacation home, located in the heavily-wooded Tahosa Valley south of Estes Park, where in 1917, Edward Steiner had purchased an all-but-abandoned 160-acre homestead for a summer retreat. Renaming it "Steiner Acres," the professor built a stream-side cottage for the family over the stone footings of the original claim cabin. On the adjacent hillside Steiner added a small study with a fireplace, where he could retire to read and write. Steiner Acres, which lay in the shadow of the region's two great peaks, Longs Peak and Mount Meeker, and bordered the new Rocky Mountain National Park, was near idyllic. Dorr Yeager thought so too, and would return years later to build a small cabin on land that Edward Steiner had given him.[8]

After graduating from Grinnell High School in 1921, Yeager followed Richard Steiner to Grinnell College, where he majored in botany and philosophy, averaging grades of B in both. Though his transcript does not tell us, the interest in philosophy may well have reflected Edward Steiner's influence. Steiner had come to Grinnell in 1903. During a long and distinguished 38-year teaching career, he was well remembered for his "half hours," during which students were invited into the Steiner home, seated in a large chair in Dr. Steiner's small study and encouraged to talk about themselves and describe the kind of men or women they hoped to become. Dorr Yeager enrolled in Professor Steiner's applied Christianity course in the fall of 1924, earning a respectable grade of B from a professor known to be demanding, though whether he was ever officially

summoned to Edward Steiner's study, we do not know.
We also know comparatively little about the rest of Yeager's
college years. Some men have nostalgic memories of those
days. Dorr Yeager apparently did not, perhaps because he lived
at home rather than in a campus dormitory. In fact, except for
the college literary magazine, the *Malteaser*, whose staff he
joined during his first year, and the science club, which he
joined during his last, there is no indication that he was much
drawn to college life. As far as Dorr's academic life was
concerned, his transcript suggests that he was about as good a
student as interest dictated and he chose to be. Perhaps for this
reason, we know considerably more about his relationship with
botany professor Henry Schoemaker Conard (1874-1971), a
member of the Grinnell faculty since 1906. Conard's extraordinary 49 years of service exceeded even Edward Steiner's.

Yeager encountered Professor Conard, an international
authority on mosses and water lilies, during the fall of 1923,
when he enrolled in his first course in botany, clearly liking
both subject and teacher. It was Conard, Yeager later wrote
with his customary succinctness, who not only "exerted a
great influence on my life," but was "largely responsible for my
entering the National Park Service. In 1924, Dr. Conard was
given an appointment as a nature guide at Roosevelt Camp
in Yellowstone. The following summer, on his recommendation,
I received a similar appointment and was stationed
at Mammoth."[9]

In taking up his first Park Service appointment as one of
Horace Albright's seasonal rangers in 1925, during the summer
between his junior and senior years,[10] Dorr Yeager had a
decided advantage. He had been in Yellowstone twice before,
beginning in 1921, when making use of his experience in his
father's jewelry store, he obtained a summer job as a "pack rat"
in the curio shop operated at Canyon by the Yellowstone Park
Camps Company. Though the salary was meager, there were
plenty of other attractions to occupy the leisure time of a
young man already attracted to the out-of-doors, and Yeager
willingly returned to the same job the following year.[11]

In following his mentor, Henry Conard, to Yellowstone,
Yeager knew what to expect of the day-to-day life of the

summer seasonal. Though the pay was again modest, the job itself was highly sought after, so much so that during the summer of 1923, Superintendent Albright, "swamped" with applications, devised a form letter to discourage the "casual applicant." "It has been our experience," Albright told would-be rangers:

that young men often apply for a place on the park ranger force with the impression or understanding that the ranger is a sort of sinecure with nothing resembling hard work to perform, and that a ranger's position offers an opportunity to pass a pleasant vacation amid the beauties and wonders of Yellowstone Park, and with very frequent trips about the park and innumerable dances and other diversions to occupy one's leisure hours.

Then, Albright got to the heart of the matter, employing much the same language and tone that Dorr Yeager's Bob Flame would use in addressing his own recruits:

The duties are exacting and require the utmost patience and tact at all times. A ranger's job is no place for a nervous, quick-tempered man, nor for the laggard, nor for one who is unaccustomed to hard work. If you cannot work hard ten or twelve hours a day, and always with patience and a smile on your face, don't fill out the attached blank. You have perhaps believed Government jobs to be "soft" and "easy." Most of them are not, and certainly there are no such jobs in the National Park Service. The ranger's job is especially hard. There will not be more than twenty vacancies in next year's force of rangers, and there is really very little chance of your being considered unless you possess all of the qualifications mentioned herein... If you want to come for pleasure you will be disappointed. If you want a summer in the Park as an experience in outdoor activity amid forests and a fine invigorating atmosphere, apply if you are qualified. Otherwise plan to visit the Yellowstone Park as a tourist.[12]

Dorr Yeager, one of Albright's chosen 20, enjoyed his summer as a seasonal ranger, in part because he was able to work closely in the field with Professor Conard, who was essentially in charge of Yellowstone's summer interpretive program of lectures and field trips, and with whom Yeager had arranged in advance to do a one-hour elective in botany to be transferred back to Grinnell. Yeager got a grade of A. When he returned again as a seasonal employee in the summer of 1926, it was as a newly minted college graduate.

Yeager now had to think about vocation, and sometime during that summer, he had the good fortune to meet Ansel F. Hall (1894-1962), the Park Service's chief naturalist who headed the education field division headquartered on the University of California campus in Berkeley. Though Yeager had been encouraged by Henry Conard to pursue graduate work, and was in fact headed to the University of Washington in Seattle that fall on a fellowship to begin a master's program in botany, Hall talked to him about the possibilities of a career with the National Park Service. In fact, Hall offered Yeager a concrete proposal, which Dorr summarized in a letter written from Seattle on October 3, 1926. "My dear Mr. Hall," Yeager began,

I have delayed writing you because I wanted to think over the proposition you made me in the park. However, I believe the thing is sufficiently thrashed out in my mind to give you a definite answer.

First of all, however, I want to state this proposition as I understand it, and as I think you stated it to me. I go to Yosemite next summer to work in the Naturalist Service and absorb just as much as I can of the system, style, etc. that they use there. Then at the end of the summer I take a job approximating $2100 in some park, providing you think I am capable of holding it down. If at the end of the summer, you don't feel that I can hold down a job as Park Naturalist in some park, you are to give me some job that will assure me enough to carry me over the following fall when I can get a position teaching. Also I am to be given time off sufficient to come back to Washington and finish my Master's Degree, which will probably take a quarter. (However, I'm trying to make arrangements now whereby I can do that extra work next summer and in that case I will not have to come back here at all after I leave this spring). Conard also said that it was your wish to send men in these positions to Berkley [sic] for study two or three months each school year.

I realize the above reads as if I were drawing up a contract but I do not mean it that way. I simply want to understand what I am getting into. If the above is correct and meets with your O.K. I'll be glad to enter the Ranger Nature work permanently if you still want me. I realize it is a big job and that I am young but I am going to throw myself heart and soul into the work and that is all I can do. I appreciate your interest and offer very much, Mr. Hall, and if you put me into a job of that kind I'll do my level best to make good and show my appreciation to you.[13]

Yeager ended his letter, "Yours for the Service."

Ansel Hall was as good as his word. Following the 1926-1927 school year, Yeager reported to Yosemite National Park to work under Park Naturalist Carl P. Russell (1894-1967). It was, he later recalled, "the first organized interpretive program I had seen." As Yeager discovered, Yosemite's interpretive program, featuring guided nature trips, evening talks at the valley's hotels and campgrounds, and a six-room museum opened in 1922, was a well-established one.[14] But Yeager's assignment was more than that of a seasonal. He was there to attend the Yosemite School of Field Natural History, a pioneering summer program established in 1925 that offered intensive classroom and field training in geology, botany, zoology and the conservation of natural resources to improve the interpretive skills of those with scientific backgrounds. Like so many of the school's alumni who would permeate the Park Service, Yeager became hooked. Before the summer was over he had taken, and passed, the Civil Service examination for park naturalist. That fall, while waiting for a permanent posting, he headed back to Grinnell, where he completed his master's degree under the direction of Henry Conard (writing a thesis titled "The Fleshy Fungi of Grinnell and Vicinity").[15]

Yeager's appointment came in January with orders to report to Mount Rainier. "Although I had planned on Yellowstone," he would later tell the story, "in my eagerness to accept any appointment I set out for Seattle only to receive a wire enroute signed by Sam Woodring (chief ranger) instructing me to report at Yellowstone. I arrived at the Gardiner Entrance in February 1928." Frances Pound, daughter of the district ranger (she considered herself Yellowstone's first woman ranger), was manning the gate. Her words of greeting were brief: "Diptheria is raging at Mammoth." [16]

For someone interested in becoming a park naturalist and the art of presenting the "facts" of biology, geology and human history in an informed and interesting way, Yeager could not have found a better boss than Horace Albright or more inspiring teachers, mentors and friends than Henry Conard, Ansel Hall and Carl Russell, all of whom played important roles in the evolution of the modern Park Service. Moreover, Yeager's timing was perfect. Less than a year later, in January of 1929, Albright would replace an ailing Stephen Mather as director and embark on a major reorganization program that included the establishment of a separate education branch to coordinate and supervise educational and scientific research activities within national parks, including nature guiding, lectures, museums and publications. Harold C. Bryant (1886-1968) was brought in from Yosemite as assistant director to head the new research and education branch, Carl Russell was promoted to oversee museum planning, while Ansel Hall, who had developed the museum at Yosemite, continued to direct the educational field headquarters at Berkeley. As one historian noted, these changes, and the stability and structure they provided, "allowed the Park Service by 1930 to turn inward and begin to develop and strengthen visitor-use programs and learn more about park resources." [17]

It was in context of this expanding role for naturalists that Dorr Yeager reported to Yellowstone to work with Horace Albright and soon afterwards, with veteran superintendent Roger Toll, who was brought in from Rocky Mountain to replace him. Quartered in a comfortable two-room suite above the museum building, Yeager went to work putting together a new and comprehensive interpretive program, which included, that first summer, a self-guided nature trail at Mammoth. "The summer of 1929 went well," Yeager later wrote, a bit tongue-in-cheek, "considering that the head ranger naturalist was a professor of speech and knew nothing about the other phases of interpretive work." [18] The new level of professionalism that Dorr Yeager and others would bring to the Park Service was clearly beginning to assert itself. A member of the second generation of Park Service personnel, Yeager would never be regarded as "one of Mather's men." But being one of Horace Albright's would carry much the same weight.

At Yellowstone, Yeager found himself simultaneously occupied on a variety of fronts. These included museum work that resulted in Yellowstone's unique system of rustic trail-side museums,[19] and editing and writing articles for *Yellowstone Nature Notes*, a quarterly booklet containing brief notes, essays and natural history tidbits intended mainly for park staff. He also put together the first hardcover edition of the *Ranger Naturalists Manual*, a volume filled with information he expected his 30 summer assistants to know, along with some of his own thinking about wildlife management.[20] In 1930, Yeager produced a second guide, titled *Plan of Administration and Manual for the Education Department*. All of this required considerable work and energy, for as Horace Albright reminded him years later, "your staff was small in the height of the season, and non-existent in winter!"[21]

Perhaps the most career-enhancing activity of Dorr Yeager's Yellowstone years occurred in November of 1929, when he was invited to participate with the Park Service's five other year-round park naturalists in the First Park Naturalists' Training Conference in Berkeley. It was a month-long event put together by Chief Naturalist Ansel Hall to discuss natural resource management subjects. Though the conference was attended by Park Service personnel and scientists interested in interpretive work, it was Yeager and his fellow naturalists who assumed responsibility for much of the presenting. Yeager himself gave papers on such wide-ranging topics as "The Park Visitor," "The Purpose of Educational Work in National Parks," "The Place of the Museum in the Educational Program of a National Park," "Establishment of a Nature Trail," "Principles of Guiding in the National Parks" and "The Research Program and its Part in the Park Educational Program," some 18 in all.[22]

Though these papers were short, intended as springboards for discussion rather than definitive statements, the expertise and thoughtfulness they reveal in a young man not yet 30 is remarkable. Moreover, the conference's underlying theme of how research and science might be used to define the duties of the park naturalist and inform the decisions of park officials made the event a groundbreaking one. It was partly because of this conference, environmental historian James Pritchard noted, that the education division, shortly to be reorganized under Harold Bryant as the branch of research and education, would become "one of the roots of scientific research within the NPS."[23]

Chief Naturalist Ansel Hall, also a participant, must have been impressed.[24] "If you put me into a job of that kind," Dorr had told him just three years before, "I'll do my level best to make good and show my appreciation to you." The 1929 conference was a watershed moment for both Yeager and the National Park Service, one captured in an official photograph showing Dorr Yeager and his fellow naturalists posing with Ansel Hall and Carl Russell on the steps of the University of California's Hilgard Hall.

On the basis of his performance at Berkeley alone, Dorr Yeager's position at Yellowstone seemed secure, and Dorr himself appeared fast-tracked for quick advancement. But here, at the beginning of what would turn out to be an otherwise seamless career, Yeager hit a roadblock. During the winter of 1930-1931, naturalist positions were reclassified under Civil Service and Yeager's grade was changed, unaccountably, to "associate," even though Yellowstone was eligible for a full park naturalist. "It was my feeling and that of the park personnel," Yeager recalled, "that the logical solution would be to reclassify me to the higher grade." When his appeal to Washington fell on deaf ears, Yeager was in a quandary, for having been in charge of things at Yellowstone he was understandably reluctant to take a subordinate's role. Good fortune intervened. Rocky Mountain National Park established its first park naturalist position. Dorr applied, and was accepted. There was a further measure of irony to all this. During the early months of 1931, as negotiations with Rocky Mountain were going forward, Yeager was preparing *Our Wilderness Neighbors: A Sympathetic Description of the Most Interesting Animals in Yellowstone National Park* (Chicago: A. C. McClurg, 1931), a compendium of the park's animal life he would never have the opportunity to use. It was, Yeager would modestly say, "readable in spots."[25]

Dorr Yeager reported for duty in Rocky Mountain National Park on June 21, 1931, to a "warm welcome." Edmund Rogers was superintendent, John Preston assistant superintendent and John McLaughlin was chief ranger. Yeager and "Johnny Mac," as McLaughlin (1905-1977) was affectionately called, were old friends. They had known each other since Yeager's first days at Yellowstone, where McLaughlin, a recent graduate from the forestry program at the Agricultural College of Colorado in Fort Collins (the "ranger factory," Yeager called it), was a member of the first group of college-trained Civil Service rangers recruited by Superintendent Albright. "He was one of the favorites among the new men," Yeager recalled, "everybody liked him. Although somewhat slender, he was wiry and tough as any... no matter what the job – ski patrol or fighting fires – he would come through it without a hair mussed!"[26] McLaughlin had transferred to Rocky Mountain as chief ranger in April of 1930, and one reason for Yeager's decision to apply for the transfer (and no doubt a reason he got the job) was Johnny Mac.

For someone coming down from Yellowstone, a place larger than Delaware and Rhode Island combined, Rocky Mountain National Park took some getting used to. Superintendent Rogers' permanent staff numbered only 13, and McLaughlin and his four rangers were expected to oversee the comings and goings of more than a quarter million annual visitors in a park covering nearly 400 square miles of mountains, lakes, forests and alpine tundra. Arriving on the cusp of the new tourist season, Yeager's first year was an exceptionally busy one. A small frame-and-masonry museum below park headquarters on Moraine Avenue was being completed, and Yeager had the opportunity to finish the installation of its 18 animal and bird exhibits, some of which had been donated by Coloman Jonas, one of the founding brothers of Denver's pioneering taxidermy studio, for which Estes Park artist Dave Stirling had painted the exhibit backdrops.

Yeager also went to work redesigning and reinvigorating the park's interpretive program in much the same way he had at Yellowstone. Despite the lateness of his arrival, he arranged for new lectures to be given in the campgrounds and at local

resort hotels, added new field trips and auto caravans (some all
day and others overnight) and laid out self-guided nature-trails
at Bear Lake and the new museum.[27] In addition, Yeager put the
park's small library in order and began the time-consuming
task of cataloging its collections of specimens, artifacts and
lantern slides. By July, he had also taken over editorship of
Nature Notes from Rocky Mountain National Park, the
mimeographed newsletter he would soon transform into
a small, handsomely printed magazine to which he regularly
contributed articles. That same month, he had the opportunity
to interact with scientists from the Wildlife Research Division
in Berkeley sent out to begin the first systematic survey of the
wildlife in Rocky Mountain National Park – part of a study that
within two years would produce the Park Service's first
wildlife-management policies.[28] In November, to complete a
hectic but highly successful year, Yeager invested his annual
leave in a trip back to Grinnell, where in addition to seeing his
parents and Henry Conard, he gave several talks at local schools
and on the Grinnell campus.

One other event made 1931 particularly memorable. That
year, together with local hotel man Joe Mills (1880-1935), the
younger brother of famous naturalist, author and innkeeper
Enos Mills, Yeager helped found the Rocky Mountain Nature
Association, a support group modeled after the Yosemite
Natural History Association formed eight years earlier. Its
mission statement (probably written by Joe Mills, who served
as president) was both broad and generous:

> *To unite the energy, interests and knowledge of the*
> *students, explorers and lovers of Rocky Mountain National*
> *Park; to collect and disseminate information regarding the*
> *region in behalf of science, literature and recreation; to stim-*
> *ulate public interest in our mountain area; to encourage and*
> *preserve the forests, flowers, fauna and natural history; and*
> *to render accessible the alpine attractions of this region.*[29]

The following summer, the new organization, whose
members were asked to pay a dollar a year to support park
programs, produced its first publication, *The Animals of Rocky*
Mountain National Park, a 57-page mimeographed booklet
authored by chief naturalist Dorr Yeager.

The expanding relationship between Yeager and Joe Mills was one of the highlights of Dorr Yeager's years at Rocky Mountain. The two men undoubtedly met during one of Dorr's illustrated evening talks at the Crags, the hotel on the lower slope of Prospect Mountain Mills had built and opened in 1914. Both quickly found they had much in common. Mills had been a star athlete at Agriculture College of Colorado, and served as athletic director and head football and basketball coach at the University of Colorado. Like Yeager, he loved the out-of-doors and national parks. Although destined to live in the shadow of an older brother widely celebrated as the "Father of Rocky Mountain National Park," Joe Mills was an accomplished mountaineer, photographer and writer-lecturer, talents that Yeager admired and even emulated. Joe Mills was also, as Yeager soon discovered, arguably the most popular man in Estes Park because of the time and leadership he invested in community affairs.

Additionally, there was the matter of Joe and Ethel Mills' daughter, Eleanor Ann, a chemistry graduate of Massachusetts' Wellesley College come home to Colorado. Romance ensued, and although Eleanor Ann, or "Peg" as Dorr called her, vowed she would never marry one of "them" – meaning a conservation enthusiast like her father and uncle[30] (according to a well-massaged family story), the two were married in Denver on May 18, 1935, with John McLaughlin serving as best man.

The early 1930s were important years for Rocky Mountain National Park. The successful conclusion of a jurisdictional dispute from the previous decade over the policing of park roads (one that became serious enough to threaten the existence of the park itself) brought additional funding, including monies to complete Trail Ridge Road by 1932. The so-called "eighth wonder of the world," Trail Ridge Road linked Estes Park with Middle Park and Grand Lake across the Continental Divide. A year later, in May of 1933, during a bitter spring snowstorm, the first Civilian Conservation Corps (C.C.C.) camp arrived in Little Horseshoe Park. Other camps followed, and before the last one closed in October 1942, the victim of the manpower needs of war, the young men of the C.C.C. had not only helped "de-louse" the forests from the

ravages of the Black Hills pine beetle, but had devoted
thousands of man hours to fire prevention, erosion control, trail
maintenance and construction, the landscaping of new roads
and the obliteration of abandoned ones, tasks that advanced
park development, it was said, by as much as two decades.

During these years, Yeager continued his museum and
naturalist activities, which as in Yellowstone, he codified in a
manual for the benefit of his own seasonal naturalists and other
rangers. The museum at headquarters proved to be extremely
popular, so much so that by the end of the 1932, two more had
been established: one a small branch museum in the ranger
station at Bear Lake, then as now a tourist magnet; the other a
somewhat larger facility in the old stone building at Fall River
Pass built as a shelter cabin a decade before. These new
museums, together with Yeager's other programs, fueled an
even greater visitor interest in interpretive programs whose
demands, Superintendent Rogers told his superiors more than
once, could not be met because of insufficient staff.

As time permitted, Yeager continued to work on the park's
various collections, including its collection of Native American
artifacts, much of which had been randomly gathered and
stored. Though he had little or no formal training in archaeology and certainly did not consider himself an authority,
Yeager pursued an avocational interest, participating with
fellow rangers John McLaughlin, John Preston and Ed Andrews
in what they loosely called "Indian hunts." Yeager brought to
their weekend field trips the perceptiveness of the naturalist,
and as a result, archaeologist James Benedict suggested, appears
to have been the first to correctly identify the puzzling rock
walls on Flattop Mountain and Trail Ridge as game drives. He
was also, Benedict indicated, the first to understand the
archaeological importance of the pottery shards and other
cultural remains found on and about the rocky knob known
as Oldman Mountain, a location that Benedict later concluded
was a vision quest site where Native Americans fasted and
left offerings.[31]

Looking back on his time in Rocky Mountain National Park,
Yeager rightly took greatest pride in the establishment of the
Moraine Park Museum (today's Moraine Park Visitor Center) in

the big two-story recreation hall on the site of the Moraine Park Lodge, a resort whose other buildings the Park Service had acquired in 1931 and removed as part of its effort to reduce the number of privately owned properties within park boundaries. The museum at headquarters had been planned well before Yeager's arrival, and the museum at Fall River Pass, with display panels illustrating the geological development of the park, was a small one. But in the flat glaciated valley known as Moraine Park, with its spectacular view of Longs Peak and other mountains of the Front Range, Yeager had a chance to be involved from the beginning in planning and installing a large-scale museum project.

While Carl Russell came in to advise, it was Yeager's project to oversee. Though the site naturally lent itself to an exhibit on glacial history, Yeager, with Russell's concurrence, decided that the museum's primary focus should be the story of the Arapaho, the nomadic people who once made their seasonal homes in Moraine Park, and in other places within the park and throughout the Estes Valley. With the help of a small but enthusiastic and talented group of C.C.C. recruits from the year-round camp on Mill Creek, Yeager made his central installation a typical Arapaho encampment, a reconstruction consisting of a full-sized tipi made of buffalo hides, a travois, back rests, a papoose cradle board and other items.[32] Not all of the museum displays could be put together on site, and Yeager spent the winter months of 1934-1935 at the Park Service's Field Division of Education in Berkeley preparing his interpretive exhibits. The new Moraine Park Museum, which opened during the 1935 season, marked the high point of Dorr Yeager's short tenure in Rocky Mountain National Park. That December, he accepted a transfer back to Berkeley and the opportunity to continue working with Ansel Hall, the mentor whose encouragement and advice a decade before brought Yeager into the National Park Service.

Sometime during these years, probably during the late fall or early winter of 1933, Bob Flame was born. Though the precise inspiration is unclear, Joe Mills, himself a published author, was surely involved, if only to give advice. Seven years earlier, in 1926, Mills had published an animal novel, *The*

Comeback: The Story of the Heart of a Dog, the tale of a collie named Jane and "Three-toes," a wolf-like predator. The story combined fiction and natural history in the manner of famed naturalist Ernest Thompson Seton. That same year, Mills also published a delightful semi-fictional autobiography titled *A Mountain Boyhood.* It can scarcely be mere coincidence that in turning his hand to fiction, Dorr Yeager would not only write books of both types, but that all three of his animal novels – *Scarface: The Story of a Grizzly* (1935); *Chita* (1939), the story of a mountain lion; and *Grey Dawn, the Wolf Dog* (1942) – would make use of the same general setting as Mills' *The Comeback.*[33] It also is no surprise that Yeager's first Bob Flame novel, *Bob Flame, Ranger,* a Junior Literary Guild selection, would bear the imprint of J.H. Sears, the same New York publishing house that issued Mills' *A Mountain Boyhood.*

Dorr Yeager's books, like those of Joe Mills, are artful blends of fact and fiction that drew heavily upon the author's own experience. Bob Flame, he unapologetically admitted, was modeled after fellow ranger John McLaughlin, his comrade since Yellowstone. "I have never been quite sure why I selected Johnny Mac as the prototype," Yeager later wrote.

At the time I didn't do it consciously but after my character began to take shape as the story progressed I realized who it was I was writing about. He fit perfectly – a young ranger, conscientious, likeable, with a good sense of humor, good looking, and really dedicated to parks. He has been my friend for over 50 years and I never had any reason to modify that early appraisal of his qualities... And there are so many things to remember – his skills as an administrator, his ability to organize, to analyze and to solve problems, his friendly nature, his enthusiasm for life. When he made mistakes, he laughed at himself for making them.[34]

Bob Flame, Ranger, with its unequivocal dedication to his Park Service comrades, established the pattern and tone for the novels that followed. Its foreword is disarmingly blunt. "If you are a seeker of plots," Yeager tells the reader,

lay this book aside, for you will find none. Bob Flame – Ranger *is a straightforward tale of the life of one of those men and his comrades whom someone more imaginative*

than I has christened "the unsung heroes of the wilderness."
The story of Bob Flame is the story of any Ranger. I have told
of the commonplace as well as the extraordinary; the bitter
as well as the sweet; for they must all be taken together before
the picture is finished.[35]

Yeager was as good as his word. *Bob Flame, Ranger* is a
somewhat romanticized – but honest – look at ranger and Park
Service life. To illustrate his thesis that the "average person"
knows surprising little about the life of the park ranger,
especially "after the great gates are closed in the fall," Yeager
takes his protagonist through a "typical" year in the life of a
new ranger. In something less than 300 pages, he manages not
only to tell a good story, but to surround it with useful and
interesting information about Yellowstone's landmark places,
natural and human history, and park lore.

Bob Flame, Rocky Mountain Ranger, published a year
later in 1935, is cut from much the same cloth. Bob Flame, now
an experienced veteran of the Service, has been transferred
from Yellowstone to Rocky Mountain to become its new chief
ranger. Once more, we follow Bob and his ranger companions
through the seasons of the year in a book that makes good use
of events that took place during Dorr Yeager's tenure to
capture and preserve an important period in Rocky Mountain
National Park history. To be sure, there is no mention of the
building of Trail Ridge Road, considered a marvel of engineering, probably because there was no direct ranger involvement,
but Yeager spends considerable time describing the activities
and successes of the C.C.C. program precisely because rangers
were involved. By design, however, most of the events in *Bob
Flame, Rocky Mountain Ranger* are the sort that repeat
themselves in the course of any ranger's year: fighting a fire
caused by careless campers, rescuing tourists stranded in their
automobiles, planting fish in high country lakes, chasing
bootleggers and poachers, looking for a lost fisherman and
taking the measurements of the movement on Tyndall and
Andrews glaciers. All of these, once again, have the ring of truth,
and many – if not most – of Bob's adventures in Rocky Mountain National Park, as in Yellowstone, can be documented in the
monthly and annual reports of the park superintendent.[36]

There would later be two additional Bob Flame books, neither as successful as their predecessors: *Bob Flame in Death Valley* (1937) and *Bob Flame Among the Navajo* (1946). The first includes a meeting between Bob and the valley's "Mystery Man," the rodeo stunt man turned con artist known as Death Valley Scotty, whose home, Scotty's Castle, had become a local landmark – a *tour de force* considering that at the time of the novel's publication, Walter E. Scott was still very much alive. Yeager's story line, which lacks the tightness of control and firm sense of place of the earlier books, also makes use of legends about Lost Gunsight Mine, triggering a search that once again, nearly costs Ranger Flame his life. *Bob Flame Among the Navajo*, published nearly a decade later, takes Bob, on leave from his job at Death Valley National Park, to the famous Wide Ruins Trading Post at the edge of the Hopi Reservation in northeast Arizona. This novel allowed Yeager to weave the knowledge of southwestern Indian life he had learned after leaving Rocky Mountain with an adventure story whose plot involves stolen pawn. The novel is dedicated to Sallie and Bill Lippincott, the couple who had come to Wide Ruins as newlyweds in 1938 and soon found themselves running a trading post.

With the publication of *Bob Flame Among the Navajo*, Dorr Yeager brought the career of his ranger hero to an end and turned his attention to other projects. In later years, Yeager was modest about the Bob Flame series and its achievements, as indeed he was about most things involving his Park Service career. From the advantage of the 21st century, however, we can understand and appreciate the historical significance of these books in ways their author could not. Bob Flame was, as historian C.W. Buchholtz observed, "an historical phenomenon," a compelling true-to-life figure through whose "eyes and actions Americans discovered the dramatic world of rangering in the Rockies."[37] To be sure, Dorr Yeager was not the first to write a popular book about park rangers. That honor belongs to a book that Yeager knew well,[38] the enormously successful *Oh, Ranger!*, published in 1928 by Horace Albright and Park Service publicist Frank J. Taylor. It is a light-hearted, frequently whimsical, collection of stories, anecdotes and tall stories about national parks, interspersed with general information for tourists and campers. Though their tone is very different, the novels of Dorr Yeager's Bob Flame series, none of which until now has ever been reprinted, provide all of this and more. Fiction at its best offers a compelling sense of reality. By focusing his books on the life and adventures of a single ranger, the man he calls Bob Flame, Yeager achieves a sense of the authentic and real in demonstrating to the reader the many ways ranger lives reflect the ideals of the Service.

* * *

Leaving Rocky Mountain National Park for Berkeley proved difficult for many reasons, not the least of which was the tragic death of Joe Mills in October of 1935, an event that left his mother-in-law, Ethel Mills, to manage the Crags alone. Dorr, nonetheless, greatly enjoyed his work with Ansel Hall. "A modern museum tells a story," he had written months before his transfer, "and each exhibit is a chapter in a fascinating book. The visitor leaves a museum of today with clear, concise ideas of what he has observed while twenty years ago his mind was a jumbled mass of vague forms and scientific terms."[39] Hall's Berkeley group, whose efforts were mainly focused on museum planning and the construction of exhibits, was a large one, some 200 individuals in all, thanks to Franklin Roosevelt's New Deal programs, which added workers from the Works Progress Administration, the Federal Writers and Federal Artists Projects and some 30 C.C.C. recruits to a supervisory staff that included specialists on leave from the best museums and universities in the country. Shortly after Yeager's arrival, the Field Division of Education became the Western Museum Laboratories to reflect its major activity, and his title was changed to assistant chief, Museum Division. These years were particularly productive ones for museum work, and Yeager had a hand in preparing new exhibits for museums throughout the western United States, including the highly regarded dioramas of Anasazi life at Mesa Verde.[40]

World War II changed much of that. The annual number of park visitors plummeted, funding was short and National Park Service offices were moved from Washington to Chicago to provide space for the war effort. With the need for interpretive

work at a minimum, Yeager was transferred back into the field
in the spring of 1943 and assigned to Utah's Zion-Bryce Canyon
National Park as assistant superintendent. While there, Yeager
wrote not only the last of the Bob Flame books, but authored a
controversial paper on the impact of development on park
resources and values. "We construct roads and trails and
buildings one moment," he pointedly noted, "and cry 'spoilation'
the next."[41] Though such comments went straight to the heart
of a dilemma that would vex the Park Service for the rest of the
century and beyond, they "created much adverse criticism
among old line superintendents, especially those who had
served in Zion." Yet Yeager later recalled, "The paper was
responsible for the study of impairment of values in
many areas."[42]

Yeager's stay in Utah was comparatively brief. In 1946, he
left the front lines of park administration and returned to California as regional naturalist. There, the next year, he published
Your Western National Parks, a short but comprehensive
guidebook dedicated to Carl Russell. Newton B. Drury, director
of the National Park Service, furnished a brief prefatory
commendation. Yeager would remain in California for rest of
his career. This was a particularly critical period for a Park
Service struggling to recover from the retrenchments of the
war years while trying, despite austere budgets and deteriorat-
ing facilities, to cope with record-setting crowds of visitors. By
1953, the condition of America's parks had become desperate
enough to provoke Western writer Bernard DeVoto, a long-
standing conservationist and park champion, to write a much-
discussed exposé for *Harper's* magazine titled "Let's Close the
National Parks."

The solution proposed in 1955 by Conrad Wirth, who was
named director four years earlier, was ambitious and costly: the
decade-long, billion-dollar program called "Mission 66,"
designed to repair and upgrade park infrastructure in time to
celebrate the 50th anniversary of the National Park Service.
Interpretation received special emphasis. Wirth's plan called for
the construction of nearly 150 new museums and visitor
centers, facilities that inevitably called upon the expertise of
people like Dorr Yeager, who in 1954 had become regional

chief of interpretation for Region Four and was responsible for parks and monuments in California, the Pacific Northwest, Alaska and Hawaii. The planning phase of Mission 66 – the first and the last system-wide program of park development in the near 100-year history of the National Park Service – was coordinated at two offices, one in San Francisco, the other in Philadelphia.

The problems faced were complex, in some cases involving issues within individual parks that had existed for years, and the timetable was short. Yet Yeager and his colleagues did their work well. The visitor centers and museums they helped design did much to foster the new sense of ecological awareness and appreciation among Americans that characterized the decades which followed. The formal submission to Congress of the Mission 66 proposal in January of 1956,[43] and the widespread public support with which it was immediately greeted, was a historic moment for the National Park Service, one that restored much of the pride and morale that the war years and their aftermath had sapped. No one understood this better than Dorr Yeager, who for 30 years had watched it all, not from the sidelines but from various vantage points close to the decision-making process. He made it a personal moment as well by deciding to retire, a decision he formally announced to his staff of Region Four naturalists on October 25, 1957. "The last thing I am doing," he told them, "is writing this memorandum to you."[44]

Dorr Yeager retired on October 31, 1957. Two weeks later, on November 14, he was given a retirement dinner at San Francisco's Via Veneto restaurant near the Yeager home in Alamo. It was a festive, if nostalgic affair, with Regional Director Lawrence C. Merriam serving as master of ceremonies. The evening, not surprisingly, there was a reprise of Yeager's years of service. Edmund Rogers, Dorr's superintendent at Rocky Mountain was there; so too were Park Service colleagues and friends Carl Russell, Tom Allen and Bill Everhart. Yeager was presented with two large albums filled with letters from individuals such as Park Service Director Conrad Wirth (who also sent a telegram), Horace Albright, Harold Bryant, John McLaughlin, John Preston and others. Many of them spoke briefly of shared moments past, going as far back as the early days at Yellowstone. Chester Thomas, Zion's Assistant Superintendent, went straight to the heart of the matter. "You know," he told Dorr,

> this is a great game we've been in. The NPS is a great conservation agency. We protect and conserve natural resources. But I always like to think that we are really in the business of conserving the most precious and valuable resource we have – our human resources! And you have been privileged to work more closely with that phase of it than many of us. You have been in that group that has been instrumental in taking the resources of scenery, history and natural wonders and converting them into terms of human satisfaction. It follows that the whole human race is a little better off for the efforts of you interpreters."[45]

There would be other honors: a Department of the Interior Distinguished Service Award in 1958 and an Alumni Award from Grinnell College in 1976. The former cited Yeager's "high personal integrity" and "unusual professional competence," the latter praised his "determined interest in illustrating to the American public the scientific and historic values of the national parks."[46] Both mentioned Bob Flame.

Dorr Yeager's retirement was a long and busy one of nearly 40 years, filled with activities, including civic ones that still left plenty of time for the mountains, parks and the out-of-doors. Though he continued to write and took time to teach creative writing courses in several adult education programs, there would be but one more book, a small volume titled *California National Parks* published in 1969. Through all of this, Peg Yeager, whatever her initial reservations had been, adapted easily to Park Service life and remained a constant.

There was also John McLaughlin, who followed Yeager to Berkeley in 1936 as assistant regional officer of Region Four to play an important role with the area's C.C.C. programs. When one of Yeager's daughters, Patricia, was born the following year, Johnny Mac was there at the hospital and became her godfather. Transferred back to Rocky Mountain as assistant superintendent in 1937, Johnny Mac, like so many Park Service people, spent the war years in the armed services, after which he served as superintendent at Grand Teton, Grand Canyon and Yellowstone national parks before following Yeager into retirement in 1973. Two years later, the McLaughlins bought a home in Oakmont, near Santa Rosa, only 20 miles or so from the Yeagers, providing occasions, Dorr recalled, "to talk over old times and bemoan (as I suppose all retirees do) the changes that had come about in the Service over the last 40 years."[47] Johnny Mac died in April, 1977; his friend, Dorr Yeager, two decades later on April 22, 1996 (Earth Day), just short of his 94th birthday.

But Bob Flame, like all genuine literary heroes, lives on, a tribute to the old-time ranger and all those who lived the ideals that Mather and Albright brought to the National Park Service during its critical early years. It is with these ideals in mind, and what they say about America's national parks and our need to protect and support them in a new century, that the Rocky Mountain Nature Association, in collaboration with the Estes Park Museum Friends and Foundation, Inc., brings *Bob Flame, Rocky Mountain Ranger* back into print. But let Johnny Mac, Bob Flame himself, have the final word. "Your knack of handling the written word," he wrote Dorr Yeager in 1957, "has stood the conservation cause, the Service, the Parks, your friends and you, in good stead; and I know some of the younger people in the Service have been influenced in their life's work by your writings. I am sure many people have been inspired to greater affection for the superb places of Nature in this country through your writings and interpretive abilities."[48] Nothing more need be said.

JAMES H. PICKERING
ESTES PARK HISTORIAN LAUREATE
ESTES PARK, COLORADO, AND HOUSTON, TEXAS
JUNE, 2009

NOTES

1. Horace M.Albright (as told to Robert Cahn), *The Birth of the National Park Service:The Founding Years, 1913-1933* (Salt Lake City: Howe Brothers, 1985), p. 137.

2. Paul S. Schullery, *Searching for Yellowstone: Ecology and Wonder in the Last Wilderness* (Helena, MT: Montana Historical Society Press, 2004), p. 140.

3. Quoted in Albright, p. 138.

4. Ibid., p. 140.

5. Ibid., pp.141-142.

6. George B. Hartzog, Jr., "Preface to the Centennial Edition," *Oh, Ranger!,* by Horace M.Albright and Frank J.Taylor (Riverside, CT:The Chatham Press, Inc., 1972), pp. vi-vii.

7. Dedication, Dorr G.Yeager, *Scarface:The Story of a Grizzly* (Philadelphia:The Penn Publishing Company, 1935).

8. For many of the details of Dorr Yeager's life not in the public record, I am indebted to his daughter, Patricia Yeager Washburn. For information on the lives of Edward and Richard Steiner and the relationship between the Yeager and Steiner families, both in Grinnell and in Estes Park, I am indebted to Richard Steiner's sons, Henry York Steiner and David Steiner. See also, John Scholte Nollen, *Grinnell College* (Iowa City, IA:The State Historical Society of Iowa, 1953), pp. 106-107. Richard Steiner shared Dorr Yeager's interest in wildlife, and Yeager thought enough of Steiner's knowledge of animals to ask him to review the manuscript of his first book, *Our Wilderness Neighbors* (1931). In his preface, Dorr thanked Steiner for his "many helpful suggestions." Dorr G.Yeager, *Our Wilderness Neighbors:A Sympathetic Description of the Most Interesting Animals in Yellowstone National Park* (Chicago:A. C. McClurg and Company, 1931), n.p.

9. Dorr G.Yeager, "Foreword," p. 2. Unpublished 17-page type-script autobiographical sketch, courtesy of Patricia Washburn. It appears that this manuscript was written at the suggestion of Herbert Evison (1892-1988), a veteran of the National Park Service who in 1946 became its chief of information. Much of the available biographical information about Yeager's Park Service career comes from this document, hereafter referred to as "Autobiographical Sketch."This sketch and other documents made available by Patricia Washburn are hereafter referred to as being part of the Yeager/Washburn Collection (Y/WC).

10. Yeager's Grinnell transcript tells us that he withdrew from school at the end of the first semester of his sophomore year (1922-1923), returned the following fall and took courses during both

semesters in 1923-1924, 1924-1925 and 1925-1926, graduating with an
A.B. on June 8, 1926.

11. That summer,Yeager met and briefly interacted with a fellow
student from Grinnell who was working that summer as a "gear
jammer," driving one of the park's big yellow open-air tour buses.
Edward James Cooper, or "Cowboy Cooper" as he was known back on
campus because he wore boots and a Stetson, would soon make his
way to Hollywood as actor Gary Cooper. Cooper (1901-1961) had
transferred to Grinnell in 1921 to study graphics and art with the
intention of pursuing a career as a commercial artist or cartoonist, but
left in the spring of 1924, without taking a degree. Ironically, on four
occasions, the tall and lanky Cooper tried out for dramatic club
productions and failed to make the cast. For information on Cooper's
days at Grinnell, see Larry Swindell, *The Last Hero:A Biography of
Gary Cooper*, (New York: Doubleday, 1980), pp. 36-50; and Jeffrey
Meyer, *Gary Cooper:American Hero* (New York:William Morrow and
Company, Inc., 1998), pp. 22-25.

12. Quoted in Albright, pp. 144-145.

13. Copy, letter, Dorr G.Yeager to Ansel F. Hall, October 3, 1926,
Y/WC.

14. For information about the development of education and
interpretative activities in the National Park Service, see C. Frank
Brockman, "Park Naturalists and the Evolution of National Park Service
Interpretation Through World War II," *Journal of Forestry*, 22 (January
1978): 24-43; Barry Mackintosh, *Interpretation in the National Park
Service:A Historical Perspective* (Washington, D.C.: National Park Serv-
ice/History Division, 1986); and Richard West Sellers, *Preserving Nature in the National Parks* (New Haven:Yale University Press, 1997).

15. Grinnell did not, of course, officially have a graduate school,
but during the fall and winter quarters of the 1927-1928 academic
year, Conard put together for Yeager courses of master's equivalency in
botany and zoology.Yeager received his M.A. degree on June 5, 1928.

16. "Autobiographical Sketch," pp. 4-5.

17. R. Gerald Wright. *Wildlife Research and Management in
National Parks* (Urbana: University of Illinois Press, 1992), p. 12.

18. "Autobiographical Sketch," p. 8.

19. Aubrey L. Haines, *The Yellowstone Story*,Volume Two
(Yellowstone Library Association/Colorado Associated University Press,
1977), p. 310.

20. James A. Pritchard, *Preserving Yellowstone's Natural
Conditions: Science and the Perception of Nature* (Lincoln: University
of Nebraska Press, 1999), p. 54. See also Carl Russell,*A Concise History
of Scientists and Scientific Investigation at Yellowstone National*

Park (Washington: Department of the Interior), p. 8ff.

21. Letter, Horace M. Albright to Dorr Yeager, November 4, 1957, Y/WC.

22. See *Proceedings of the First Park Naturalists' Training Conference, Held at Educational Headquarters, Berkeley California, November 1 to 30, 1929.* (Washington: National Park Service, 1932). Available online: National Park Service.

23. Pritchard, p. 54.

24. See Ibid., pp. 50-53.

25. Dorr Yeager, Oral Interview Tape, n.d., Y/WC.

26. Dorr G. Yeager, "Memories of Mac," Employee and Alumni Association of the National Park Service newsletter (c. 1980), Y/WC.

27. Rocky Mountain National Park, Superintendent's Monthly Report, August 1931, pp. 7-8.

28. Wright, p. 15.

29. The Rocky Mountain Nature Association, *Nature Notes from Rocky Mountain National Park,* 6 (July 1932): 1 (hereafter *NNRMNP*).

30. See Patricia Washburn, "Dorr Yeager," Estes Park Oral History Project (October 1972), transcript, Estes Park Public Library Archives.

31. James Benedict, "Archaeologists Above Timberline: The Early Years," *Southwestern Lore: Official Publication, The Colorado Archaeological Society,* 67 (Summer 2001): 6-8.

32. "Autobiographical Sketch," pp. 12-13.

33. Yeager's use of the Estes Park-Rocky Mountain National Park-Tahosa Valley region as the setting for his animal novels, two of which were written and published after he left the area, was a product, of course, of his familiarity and love of place. The Tahosa Valley was a special favorite, not only because of Yeager's experiences at Steiner Acres, but because it was there, on the western slope of Twin Sisters Mountain on what became known as Cabin Rock, that his father-in-law, Joe Mills, built a homestead cabin in the years following Mills' arrival in 1899. Though Mills abandoned the place without ever staking a formal claim, the deserted cabin and its cobblestone fireplace remained a landmark site until destroyed by fire in 1968.

34. Yeager, "Memories of Mac."

35. Dorr G. Yeager, "Foreword," *Bob Flame, Ranger* (New York: Sears Publishing Company, 1934), p. xii.

36. In March 1933, for example, Edmund Rogers describes a winter patrol trip on skis – one "that has never been made before in the history of the park" – during which Yeager, McLaughlin and Ranger Jack Moomaw made their way from the Utility Area, beginning on February 3, up Fall River Road to Chapin Pass, and then descended to

Chapin Creek and Cabin 13 at the junction of Cache la Poudre River and Hague Creek, where they spent the night in 30-degree-below weather.The next day, the three headed up Hague Creek, came over Mummy Pass, and then skied their way along the North Fork of the Big Thompson to the North Fork Patrol Cabin, returning to the Utility Area the following day, having completed a trip of some 40 miles."The most difficult part of the journey," Rogers wrote,"was over Mummy Pass, which is about 12,000 feet in altitude. Near the top of the pass, a bitter cold gale was blowing.At times it was impossible to stand up because of the terrific velocity of the wind. It was necessary to crawl on hands and knees through the gap known as "The Pass.'"Yeager uses these experiences as the basis for Chapters XIX and XX, in which Bob Flame and the ranger he calls Judd Hughes complete exactly the same trip, though theirs, in the interest of romantic adventure, includes a near-fatal snowslide near the top of Mummy Pass. In much the same way, Bob's search for a missing hiker on Taylor Peak, which occupies Chapters X and XI, was inspired by the massive manhunt that followed the disappearance on August 15, 1933, of a 22-year-old from Chicago.To quote Superintendent Rogers once again (September, 1933):"From August 15 to 21 every ranger that could possibly be spared was used in the search for Joseph Halpern who disappeared while climbing Taylor Peak.An intensive search was made of the rugged country in that vicinity but no trace of the missing young man was ever found. It is estimated that members of the force walked over 300 miles while carrying on the search."

37. C.W. Buchholtz, *Rocky Mountain National Park:A History* (Boulder: Colorado Associated University Press, 1983), p. 171.

38. *Ob! Ranger*, published in 1928 by Stanford University Press, was reprinted in 1929, 1934 and in 1972 (in a new Centennial Edition). First published the year that Yeager arrived in Yellowstone as a permanent ranger-naturalist, the Albright-Taylor book specifically referenced (and on the same page) the contributions of Henry Conard of Grinnell College and Enos A. Mills of Rocky Mountain National Park.

39. Dorr Yeager,"Museums," NNRMNP, 7 (April 1934), p. 167.

40. Benedict, p. 7.

41. Quoted in Alfred Runte, *Yosemite:The Embattled Wilderness* (Lincoln: University of Nebraska Press, 1990), p. 175.

42. "Autobiographical Sketch," p. 16.

43. The Mission 66 program and its contribution to interpretive activities throughout the national park system are well chronicled in Ethan Carr, *Mission 66: Modernism and the National Park Dilemma* (Amherst, MA: University of Massachusetts Press, 2007).

44. Memorandum, Dorr G.Yeager to Park Naturalists, October 25,

316

1957, W/YC.

45. Letter, Chester A. Thomas to Dorr Yeager, October 25, 1957, W/YC.

46. A copy of Yeager's Distinguished Service Award is in the Yeager/Washburn Collection; a copy of the 1976 Alumni Award citation is in the Grinnell College Archives.

47. "Memories of Mac," p. 29.

48. Letter, John S. McLaughlin to Dorr Yeager, October 21, 1957, W/YC.

JAMES H. PICKERING